Turkey's Syrians:
Today and Tomorrow

TRANSNATIONAL PRESS LONDON

Books by TPL

Turkey's Syrians: Today and Tomorrow

A Defining Moment - Transnational Nursing Education

Revisiting Gender and Migration

Civil Society Impact on the European Union Climate Change Policy

Economic Survival Strategies of Turkish Migrants in London

International Operations, Innovation and Sustainability

Overeducated and Over Here

Image of Istanbul: Impact of ECOC 2010 on the city image

Women from North Move to South: Turkey's Female Movers from the Former Soviet Union Countries

Turkish Migration Policy

Conflict, Insecurity, and Mobility

Family and Human Capital in Turkish Migration

Little Turkey in Great Britain

Politics and Law in Turkish Migration

Turkish Migration, Identity and Integration

Göç ve Uyum

Journals by TPL

Migration Letters

Remittances Review

Göç Dergisi

Border Crossing

Journal of Gypsy Studies

Kurdish Studies

Transnational Marketing Journal

Turkey's Syrians:
Today and Tomorrow

Edited by

Deniz Eroğlu UTKU

K. Onur UNUTULMAZ

Ibrahim SIRKECI

TRANSNATIONAL PRESS LONDON
2017

Turkey's Syrians: Today and Tomorrow

Edited by Deniz Eroğlu UTKU, K. Onur UNUTULMAZ, Ibrahim SIRKECI

First Published in 2017 by TRANSNATIONAL PRESS LONDON in the United Kingdom, 12 Ridgeway Gardens, London, N6 5XR, UK.

www.tplondon.com

Paperback

ISBN: 978-1-910781-74-6

Cover Design: Gizem Çakır .

Cover Photo: Tahire Erman

www.tplondon.com

Contents

About the Authors

Deniz Eroğlu Utku is Assistant Professor in the Department for Public Administration in Trakya University and former deputy director of the Institute for Roman Language and Culture, Trakya University. She holds a PhD and a Master degree in Government Department at the University of Essex. She obtained her BA in International Relations from Hacettepe University. Her PhD thesis is titled 'The Making of Asylum Policies in Turkey: Analysis of Non-Governmental Organizations, Political Elites and Bureaucrats'. Currently her fields of academic interest include asylum policies of Turkey, mass migration movements and policy making processes. She is one of the founding editors of the *Journal of Gypsy Studies* while also serving in the editorial boards of *Göç Dergisi* and *Border Crossing*.

Ibrahim Sirkeci is Professor of Transnational Studies and Marketing and the Director of the Regent's Centre for Transnational Studies (RCTS) at Regent's University London (UK). Sirkeci holds a PhD in Geography from the University of Sheffield (UK) and a BA in Political Science and Public Administration from Bilkent University (Turkey). Prior to joining Regent's University London in 2005, he worked at the University of Bristol. His main areas of expertise are human mobility, Transnational Marketing and consumers, minorities, labour markets, remittances, and integration. He is the editor of several journals including *Migration Letters* and *Remittances Review*. He is authored several books including *Little Turkey in Great Britain* (Transnational Press London, 2016), *Transnational Marketing and Transnational Consumers* (Springer, 2013), *Migration and Remittances* during *the Global Financial Crisis and Beyond* (World Bank, 2012 with J. Cohen and D. Ratha), and *Cultures of Migration, the global nature of contemporary mobility* (University of Texas Press, 2011 with J. Cohen). He has been chairing The Migration Conference series since 2012.

Kadir Onur Unutulmaz is currently the Deputy Head of Department of International Relations, Social Sciences University of Ankara. He received his doctorate from the University of Oxford in Social and Cultural Anthropology in 2014. His doctoral research focused on the Turkish-speaking communities in London and relied on a 1.5-year ethnographic fieldwork conducted in North London focusing on the ethnic community football leagues established by these communities. He received a Master's Degree from Oxford in Migration Studies (2009) and a Master's Degree in International Relations from Koç University (2007). Unutulmaz also holds two undergraduate degrees, in Political Science & International Relations and Sociology, from Boğaziçi University (2005). He is currently involved in several projects concerning mostly Syrian refugees, including one EU Horizon 2020 funded project and an IOM project with the Directorate General of Migration Management on supporting Turkey to create a Strategic Document and Action Plan on its emerging integration policy. Unutulmaz has published many book chapters and articles, and he has co-authored *Little Turkey in Great Britain* (Transnational Press London, 2016).

H. Yaprak Civelek is an Assistant Professor in the Department of Sociology at Istanbul Arel University, where she has been a faculty member since 2012. She completed her MSc at Middle East Technical University Department of Sociology, also the time she left her job at the State Institute of Statistics which continued two years in the Department of Social Statistics. She applied to Hacettepe University Institute of Population Studies in 2002, became a research assistant there and completed her PhD in Economic and Social Demography. Then, between 2006 and 2012, she worked at Yeditepe University, Department of Anthropology as a full-time faculty. Her areas of interest include cultural demography especially focused on migration, ethnicity, identity, language, family formation and women studies.

M. Murat Yüceşahin is an associate professor at Ankara University, Faculty of Language and History-Geography, Department of Geography, Turkey. After received his PhD from the Institute of Social Sciences at Ankara University in 2002, Dr Yüceşahin's major research interest focused on population geography. In 2011, as a collaborator researcher, Dr Yüceşahin participated to the World Population Programme at the International Institute for Applied Systems Analysis (IIASA), Laxenburg, Austria and worked on Turkey's fertility, mortality and migration trends and sub national level population projection. His current research primarily focuses on feminist geography, population geography, and urban social geography. In addition to his many currently academic works, Dr Yüceşahin is a managing editor of the international *Göç Dergisi* (Journal of Migration).

Funda Ustek-Spilda is a post-doctoral researcher on the ERC-funded project: ARITHMUS (How data make a people) at Goldsmiths, University of London. She works on the missing people in official statistics. Previously, she completed a DPhil at University of Oxford, Department of Sociology (2015) on the invisible women workers in Turkey's informal labour market. Ustek also holds an MSc degree from the University of Oxford in Comparative Social Policy (2010) and Political Science & International Relations and Philosophy from Boğazici University (2009). She also writes on gender issues on Turkish popular media.

Şevin Gülfer Sağnıç works as a researcher and project assistant at Citizens' Assembly-Turkey. She graduated from Marmara University and received an M.A. degree from the University of Kent - Brussels School of International Studies on International Migration. She is currently in the final stages of her second master in comparative refugee laws at Bogazici University.

Helen Mackreath is a researcher at Citizens' Assembly. She was educated at the University of Cambridge and the American University of Beirut and has previously conducted research into Syrian refugees and hosting communities in the North of Lebanon.

Mustafa Utku Güngör has been working as Project Assistant in Citizens' Assembly (formerly, Helsinki Citizens' Assembly) for three years. His main research focus is civil society, security, and social movements. He is currently finishing his thesis on the conceptualization of security during the Gezi Park Resistance and police force in Turkey, titled as "Security at Two Levels: the Gezi Park Resistance and Police".

Aslı Ilgıt is Associate Professor in the Department of Political Science and International Relations at Cukurova University, Turkey. Her research interests include politics of identity, migration, theories of state identity and foreign and security policy. Her work has been published in *Review of International Studies*, *Security Dialogue*, *Mediterranean Politics* and MERIP.

Fulya Memişoglu is research officer at the Refugee Studies Centre, University of Oxford and assistant professor in the Department of Political Science and International Relations, Çukurova University. She holds a MA in International Studies from the University of Warwick and a PhD in Politics from the University of Nottingham. Her general area of research is comparative politics with particular emphasis on the European and domestic policy-making processes related to international human rights issues. Her current research focuses on the analysis of institutional and public policy responses to migration across multiple layers of governance.

Tahire Erman received her Ph.D. from the City University of New York, USA. Her main research interests are in urban ethnography and urban sociology, migration studies and gender studies. She contributed to such journals as Environment and Planning A, International Journal of Urban and Regional Research, Urban Studies, Gender & Society, Women's Studies International Forum, International Journal of Middle East Studies, Middle Eastern Studies, Environment and Behavior, Habitat International, International Journal of

Turkish Studies, Urban Anthropology and Ethnologie Française. She was awarded the 'Donald Robertson Memorial Prize' for the best paper published in Urban Studies (2001). She was a Fulbright scholar at the Social Anthropology Department of Harvard University (2005-2006), and the principal investigator of TÜBİTAK 1002 (2007-2008), MiReKoç (2010-2011) ve TÜBİTAK 1001 (2010-2013) projects. Her book *"Mış Gibi Site": Ankara'da bir TOKİ-Gecekondu Dönüşüm Sitesi* was published by Iletişim (2016).

Güneş Gökgöz is a graduate student in Global Migration and Policy Program at Tel Aviv University. She is writing her dissertation on the interconnectedness of the perceptions of the Syrian conflict and public attitudes towards Syrian refugees among the Turkish population.

Alexa Arena is a graduate student in Global Migration and Policy Program at Tel Aviv University. She is writing her dissertation on state-diaspora relations, examining the way the Eritrean regime engages its diaspora in Israel.

Cansu Aydın received her Master of Public Administration with a focus on Human Rights and Social Justice from Cornell University in 2015. She is now leading a Sexual and Gender-Based Violence project being implemented inside Syria.

Bilge Deniz Çatak is research assistant and PhD student in the Department of Sociology at Mersin University. The topic of her master thesis was 'The effects of sectarian differences on the relationships of married couples: Berlin and İstanbul example'. Her doctoral thesis bases on in depth interviews with Syrian refugees and local people and focuses on everyday dynamics of Syrian refugees and local people who are living in Mersin. Her research interests are migration, Syrian and Palestinian refugees, everyday life and identity.

Nagihan Taşdemir is Assistant Professor of Psychology at Anadolu University, Eskisehir, Turkey. She holds a PhD in Psychology from Middle East Technical University, Ankara. Her work has been published in journals including *Nations and Nationalism, Review of General Psychology,* and *Sex Roles.*

Chapter One

Syrian Communities in Turkey: Conflict Induced Diaspora

K. Onur Unutulmaz[¥], Ibrahim Sirkeci[Υ], Deniz Eroğlu Utku[±],

Six years on, the conflict in Syria continues to displace people in the region. This is no surprise as the previous major conflict in the region (i.e. Iraq war) has continued to unsettle for over three decades. The root causes of the conflict, the ways in which crisis was triggered and handled will continue to be analysed and debated. Human mobility, though, undoubtedly has been a function of conflict in this geography (Sirkeci, 2003; 2005; 2006; 2017; Sirkeci & Cohen, 2016). In a series of conferences, Sirkeci[1] has outlined a model he calls "3Ds of human mobility" further adding to the conflict model of migration. Three Ds refer to *Demographic Deficit*, *Development Deficit* and *Democratic Deficit,* which are described as root causes of human mobility.

Population movements in Syria have been caused by these 3Ds, too. Syrian regime has been known for its denial of ethnic minority rights while the country has been plagued by inequalities across the society and geography. As shown in Chapter 4 of this volume, country's demography was also characterised by high fertility and rapid population growth. These all

---

[¥] K. Onur Unutulmaz, Social Sciences University of Ankara, Turkey.
E-mail: onur.unutulmaz@asbu.edu.tr.
[Υ] Ibrahim Sirkeci, Regent's University London, United Kingdom.
E-mail: sirkecii@regents.ac.uk.
[±] Deniz Eroglu Utku, Trakya University, Edirne, Turkey.
E-mail: denizeroglu@trakya.edu.tr.

[1] 3Ds of human mobility as a theoretical construct has been elaborated at several speeches at conferences including the *Turkish Migration Conference* at the University of Vienna, 12-15 July 2016; *International Symposium on Migration and Children* at Üsküdar University, İstanbul, Turkey, 17-18 November 2016, and at OSU Global Mobility Programme, Mershon Center for International Security Studies, Ohio State University, Columbus, OH, USA, 24 October 2016; and most recently at the 75th Year Congress of Turkish Geographical Society in Ankara, Turkey, 8 November 2017 .

contribute to the three deficits facilitating out-migration. The key point here is that Syrian out-migration is not solely a product of what happened in 2011 or after. Although the civil war speeded up the process, even prior to the conflict, there was a strong desire for emigration as Gallup World Poll indicated (Esipova & Sirkeci, 2013). Democratic deficit caused by high levels of representation issues –lack of representation for sizeable groups- often causes such out-flows. Heightened levels of insecurity marked by significant risk of death and persecution simply have increased the migration pressures since 2011 when the violent armed conflict began.

Consequently, the conflict evolved into a complex war involving many countries, jihadists and other armed groups making masses of civilians in Syria vulnerable. In the early stages of the conflict, the Syrian crisis was also considered as part of a series of domestic upheavals in the Arab world, the so-called 'Arab Spring' or 'Arab awakening'. This process has surprised the world as well as the experts (Gause III, 2011).

The reasons for the consecutive protest movements in the Arab world have sparked much concern. Demographic factors (Kuhn, 2012), socio-economic and socio-political reasons (Ansani & Daniele, 2012; Ozekin & Akkas, 2014), and even EU policies (Hollis, 2012), were examined as triggers for the protests in the region.

Besides these studies focusing on root causes, there were also other studies focusing on the factors facilitated the Arab Spring. The roles of media and social media were mentioned as these were seen critical in organising the street protests in several Arab countries (Andén-Papadopoulos & Pantti, 2013; Howard et al., 2011; Khondker, 2011; Lotan et al., 2011; Wolfsfeld et al., 2013). Johnstone and Mazo (2011) pointed at the 'global warming' as a factor boosting already existing causes for these conflicts along with a series of social, economic and political factors underneath these crises. As we formulate human mobility as a function of 3Ds referring to a multitude of factors contributing to these conflicts and insecurities, it is difficult to pin down a single cause for these upheavals in Arab countries. One thing is sure that these conflicts have produced ever-growing number of refugees causing "the biggest humanitarian and refugee crisis of our time" (UNHCR, 2016b).

It has been six years since the first refugees began to move out of Syria in large numbers in 2011. So far, millions have been deeply affected by the conflict and had to be displaced (Yazgan et al., 2015). These refugee flows mostly affected the neighbouring countries, namely Turkey, Lebanon, Jordan, Iraq and Egypt. At least 4,810,710 Syrians (2,823,987 in Turkey alone) were registered as refugees[2] abroad by 26 September 2016 (UNHCR, 2016). While 494,411 of these refugees lived in camps, the overwhelming majority remained outside camps and relied on their own means. According to the UNHCR, 1,177,914 Syrians filed asylum applications in Europe and about two thirds of these were lodged in Germany (449,770), Serbia and Kosovo (314,852), Sweden (109,664), and Hungary (76,116) (Sirkeci, 2017). There are 4,961,300 registered Syrians to the UNHCR from Turkey, Lebanon, Iraq, Jordan, Egypt and North Africa (UNHCR, 2017a) and this number increases with each passing day.

As the refugee issues are becoming ever more challenging and influential in politics across Europe and North America, Turkey's question is whether it is right to consider these people as temporary 'guests'. Should nations get ready to prepare a future with them? An accumulating set of studies, albeit still not enough, focuses on the lives of Syrian refugees in the host countries, and discuss a variety of subjects, such as political discourse towards Syrians, their social rights, integration problems, and gender issues.

Since the very beginning of the crisis, it has attracted considerable academic interest, particularly from those who are specialising on issues such as human rights, international migration, and refugee law. Journals devoted special issues on the plight of the Syrians, fieldwork reports focusing on the crisis came out, and both INGs and NGOs issued certain reports to indicate human rights violations that refugees are faced with. As time passes by and actors in the conflict got diversified, the number of scholars dealing with the topic from different disciplines has also expanded.

Academic interest has been significant since the early stages of the conflict in Syria and we have edited the first volume on the topic with *Migration Letters* releasing a special issue titled *the Syrian Crisis and Migration* in 2015 building on two years of preparation. This special issue brought together a selection of articles that critically tackle human mobility in relation to the Syrian crisis. Contributions covered migration and foreign policy dimension (Aras & Mencutek, 2015), critical analysis of Turkey's open door policy (Toğral 2015), socio-economic aspects of hosting refugees (Bircan & Sunata, 2015; Dalal, 2015), media coverage of Syrians (Yaylaci & Karakus, 2015) and

---

[2] We should note though that Turkey is one of the very few countries that impose a geographical restriction on the 1951 Geneva Convention by not accepting refugees from outside Europe. Therefore, Syrian refugees in Turkey are officially registered under the temporary protection regime and often referred to as "guests". For details see Öner & Genç (2015), pp.254-255.

Syrian refugees' motivations for leaving Turkey (Öner & Genç, 2015). While offering insights and clarity on certain aspects, contributors of the special issue have also pointed at the areas in need of further investigation and while encouraging others to continue work in this line of investigation.

The special issue of *Migration Letters* journal in 2015 was followed by other journals' special issues on the Syrian refugee crisis. For example, towards the end of 2016, *New Perspectives on Turkey* released a special issue titled 'Precarious Lives and Syrian Refugees in Turkey'. Articles in this issue mainly emphasised the reluctance of the international community to take responsibility regarding the refugee crisis, legislative failures to provide rights and, consequently, the situation of refugees in Turkey.

Along with growing academic interest, several NGOs have also published reports on Syrian refugees and the challenges posed to local, national and international levels. These reports often tackle global and national reaction to the refugee issues with some criticism, drawing attention to the rights of refugees. For example, Amnesty International released several reports underlining human rights violations in the region from the beginning of the crisis in Syria. Protesting the detention of the human rights lawyer Raadef Mustafa (Amnesty International, 2011), the organisation published reports to point out the struggle of prisoners who had criticised the Syrian government. While the early reports of 2011 mostly focused on torture and ill treatment of opposition group members among the prisoners, later investigations were dedicated to refugees and displaced people, detention and deportation of Syrians in neighbouring countries, condition of refugees from Syria in the main countries (Lebanon, Turkey, Jordon, Iraq and Egypt), and lacklustre response of the international community to provide protection for Syrians (Amnesty International, 2013, 2014a, 2014b, 2016). These reports are important in shaping the public opinion as well as offering evidence for policy formulation.

The UNHCR and the IOM (International Organisation for Migration) also aim to raise awareness of the refugee issue in host countries and beyond. The representatives of these organisations express their concerns about increasing xenophobia and racism that can make lives of Syrian refugees harder. In this regard, the UNHCR's campaign against 'the climate of xenophobia' has to be noted (Grandi, 2016).

The UNHCR and the IOM have published several reports and draw attention to the difficult circumstances in which refugees live. They intended to promote global and national actions to protect the refugees. UNHCR's annual Global Trends Reports also paid a particular attention to the case of Syria. The 2016 report, for instance, empirically explored the conflict in the Syrian Arab Republic that has significantly contributed to the total number of refugees in the world (UNHCR, 2016a). Apart from their routine tasks in providing support for displaced people around the world, both the UNHCR and the IOM also produce data which are useful for further analysis within and outside academia.

On the other hand, the European Union also released some reports which were rather concerned about the European countries than the Syrian refugees. There were more discussions about who is refugee and who 'economic migrant' is. This kind of debates set the tone for the member states' stance over accepting or refusing refugees:

"... not everyone coming to Europe needs protection. Many people leave their home country in an attempt to improve their lives. These people are often referred to as economic migrants, and if they are not successful in their asylum application then national governments have an obligation to remove them to their home country, or another safe country which they have passed through" (European Commission, 2016a).

The discourse of the EU institutions is also quite distinct, as the frequently used terms are 'crisis', (European Commission, 2016a, 2016c, 2017) 'burden' (EURACTIV.com, 2013), 'readmission' 'protecting the EU's border' (European Commission, 2016a) and the Commission perceives the migratory flows as 'disorganized, chaotic, irregular and dangerous' moves (European Commission, 2016b). The Syrian movers do not only put significant strain on neighbouring countries (Ostrand, 2015; Oytun, 2014), but also force the EU countries to find new ways to prevent Syrians to enter. Although the number of refugees accepted by the EU is relatively small compared to Turkey, Lebanon and Jordan, the EU seeks more efficient instruments to prevent asylum applications within the union. The most radical attempt is the inclusion of Syrians into previously discussed readmission agreement negotiations with Turkey:

"The statement following the informal European Union summit on 23 September 2015, while promising welcome and much-needed increases in support to countries of first asylum and transit and humanitarian agencies, focuses on keeping refugees out or at the periphery of the European Union. Beyond that, however, it reveals a

> *reluctance to accept protection responsibilities, with no mention of resettlement, and a lack of solidarity in burden sharing between states. This suggests that, overall, action will remain inadequate and ineffective" (Parliamentary Assembly, 2015).*

Although negotiations over readmission agreements between Turkey and the EU date back to 2005, it was 2011 when the Justice and Home Affairs Council declared the conclusion of negotiations of the EU-Turkey Readmission Agreement (Sözen, 2016, p. 157). As was critically assessed by many, the agreement's carrot for Turkey is 'visa facilitation' (Sözen, 2016; Toygür & Özsöz, 2016). When it came to 2015, the readmission agreements, were once again a hot topic between two sides as a result of EU leaders' aim to solve the Syrian refugee problem as soon as possible (Didem, 2016). Syrians seeking 'an environment of security'[3] tried to leave Turkey in large numbers and the EU used all means to avoid this and return them to non-European countries (Genç & Öner, 2016). This is pretty much the outcome of those deals. These efforts by the EU are just an attempt to transfer the 'burden' to other countries (Yazan, 2016).

As the EU's main concern seems to hold refugees outside the Europe and reduce the burden, the Union tries to fulfil humanitarian responsibility by providing financial assistance. As Carrera et. al. (2015) empirically reveals, while the reallocation programmes talk about sharing tens of asylum seekers, there is a rather observable output in terms of funding. The union established Trust Funds for the Syrian crisis in 2014 and the Fund reached a total volume of close to €1 billion thanks to the contributions from 22 EU member states, Turkey and various EU budget instruments (European Union, 2017). It is possible to see the same tendency from individual member states as, very recently, Theresa May said, "We have always taken the view that we can help more Syrian refugees by putting aid into the region" (Guardian, 2017). Even if European leaders declare their support for Syrian refugees, they call for some quotas to accept them (Sirkeci, 2017). By focusing on three EU countries, (Germany, Sweden, and the UK, as well as the US), Ostrand shows that the degree of protection provided by these countries are inadequate. According to him, states should share the refugee responsibility with neighbouring countries by increasing refugee resettlement, facilitating family reunification and other forms of legal admission, and allowing

---

[3] For detail of this concept see; Cohen and Sirkeci (2011). *Cultures of migration: The global nature of contemporary mobility*, University of Texas Press.

refugees to seek protection through embassies in the region (Ostrand, 2015, p. 256). Furthermore, the practice of deliberative selection of asylum seekers, *so-called cherry picking of asylum seekers*, has also been discussed, albeit state leaders still reject it. Eventually, the numbers are less than expected and country leaders prefer to keep Syrians in the region. The most sarcastic comment for this reluctance of the countries to implement efficient solutions comes from the New York Times columnist Andrew Higgins. He indicates the slow pace of the EU resettlement programme and says: "It would take more than 750 years to relocate the 160,000 asylum seekers covered by a now-expanded resettlement plan" (Higgins, 2015).

Europe's visible reluctance to host refugees permanently and share responsibility with neighbouring countries paved the way for the accumulation of literature which tackle the EU's approach to the Syrian refugee case (Fargues, 2014; Fargues & Fandrich, 2012; Karageorgiou, 2016). What is remarkable with these studies is that they also attempt to suggest ways for burden-sharing. In other words, the burden discourse of the EU is also reflected in the studies. While these studies focus on the cost of refugees, there has been a common understanding that a fair share of responsibility for hosting refugees is necessary and refugee responsibility is not just one country's (Kirişçi, 2015). However, 'common understanding' is not an effective way to motivate states to achieve international responsibility sharing. Achiume (2015) argues that states' failure to share cost and responsibility in the field of migration is rooted in a lack of international institutions to ensure cooperation. His study suggests adopting the international doctrine of the responsibility to protect in the context of the Syrian refugee issue in order to provide a mechanism motivating decision-makers to share the cost of protecting these refugees.

Despite Achiume's optimistic suggestion regarding burden sharing and international solidarity in the field of migration, it appears obvious in the Syrian case that neighbouring countries shoulder much more responsibility than other countries as they are currently hosting over 4.8 million Syrian refugees (European Commission, 2017). European countries' unilateral decisions regarding Syrian refugees also pave the way for an uneven burden within the European Union as Professor Crawley rightly points out: "The UK's initial refusal to resettle refugees who had already crossed into Europe was "appalling" as an estimated 60,000 migrants remain trapped in Greece alone" (Independent, 2016).

Roberts et al. (2016) define this as 'Europe's collective failure to address the refugee crisis'. In this regard, rather than focusing on the financial cost of hosting refugees, Roberts et al. tackle the subject as a humanitarian issue and critically examine the responses of European countries to the plight of refugees fleeing danger. They highlight that refugees continue to suffer even if they eventually escape from war and reach Europe, because of the inadequate policies of European countries. The study precisely indicates a leadership problem in these countries. In many European countries, political leaders prefer to pursue a political discourse fostering to xenophobia rather than acting towards the common good of all Europe (Roberts et al., 2016, p. 4).

As Roberts et al. (2016) underline, another important issue becomes the face of European politics: xenophobic and racist discourses. European leaders attribute blame to countries' economic hardship, lack of sufficient health care and failures in the education system on Syrian refugees. Hungary's prime minister, Viktor Orbán, called countries that plan to accept refugees as 'mad' (Culik, 2015), The UK's former prime minister David Cameron insisted "Britain should not take more refugees" (Dominiczak, 2015). While anti-immigration discourse is remarkable in several European politicians' discourse, similar framing is also distinct in neighbouring countries' politics. As can be remembered, Lebanese President Michel Aoun defined Syrian refugees as 'serious danger'(Chit & Nayel, 2013), and Turkish MP , Öztürk Yılmaz, very recently hailed Syrians to return to their country. He believed that Syrians deeply affect the national security and that, consequently, all the bomb attacks in Turkey happened (Cumhuriyet, 2017).

Anti-immigrant discourses and state policies further aggravate hardship that refugees have to endure. Furthermore, state policies also affect Syrians' relations with the local population. Osseiran (2016) evidences this by investigating the relation of kin communities: Kurds from Syria and Kurds in Turkey living in İstanbul. Accordingly, different citizenship policies towards Kurds affect perception of two communities' approach to each other. In other words, these policies are a much more important determiner than is culture to influence refugee and local community relations. Again focusing on state policies, namely ideological-sectarian policies towards Syrians in Turkey, Gümüs and Eroğlu (2015) also argued that there is only partial integration of Syrian people in Turkey and several daily living problems based on this still continue. Besides state policies, socio-economic variables also affect refugees, such as public relations, as they are an important factor to shape public attitudes towards refugees. Keleş's (2016) analysis found that, while the education level of the participants and cities in which they live affect public opinion, income and gender do not result in a significant difference in attitude towards Syrian refugees.

Following on from examining host countries' own dynamics that cause anti-immigration feelings, scholars have gone a step forward and scrutinised the role of the media. While there has been salient anti-immigration political discourse, media coverage also has a role in provoking similar sentiments. Therefore, it has been scrutinised by a number of scholars (Hoyer, 2016; Kamenova, 2014). Particularly, favoured language has a role in influencing public opinion. This was evidenced by Hoyer's research (2016) on Spanish news framing. According to this study, the use of particular terms in the media has a 'humanising' or 'othering' effect. The identification and division created by news language, also shape attitudes towards accepting refugees, as well as how they are treated in the host countries (Hoyer, 2016, p. 27). Berry et al. (2016) also prepared a detailed report for the UNHCR and highlighted the importance of language used in the news. The analysis explored news coverage in five EU states, namely the UK, Germany, Spain, Italy and Sweden throughout 2014 and early 2015. Accordingly, sources journalists used (domestic politicians, foreign politicians, citizens, or NGOs), the language they employed, the reasons they gave for the rise in refugee flows, and the solutions they suggested are different. The report argues that news coverage in the UK has the most negative discourse, while the Swedish press is relatively the most positive towards refugees and migrants. (Berry et al., 2016). This report is somewhat significant in terms of showing the need to examine each country separately. Just like the variation from one country to another, different media sources in one country also can strike different attitudes towards refugees, as we understand from their news. In this sense, the political stance of media outlets has crucial importance. This was shown by Yaylacı and Karakuş' (2015) study as they show that ideological difference and attitudes towards government have a shaping role in newspapers' framing of Syrian refugees. Therefore, this study bridges political position and media discourse regarding the issue of migration. While many scholars indicate the relation between ideology, public opinion and media discourse relation, Holmes and Castaneda (2016) significantly contribute to the understanding of media role in public opinion as well as response to the refugees. According to this research, representation of refugees in the media through symbolic, social, political, and legal categories of inclusion and exclusion affect Europe's responses to the people arriving at their borders.

They indicate that the representation of refugees in the media is quite critical to changing responsibility feelings to fear of ethnic and religious difference.

A review of the literature regarding media role also reveals widespread interest in the specific type of media, *social media*, as showing public opinion towards Syrian refugees in their adopted countries. In their short commentary, Rettberg and Gajjala focus on this point by examining images and words shared on the Twitter hashtag #refugeesnotwelcome. They found out that Syrian refugees are associated with potential terrorists in a post 9/11 context. In addition to this, several accusatory statements, such as rapist and coward, are directed at refugees through Twitter groups (Rettberg & Gajjala, 2016). While Rettberg and Gajjala's analyses focus on the representation of male refugees, Alhayek (2014) critically investigates the role of social networking websites to promote stereotypical and/or hegemonic discourse in relation to Syrian refugee women. This study compares the Facebook campaign 'Refugees Not Captives' data with her own interview data from the field. Based on data diversification and comparison, she could uncover 'disconnection between online representations and offline realities'. Accordingly, she argues that although this local authentic online campaign aims to end the suffering of Syrian refugees, it actually tackles the issue by marginalising underprivileged refugee women and their experiences. Therefore, this campaign actually pursues the process of orientalist and self-orientalising representations.

Besides the social media factor, Alhayek' research (2014) touches upon another important point, which migration studies have long been aware of: gender and migration. According to the recent data of the United Nations Population and Fund (UNFPA, 2016), there are 1,2 million refugee women and girls of reproductive age (15-49) in hard to reach and besieged locations. There are also 80.500 pregnant refugee women. Since the numbers just show the registered Syrians, there are good grounds for believing that women and children are affected by the war more drastically than are men. Hence, a growing body of work has analysed the importance of gender in relation to the refugee question, and emphasised that taking refuge does not end the suffering of women refugees. Boynukara and Altıntaş (2016) indicate the exploitation of Syrian women in Turkey in many ways, such as becoming the second wife of a man – so-called *kuma* – and facing sexual assault. This study importantly emphasises that the exploitation of women is not only coming from outsiders, but from the Syrian community as well (Boynukara & Altıntaş, 2016, p. 174). Analysts have found that such harassment and the practice of early marriage continue to take place in Lebanese refugee camps

(Charles & Denman, 2013; Masri et al., 2013; Yasmine & Moughalian, 2016) as well as in Jordan (UN Women, 2013). As Stefanie Parker says: "gender-based violence predated the crisis within the Syrian community and is now one of the most salient features" (Parker, 2015). Besides gender-based violence, which women refugees are constantly faced with, the coverage of primary health care for women refugees is quite insufficient (Sami et al., 2014, p. 2341). Unfortunately, the plight of women refugees' lives does not end when they eventually reach a European country. Freedman (2016) emphasises that women refugees arriving at Kos, Greece island, face exactly the same kind of experiences.

While the lives of Syrian refugees, particularly of Syrian women and children, are somewhat difficult and, moreover, exacerbated by policies of the countries, we should not overlook raising awareness about the plight of Syrian refugees. Particularly, tragic images of Syrians have revealed hitherto the veiled face of the Syrian war. Pictures of the drowned three-year-old Syrian boy Aylan Kurdi and images of five-year-old Omran Daqneesh in an ambulance have bitterly shaken the world and affected the world's perception towards asylum seekers. Lenette and Sienne (2016) argue that these visual representation of pictures shifted the public mood and created an awakening to take worldwide responsibility to respond to the refugee crisis. Furthermore, these pictures motivated governments to approach the subject in a more humanitarian manner.

In 2015, Germany showed relatively better hospitability, by supplying food and shelter towards refugees coming to its borders. Many became volunteers to welcome refugees into the country. Unfortunately, this warm welcome to refugees yielded its place to hostile attitudes because of two dramatic events happening in Europe. The terror attack in Paris that killed 130 people and asylum seekers' attack on German women in the train station at Cologne paved the way for protests towards newcomers to Europe (Martin, 2016, p. 125). In this regard, securitisation of refugee policies comes to the fore. Recent critical studies handle this policy shift and explore how states have turned migration into a security question (Toğral, 2012). Scholars also rightly point out that even neighbouring countries that used to be proud of implementing an open door policy have shifted from their policy of hospitality due to securitisation of refugees (Gökalp-Aras & Şahin-Mencütek, 2016)

All in all, an accumulating body of theoretical and empirical evidence has shown us that there are changing dynamics affecting Syrian refugees' presence in their destination countries. Therefore, there is a need for further study on this question and to explore different aspects of refugees' lives. Accordingly, this edited book offers a multidisciplinary perspective and includes surveys of sociology, anthropology, law and political science, undertaken by notable scholars who have long specialised in migration. Therefore, recent developments in the field are critically examined by focusing on distinctive problem areas.

Content of the Book

In this edited book, we aim to discuss Syrian refugees comprehensively by assembling articles from a variety of disciplines. We aim to limit our interest within Turkey because Turkey's position is considerably important as a neighbour as well as a 'gate keeper' for the EU countries. Turkey is at the centre of current debates because of its role to prevent refugees travelling to Europe (Sirkeci, 2017; Yucesahin & Sirkeci, 2017). Currently Turkey hosts 3,320,814 Syrians (DGMM, 2017)[4] as well as irregular Syrian migrants.

The chapters are organised in three main parts. In the first part, there are studies that either offer theoretical insights concerning how to understand and analyse the issue of Syrian refugees in Turkey or engage in a conceptual discussion over the situation of Syrians in Turkey. The studies in the second part, in turn, provide analysis of primary data collected through various methods on selected case studies. The last part briefly looks at the future prospects for the Syrian communities in Turkey.

Following this brief introduction, Chapter 2 constructs a theoretical framework for biopolitical analysis of the Turkish politics working on the refugee population. Biopolitics refers to the politics that problematizes life; according to some sources life equals to politics, to some life is an object of politics. One way or another, biopolitics is based on demographic action and aims to control life experiences (vital statistics) in populations. In a Foucauldian manner, when life turns into the object of the political power, we possibly observe how power surrounds it and how politicians in charge incorporate natural human life and abilities into the math of power. The chapter, thus, aims to find an answer to the question "how will these people be integrated into the society?" while developing perspectives on social position of the refugee subject, how "integration" can be associated with "state of exception", which is Agamben's key concept and, fiction/fear of "other" in the society.

---

[4] See http://www.goc.gov.tr/icerik3/temporary-protection_915_1024_4748

Chapter 3 engages in a conceptual discussion concerning asylum categories and the current situation in Turkey. It aims to understand the official social classification of 'refugee' categories in Turkey, with a special focus on Syrians. The main argument of the chapter is that asylum categories in Turkey build upon an imaginary of Turkish culture and ancestry, and hence make value-laden decisions about who to include and who to exclude from the refugee category, with a hierarchical ordering of those 'deserving' and 'undeserving'. The invented category of 'guests' for Syrians is one important example in introducing a yet another level of differentiation of 'deservingness' between asylum seekers coming from the Eastern borders of the country, who do not have legitimate rights to claim asylum in Turkey.

The second part of the volume begins with Chapter 4, which provides an analysis of the civil society working on Syrian refugees in Turkey. It focuses on the extent to which civil society actors in Turkey are responding to the Syrian influx, assisting in some cases, and in other cases contesting their presence, along a human security framework. Civil society plays a significant role in the ability of refugees to secure assistance and a dignified standard of living. This works both ways – the way civil society within a host community responds to a refugee presence has a significant impact on its own character and dynamics. In Turkey, given the constant flux which the character and dynamics of civil society are going through, the multiplicity of other issues concerning identities and domestic politics which are stratifying the response to Syrians, and the increasingly centralized political decision making, this is a significant period of time to document how changes in civil society are manifesting themselves in relation to Syrians.

Chapter 5 explores how Turkey's refugee-hosting fatigue is reflected and framed in domestic political debates. While the current Syrian conflict and subsequent refugee crisis has become a crucial foreign policy tool of the Turkish government since the beginning of the Syrian crisis, the refugee issue has also been a high-priority topic in domestic political debates considering that the country has experienced two national elections, one local election, and one presidential election since 2011. The official refugee policies and discourses of the Turkish state have fluctuated over the course of five years since the arrival of first Syrians in March 2011 due to external and internal changing dynamics. While there emerged abundant information about Turkish government's main stance and policies concerning the refugee crisis (based on regular press releases and government officials' statements), a systematic understanding of where the opposition parties stand in Turkey's refugee debates and how they shape responses to the challenges the country has been facing does not get sufficient attention from the academic or political circles. Thus, this chapter focuses on discursive continuities and shifts of three major opposition political parties that are represented in the Turkish Parliament.

Based upon a field study carried out in the Önder neighbourhood (*Siteler*) of the Altındağ district in Ankara, which is now called the 'Little Aleppo', Chapter 6 focuses on the interaction between the Turkish residents and Syrian refugees in one of the most diverse districts of the Turkish capital. More specifically, the chapter investigates the relationship between old migrants in the locality, who are the very poor and the excluded, and the newcomers to the neighbourhood, mostly Sunni Arabs from the war-torn Syria. It demonstrates that the relationship between old and new migrants is shaped by a number of factors, including the type of jobs they have and the way of life they pursue, as well as the kind of response they get from the government and civil society organizations, formal and informal alike. The chapter argues that, while in discourse Syrian refugees may be described as Muslim brothers in agony, in reality the conflict of interests arising as much from cultural differences as from competition in business and jobs, and over social assistance, are causing tensions in the relationship between the two groups.

Grounded in the concept of perceived threat, Chapter 7 examines the willingness of Turkish people to give social and economic rights to Syrian refugees. Specifically, the chapter considers the impact that relative size of the refugee population has on perceived threat and consequently on exclusionary attitudes. To this end, public attitudes in the Turkish cities of Ankara and Hatay are compared, utilizing quantitative research methods; data is collected via surveys with a structured questionnaire administered to a sample of 1514 university students in Ankara and Hatay. Findings reveal an overwhelming propensity to exclude Syrian refugees from social and economic rights in Turkey, with slight cross-city variations shaped by relative refugee population size and differing levels of perceived threat.

Chapter 8 focuses on the issue of education of Syrian refugees. Specifically, it examines the so-called Temporary Education Centres (TECs), which were established to meet the needs of Syrian youth whose education was interrupted by the war and forced migration to Turkey. TECs provide education in Arabic delievered by Syrian teachers using a slightly modified Syrian curriculum. This chapter investigates the effectiveness of these centers through focusing on the case of Mersin. It suggests that while TECs provide a temporary solution, the issue of education of Syrian refugees in Turkey requires a longer-term vision and commitment.

Chapter 9 contributes to the book by providing an analysis that shows how national identification and Turkish identity boundary definitions mediate the relationships between social identity motives and attitudes towards Syrian refugees in Turkey. After a series of multiple regression analyses, the research displays that social identity motives are linked with the definitions of national in-group boundaries and thus attitudes towards immigrants.

Chapter 10 offers us a detailed demographic analysis of Syrian populations with a discussion of prospects regarding demographic features, which are contrasted with Turkey's own characteristics. The chapter attempts to offer a comprehensive demographic analysis of the Syrian population, focusing on the demographic differences (from 1950s to 2015) and demographic trends (from 2015 to 2100) in medium to long term, based on data from World Population Prospects (WPP). It offers a comparative picture to underline potential changes and convergences between populations in Syria, Turkey, Germany, and the United Kingdom. It frames the discussion with reference to the demographic transition theory to help understanding the implications for movers and non-movers in receiving countries in the near future.

Chapter 11 focuses on the issue of integration and its politics in Turkey. It, firstly, provides a brief selective analytical background for the significance of the concept of integration in the Western world by describing how the current 'backlash against diversity' has culminated into being. Secondly, the chapter discusses, also briefly, the concept of integration with respect to some of the common elements that could be identified in effective integration schemes. Then, it aims to bring the discussion of Syrian communities in Turkey into focus by discussing why their integration particularly poses such a huge challenge. Lastly, the chapter attempts to make a case for the urgent need to adopt a sound integration vision and create effective schemes for its achievement in Turkey by arguing that the issue so far enjoyed a relatively low level of politicisation. After explaining how politicisation of a controversial issue makes a significant restricting impact on its governance, the chapter discusses the reasons for low level of politicisation and why this is quickly changing today.

The last chapter, finally, provides an overall evaluation of the current situation and future prospects of Syrian communities in Turkey. While the complexity and dynamism of the topic certainly makes it impossible to predict the future with confidence, a long-term vision is crucial in shaping today's policies that would hopefully contribute in the creation of a peaceful and prosperous society out of existing ethnic, cultural, and linguistic diversity.

A Note on Terminology

It is important to note that we leave authors free to refer to Syrians as asylum seekers / migrants / refugees as they wish, even though we prefer the term 'refugee' in this introduction chapter. We believe that the term usage completely depends upon authors' approach to the subject since there is not an internationally constant and accepted definition for Syrians. We are fully aware that Syrians in Turkey are not refugees in the legal sense due to Turkey's geographical limitation on the Geneva Convention on Refugees. Since 2014, a vast majority of Syrians in Turkey are 'persons under temporary protection'. However, it is also quite clear that for all analytical purposes they are refugees who had to move to another country for safety escaping a bloody conflict and who are granted official protection by that country

REFERENCES

Achiume, T. (2015). Syria, Cost-Sharing and the Responsibility to Protect Refugees.

Alhayek, K. (2014). Double Marginalization: The Invisibility of Syrian Refugee Women's Perspectives in Mainstream Online Activism and Global Media. *Feminist Media Studies, 14*(4).

Amnesty International. (2011). Syrian human rights lawyer Radeef Mustafa faces life ban. *Amnesty International Public Statement*.

Amnesty International. (2013). An International Failure: The Syrian Refugee Crisis. *Amnesty International Briefing*.

Amnesty International. (2014a). Left out in the Cold: Syrian Refugees abondoned by the International Community. London.

Amnesty International. (2014b). Struggling to survive: Refugees from Syria in Turkey. London.

Amnesty International. (2016). No Safe Refuge Asylum Seekers and Refugees Denied Effective Protection In Turkey. London.

Andén-Papadopoulos, K., & Pantti, M. (2013). The media work of Syrian diaspora activists: Brokering between the protest and mainstream media. *International Journal of Communication, 7*, 22.

Ansani, A., & Daniele, V. (2012). About a revolution: The economic motivations of the Arab Spring. *International Journal of Development and Conflict, 2*(03), 1250013.

Aras, N. E. G., & Mencutek, Z. S. (2015). The international migration and foreign policy nexus: the case of Syrian refugee crisis and Turkey. *Migration Letters, 12*(3), 193.

Berry, M., Garcia-Blanco, I., & Moore, K. (2016). Press coverage of the refugee and migrant crisis in the EU: a content analysis of five European countries. Retrieved 05.01.2017, from http://www.unhcr.org/56bb369c9.html

Bircan, T., & Sunata, U. (2015). Educational assessment of Syrian refugees in Turkey. *Migration Letters, 12*(3), 226.

Boynukara, H., & Altıntaş, U. (2016). Turkish Migration 2016 Selected Papers. In D. Eroğlu, J. H. Cohen & I. Sirkeci (Eds.), *Turkish Migration 2016 Selected Papers* (pp. 171). London: TP London.

Carrera, S., Blockmans, S., Gros, D., & Guild, E. (2015). The EU's Response to the Refugee Crisis: Taking Stock and Setting Policy Priorities.

Charles, L., & Denman, K. (2013). Syrian and Palestinian Syrian refugees in Lebanon: the plight of women and children. *Journal of International Women's Studies, 14*(5), 96.

Chit, B., & Nayel, M. A. (2013). Understanding racism against Syrian refugees in Lebanon. Retrieved 17.10.2016, from http://civilsociety-centre.org/pdf-generate/12350

Cohen, J. H., & Sirkeci, I. (2011). *Cultures of migration: The global nature of contemporary mobility*: University of Texas Press.

Culik, J. (2015). *Anti-immigrant walls and racist tweets: the refugee crisis in central Europe.* Paper presented at the Conversation.

Dalal, A. (2015). A Socio-economic perspective on the urbanisation of Zaatari Camp in Jordan. *Migration Letters, 12*(3), 263.

Didem, D. (2016). Türk Göç Politikasında Yeni Bir Devir. *Saha Helsinki Yurraşlar Derneği*, 6-11.

Dominiczak, P. (2015). The Telegraph. Retrieved 03.03.2017, from http://www. telegraph.co.uk/news/uknews/immigration/11839283/David-Cameron-Britain-should-not-take-more-refugees.html

EURACTIV.com. (2013). EU ministers discuss burden-sharing for Syrian refugees, African migrants. Retrieved 21.02.2017 http://www.euractiv.com/section/ justice-home-affairs/news/eu-ministers-discuss-burden-sharing-for-syrian-refugees-african-migrants/

European Commission. (2016a). The EU and the Refugee Crisis. from http://publications.europa.eu/webpub/com/factsheets/refugee-crisis/en/

European Commission. (2016b). Implementing the EU-Turkey Agreement – Questions and Answers. Retrieved 14.02.2017, from http://europa.eu/ rapid/press-release_MEMO-16-1221_en.htm

European Commission. (2016c). Managing the Refugee Crisis: Commission reports on progress made in the implementation of the EU-Turkey Statement. *Press Release*.

European Commission. (2017). Humanitarian Aid and Civil Protection Syria crisis Fact Sheet.

European Union. (2017). Europe's support to refugees and their host countries. Eu regional trust fund in response to the syrian crisis. from https://ec.

europa.eu/neighbourhood-enlargement/sites/near/files/eutf_syria
_factsheet.pdf

Fargues, P. (2014). Europe must take on its share of the Syrian refugee burden, but how? *Robert Schuman Centre for Advanced Studies European University Institute, Migration Policy Centre*.

Fargues, P., & Fandrich, C. (2012). The European Response to the Syrian Refugee Crisis: What next? *MPC Research Report 2012/14*. Migration Policy Centre

Freedman, J. (2016). Engendering Security at the Borders of Europe: Women Migrants and the Mediterranean 'Crisis'. *Journal of Refugee Studies*, few019.

Gause III, F. G. (2011). Why Middle East studies missed the Arab Spring: The myth of authoritarian stability. *Foreign Affairs*, 81-90.

Genç, H. D., & Öner, N. A. Ş. (2016). Stuck in the Aegean: Syrians leaving Turkey face European barriers. In I. Sirkeci & B. Pusch (Eds.), *Turkish Migration Policy* (pp. 127-149). London: TP London.

Gökalp-Aras, N. E., & Şahin-Mencütek, Z. (2016). From assertive to opportunist usage of mass migration for foreign and asylum policy: Turkey's response to the refugees from Syria1. In I. Sirkeci & B. Pusch (Eds.), *Turkish Migration Policy* (pp. 91). London: TP London.

Guardian, T. (2017). Theresa May resists calls for UK to accept more Syrian refugees. from https://http://www.theguardian.com/uk-news/2016/sep/ 19/ theresa-may-resists-calls-uk-accept-syrian-refugees-aid

Gümüş, B. & Eroğlu, D. (2015). "Partial integration of Syrian 'escapees' under the rule of Turkey's Justice and Development Party (JDP)", *Contemporary Arab Affairs*, Vol. 8, No 4, s. 469-486.

Higgins, A. (2015). European Leaders Look Again for a Unified Response to Migrant Crisis. Retrieved 03.02.2017, from https://http://www.nytimes.com/ 2015/10/26/world/europe/merkel-and-east-european-leaders-discuss-migrant-crisis-in-brussels.html

Hollis, R. (2012). No friend of democratization: Europe's role in the genesis of the 'Arab Spring'. *International Affairs, 88*(1), 81-94.

Holmes, S. M., & Castaneda, H. (2016). Representing the "European refugee crisis" in Germany and beyond: Deservingness and difference, life and death. *Journal of American Ethnologist, 43*(1), 12-24.

Howard, P. N., Duffy, A., Freelon, D., Hussain, M. M., Mari, W., & Maziad, M. (2011). Opening closed regimes: what was the role of social media during the Arab Spring?

Hoyer, A. (2016). Spanish News Framing of the Syrian Refugee Crisis Paper 26. *WWU Honors Program Senior Projects*.

Independent. (2016). Refugee crisis: European leaders blamed for record high deaths in the Mediterranean. Retrieved 20.02.2017, from http://www. independent.co.uk/news/uk/home-news/refugee-crisis-closing-borders-people-smugglers-human-trafficking-mediterranean-deaths-record-a7391736.html

Johnstone, S., & Mazo, J. (2011). Global warming and the Arab Spring. *Survival, 53*(2), 11-17.

Kamenova, D. (2014). Media and Othering: How Media Discourse on Migrants Reflects and Affects Society´ s Tolerance. *Politické vedy*(2), 170-184.

Karageorgiou, E. (2016). Solidarity and sharing in the Common European Asylum System: the case of Syrian refugees. *European politics and society, 17*(2), 196-214.

Keleş, S. Ç., Aral, T., Yıldırım, M., Kurtoğlu, E., & Sunata, U. (2016). Attitudes of Turkish youth toward Syrian refugees in respect to youths' gender, income, education, and city: A Scale Development Study. In I. Sirkeci, D. Eroglu & J. H. Cohen (Eds.), *Turkish Migration 2016 Selected Papers*. London: TP London.

Khondker, H. H. (2011). Role of the new media in the Arab Spring. *Globalizations, 8*(5), 675-679.

Kirişçi, K. (2015). Why 100,000s of Syrian refugees are fleeing to Europe. Retrieved 10.02.2017, from https://http://www.brookings.edu/blog/order-from-chaos/2015/09/03/why-100000s-of-syrian-refugees-are-fleeing-to-europe/

Kuhn, R. (2012). On the role of human development in the Arab Spring. *Population and Development Review, 38*(4), 649-683.

Lenette, C., & Cleland, S. (2016). Changing faces: Visual representations of asylum seekers in times of crisis. *Creative Approaches to Research, 9*(1), 68.

Lotan, G., Graeff, E., Ananny, M., Gaffney, D., & Pearce, I. (2011). The Arab Spring| the revolutions were tweeted: Information flows during the 2011 Tunisian and Egyptian revolutions. *International journal of communication, 5*, 31.

Martin, P. L. (2016). Amerikan gözüyle Avrupa'nın göç krizi. *Göç Dergisi, 3*(1), 121-134.

Masri, R., Harvey, C., & Garwood, R. (2013). Shifting sands: changing gender roles among refugees in Lebanon. . *OXFAM.*   Retrieved 20.11.2016, from http://www.oxfam.org/sites/www.oxfam.org/files/rr-shifting-sands-lebanon-syria-refugees-gender-030913-summ-en.pdf

Osseiran, S. (2016). Distance beyond the border : Kurds of Syria and Turkey in İstanbul. In I. Sirkeci, J. H. Cohen & P. Yazgan (Eds.), *Conflict, Insecurity and Mobility* (pp. 19-34). London: Tp London.

Ostrand, N. (2015). The Syrian refugee crisis: A comparison of responses by Germany, Sweden, the United Kingdom, and the United States. *J. on Migration & Hum. Sec., 3*, 255.

Oytun, O. (2014). The Situation of Syrian Refugees in the Neighboring Countries: Findings, Conclusions and Recommendations. *Orsam Report.*   Retrieved 189, from http://www.orsam.org.tr/files/Raporlar/rapor189/189eng.pdf

Ozekin, M. K., & Akkas, H. H. (2014). An empirical look to the Arab spring: Causes and consequences. *Alternatives: Turkish Journal of International Relations, 13*(1&2).

Öner, N. A. S., & Genç, D. (2015). Vulnerability leading to mobility: Syrians' exodus from Turkey. *Migration Letters, 12*(3), 251.

Parker, S. (2015). Hidden crisis: violence against Syrian female refugees. *The Lancet, 385*(9985), 2341-2342.

Parliamentary Assembly. (2015). Resolution 2073: Countries of transit: meeting new migration and asylum challenges. Retrieved 21.03.2017, from http://www.assembly.coe.int/nw/xml/XRef/Xref-XML2HTML-en.asp?fileid=22175&lang=en

Rettberg, J. W., & Gajjala, R. (2016). Terrorists or cowards: negative portrayals of male Syrian refugees in social media. *Digital Feminisms: Transnational Activism in German Protest Cultures, 16*(1).

Roberts, B., Murphy, A., & McKee, M. (2016). Europe's collective failure to address the refugee crisis. *Public health reviews, 37*(1), 1.

Sami, S., Williams, H. A., Krause, S., Onyango, M. A., Ann Burton, M., & Tomczyk, B. (2014). Responding to the Syrian crisis: the needs of women and girls. *The Lancet, 383*(9923), 1179–1181.

Sirkeci, I. (2017). Turkey's refugees, Syrians and refugees from Turkey: a country of insecurity. *Migration Letters, 14*(1), 127-144.

Sözen, Ü. S. (2016). Fragile balance of EU-Turkey readmission agreement. In İ. Sirkeci & B. Pusch (Eds.), *Turkish Migration Policy* (pp. 149-168). London: , London: Transnational Press London.

Toğral, B. (2012). Securitization of migration in Europe: critical reflections on Turkish migration practices. *Alternatives: Turkish Journal of International Relations, 11*(2).

Toğral , K. B. (2015). Deconstructing turkey's" open door" policy towards refugees from Syria 1. *Migration Letters, 12*(3), 209.

Toygür, İ., & Özsöz, M. (2016). *Reshaping Relation In The Midst Of Crisis: A Bitter Anniversary For Turkey-EU Accesion Negotiation*: Istanbul Policy Center-Sabancı University-Stiftung Mercator Initiative.

UN Women. (2013). Gender-Based Violance and Child Protection Among Syrian Refugees in Jordan, with a focus on Early Marriage *Inter-Agency Assessment*. Jordan.

UNFPA. (2016). More than Numbers. Retrieved 20.02.2017, from http://www.unfpa.org/sites/default/files/pub-pdf/unfpa_gbv_take10-may17-single41.pdf

UNHCR. (2016a). Global Trends: Forced Displacement in 2015. from http://www.unhcr.org/576408cd7.pdf

UNHCR. (2016b). Syria conflict at 5 years: the biggest refugee and displacement crisis of our time demands a huge surge in solidarity. from http://www.unhcr.org/news/press/2016/3/56e6e3249/syria-conflict-5-years-biggest-refugee-displacement-crisis-time-demands.html

UNHCR. (2017a). Syria Regional Refugee Response. Retrieved 21.03.2017, from http://data.unhcr.org/syrianrefugees/regional.php

UNHCR. (2017b). Syrian Regional Refugee Response. Retrieved 21.03.2017, from http://data.unhcr.org/syrianrefugees/country.php?id=224

Wolfsfeld, G., Segev, E., & Sheafer, T. (2013). Social media and the Arab Spring: Politics comes first. *The International Journal of Press/Politics, 18*(2), 115-137.

Yasmine, R., & Moughalian, C. (2016). Systemic violence against Syrian refugee women and the myth of effective intrapersonal interventions. *Reproductive health matters, 24*(47), 27-35.

Yaylaci, F. G., & Karakus, M. (2015). Perceptions and newspaper coverage of Syrian refugees in Turkey. *Migration Letters, 12*(3), 238.

Yazan, Y. (2016). European Union's Irregular Migration "Paradox": The Case of EU-Turkey Readmission Agreement. In D. Eroglu, J. H. Cohen & I. Sirkeci (Eds.), *Turkish Migration 2016 Selected Papers*. London: TP London.

Yazgan, P., Utku, D. E., & Sirkeci, I. (2015). Syrian crisis and migration. *Migration Letters, 12*(3), 181-192.

Yucesahin, M. M., & Sirkeci, I. (2017). Demographic gaps between Syrian and the European populations: What do they suggest? *Border Crossing, 7*(2), 207-230.

Unutulmaz, Sirkeci, Eroğlu Utku

Chapter Two

Biopolitical Problematic: Syrian Refugees in Turkey

H. Yaprak Civelek*

Introduction

In Turkey, based on Geneva Convention in 1951 and Geneva Protocol in 1967[1], only those who come from European countries can be accepted as "refugees" by the government due to a geographical limitation. However, because of the increase in number of refugees in 1990s, a 1994 regulation revised the national law which was adopted in 1961[2] (Erdoğan, 2015, p. 46). As for Syrian refugees, before delving into a theoretical discussion, and the need to summarize the background of their influx into Turkey, it should be noted that this has been occurring since April 2011. This influx can be attributed to the authoritarian regime of Bashar al-Assad and the expansion of the civil war to the large parts of Syria. However, as a country embracing the casual relationship between authority and "one-dimensional man" (Meyer-Emerick, 2004,p.1), Turkey seems to have developed and applied a more humanitarian approach to the Syrians compared to European countries, the United States, and Australia. These countries place Syrians in detention centers that are governed by tough laws, which even ignore the immigrants' political and social rights (Tyler, 2006; Ahmed, 2004). Turkish government firstly recognized the Syrian National Council[3] as a political

---

* Assist. Prof. at Istanbul Arel University, Department of Sociology. Tepekent, Büyükçek-mece, Istanbul. E-mail: yaprakcivelek@arel.edu.tr.

[1] Officially the 1951 UN Convention Relating to the Status of Refugees, also known as the UN Convention on Refugees and often referred to as the Geneva Convention, it covers the asylum-seekers and refugees who have experienced the events happening before 1951, 1961 Geneva Protocol is a revision of Geneva Convention, abolishing date-limitation, however, it brings out geographical limitation.

[2] Date of Law: 29/08/1961 – Act: 359.

[3] According to the Middle East Security Report 4, Syria's Political Opposition, 2012, by Elisabeth O'Bagy, the Syrian National Council (SNC) is the widely known political opposition coalition which is made up of seven different blocs: the Muslim Brotherhood, the Damascus

power in Syria, and then the "open-door" policy is put into effect. "Temporary Protection Regulation" ensuring non-refoulement came to be the second official policy (Kirişçi, 2014).

Nevertheless, about "Temporary Protection Regulation" of today, some written sources claim that the applications are so flexible that Syrian men can return to their country whenever they want (especially young men for fighting), however, for some, if they do return to their country they can never come back again[4] (Yıldız, 2013). Such contradictory circumstances and the agreements mentioned above make the use of "refugee" concept complicated for the new-comers. Moreover, such "flexible" policy does not seem appropriate for principles of emergency protection, human rights protection and non-refoulement; contrary to the condition of "a refugee never becomes an active side of the war in his/her very own country" (Yıldız, 2013; Çiçekli, 2009).

Under antinomies, total number of Syrian refugees in Turkey in 2017 exceeded 3 million (Yucesahin and Sirkeci, 2017). The Disaster and Emergency Management Authority (DEMA) announced in June of 2016 that a total of about 260,053 Syrian refugees live in the housing centers categorized as tent cities and container cities.[5] According to the Directorate General of Migration Management there are 258,597 Syrians[6] were living in 26 housing centers. On the other hand, there is a population growing really fast and living outside of these camps which are estimated to be over 2,5 million[7]. Thus, it is obvious that this intense cross-border population movement from Syria refers to a mass migration and has spread to various geographic regions of Turkey.

Declaration, the National Bloc, the Local Coordination Committee (as representatives of the grassroots movement), the Kurdish Bloc, the Assyrian Bloc, and Independents. Its center is in Istanbul, however, it cannot encourage the local forces as it used to be at the beginning of the conflict because of the increasing influence of the military force. See, Middle East Security Report 4, Syria's Political Opposition, 2012, by Elisabeth O'Bagy. pages 10-36.

[4] Some conversations with the Syrian refugees in Istanbul, Gaziantep and Hatay point out such arrivals and departures. However, none of them are official. The Geneva Convention includes basic standards for the refugee travels. See http://www.unhcr.org/1951-refugee-convention.html, http://www.unhcr.org/3b66c2aa10.

[5] https://www.afad.gov.tr/TR/IcerikDetay1.aspx?IcerikID=848&ID=16. Last update: 30.10.2017. Visited:18.02.2017.

[6] Sirkeci (2017):136.

[7] http://www.goc.gov.tr/icerik6/syrian-nationals-benefiting-from-temporary-protection-in-turkey_917_1064_4773_icerik. (Sirkeci, 2017:136)

The tent cities and container cities which recognizably refer to an organized camp life and, that life and the influx of Syrian refugees into Turkey as a mass of "foreign" identities, their political positions, expectations, and humanitarian reception provide social scientists -mostly in Turkey- with a methodologically attractive field. And this is why one can find numerous articles and reports -all recent and based on field research- in the literature. Most of the studies focus on governmental approaches to the refugees and (mostly negative) attitudes of the locals to the new-comers (Yazgan et al., 2015, p.186). Besides, discussions and publications on human rights, freedoms, and legal practices are available. Research reports open up new paths for discussion as well as playing a key role in generating data, re-thinking, and producing the theoretical background.

With its nationalist character, Turkey grants its *citizens* some moral and respectable codes to save and to defend, which also defines *civil* types of human behaviour and relations, which are all the time culturally and politically approved but put a kind of *fear* inside people. That is why while the first part of this study presents a description of the position of the refugee as viewed by the political power that s/he is forcibly confronted with, the reminder of the chapter problematizes the integration issue in terms of consequences of the Syrians' inland movements in Turkey; their noticeable presence in almost every region and the *fear* of the locals. Agamben's concepts of *the camp*[8], *bare life,* and *state of exception,* and Foucault's opinions on the relationship between *security, territory* and *population* as associated to the socio-political practices, and Furedi's *culture of fear* are the key concepts of the theoretical process.

Biopolotical Context and Appearance of Refugee Subject

For a firmer theoretical and political understanding, one needs to grasp the relationality between population and politics. Biopolitics deals with population, which is beyond any doubt a political *problematique* as well as a demographic concept. Population dynamics (birth, death, migration) (no "etc.," population has only three dynamics) are historically subject to supervision of the state and the discourses in order to perpetuate the

---

[8] Also Tuncer-Gürkaş (2014) analyzes the region surrounding the border between Syria and southeastern Turkey based on Agamben's concept of "camp", that is the realm of existence for spatial and social polarization. Elaborating on *"state of exception"* in southeastern Turkey, she defines "camp" as a representation of a life marked by the binary oppositions of citizenship-foreignness, national identity and otherness, belonging-unbelonging, inclusion and exclusion. They are governed by security discourses, and the sovereign envisages them as spaces of crisis and tension.

political existence, which is driven by ambition of power and growth (just a simple introduction to the following argument). When the intellectual development of individuals, along with wars, epidemics, and death (factors affecting those individuals) are constantly controlled in a social structure conforming to the expectations and targets of an administration, the power emerges. This way, political economy starts functioning as biopolitics; moreover, the population turns into the biopolitics of power (Foucault, 2010; Wallerstein, 2013; Oksala, 2013).

In a study Ruth Judge (2010, p.6)[9] asks "how power-knowledge relations in contemporary Britain produce the refugee subject...What behaviours are expected of them?" These questions refer to where the acts of power are positioned as a methodological attitude fully encircling the society, turning it into a representation of itself. This is why population equals to biopolitics; and according to Foucault, it refers to a dynamic, representational mass identified by administration strategies rather than describing a mass of ruled people.

 The main objective of biopolitics is to categorize and re-evaluate population by communities and such an act should be understood as a kind of commodification: Murtola talks about "a social reality in which attempts are made to turn most any form of human experience into a commodity or a means of capital accumulation" (2014, p.836) and correlates this reality with commodification. Sharp mentions that commodification refers to objectification which transforms human bodies into objects of economic desire (2000, p.293). With reference to these approaches, a political desire of formalization can straightforwardly be found out; population is something that power can re-organize, administer, and manipulate. Population also produces the power's knowledge and the area of supervision (Foucault, 2013). For instance, rather than being treated as a "citizen", an individual within such a population is categorized at once; s/he is given a special form and position to re-produce in a political economy defined by the art of liberal administration; s/he protects both her/his own and the power's authority; and s/he aims to merge, be active, and progress with that power. Then, as opposed to the "citizen" whose national identity and belonging are - externally- defined by borders, what is the status of the refugee who crosses

---

[9] Refugee advocacy and the biopolitics of asylum in Britain. The precarious position of young male asylum seekers and refugees. Paper submitted in partial fulfilment of the requirements for the Degree of Master of Science in Forced Migration at the Refugee Studies Centre, University of Oxford, May 2010. Working Paper Series 60. Refugee Studies Centre Oxford Department of International Development University of Oxford. p. 6.

borders? How should one define the "subjectness" dilemma and the political position of the refugee?

While passing through the border is the only way for a refugee to win an ontological struggle, the local resident considers "allowing transit" almost as "breaking tradition", a matter of "codes" and "fear". The irony here is between a granted transit and a discourse defining the fiction of a second subject: The fiction of a subject desired by the power emerges right through the discursive exercises re-constructing subjects. As the power fully violates the privacy of its subjects and thus, is responsible for the protectionist-conservative or liberal-humanist stance with regard to the "other" via its "subjectification" strategies, one needs to deal with it politically and discursively.

Above all, the refugee-subject is in a void, a victim to political targets and conditions: Politically and socially isolated, s/he dwells on a threshold. Within the state-individual relationship as Badiou defined and Agamben re-argued, "singularity and excrescence" are unrepresented in the society they belong to, but do not belong to the whole in which they are represented (Badiou, 2007).[10] The refugee is in most cases still a "citizen", but devoid of the territory (homeland) in which her/his belonging is represented; s/he is a member of a camp[11] where s/he resides now, taking refuge under a new sovereign's rule and authority. Economically in a void, s/he is also devoid of certain kinship due to war and migration. If we refer to Turner's concepts of *liminality* and *communitas*, the refugee is a *liminal subject*; one who can envisage a "life in-between" and talk about a *transformative experience* (Turner, 2002). Her/his social role is ambiguous, identity formation is disrupted, and personal relations are uncertain and unstable. The refugee is in a situation where one cannot look back to those left behind, and the new has not fully emerged yet; living on a threshold where one has almost completely detached herself/himself from the past, and the future has yet nothing to promise. For threshold dwellers, new opportunities and available spaces are all temporary. They represent an unstructured and unhierarchised history, and experiential collectivism (Turner, 2009). What is called the "transition" period, however, seems as a great unknown to the

---

[10] According to Badiou, *singular multiples of a situation are presented in it, but are not represented. They belong to the situation but, are not included. Normal multiples are both represented and included. To change a situation radically the aim is to have what belongs to it (singularity) included in it* (cited by Lechte, 2008: 237)
[11] or tent or container city as in Turkey.

refugee due to future uncertainties. Therefore, the refugee's existence is surrounded by contradictions, her/his subject position is politically and socially constructed beforehand, s/he has lost her own political characteristics, and has been isolated by all external factors -good or bad- highlighting her/his foreignness. The designation "refugee" suffices alone to isolate her/him in the socio-political field. Moreover, as a member of a subpopulation, the refugee poses a "problem" to the upper-population.

Approaching masses of refugees as a wide area for further problematization, one can consider -from a sheer political perspective- accepting a very high number of refugees and facilitating proper and rapid integration processes as good steps for a government to achieve a firmer position in its foreign policy in terms of human rights and humanitarian aid. For instance, this can for sure help Turkey's accession process to the EU. Success of an integration policy, however, cannot be directly related to the number of new refugees but reasons and conditions under which one migrates, and efforts to protect refugees' rights and freedoms are just as important (Arango, 2006). Based on Agamben's understanding of biopolitics, the key step of integration is to bring populations closer by abolishing spatial differences between different lives, gradually make them participate in the political life, and ensure the functioning and stability of control mechanisms (Baştürk, 2006). Especially, war refugees are in a long term escape; their exposures to integration processes depend on the duration of their intended stay in a new country. The power's systemic agenda, biopolitics, will thus orient, transform, and coordinate them under the subordinating and controlling mechanisms just as much as the pre-configured local subjects. Surrounded by new political-discursive practices, the refugees face another *governmentality*, subject formation, and controlling mechanism. Following a change in their bonds, if we borrow Butler's concepts (2005), each of the refugee subjects is on a threshold towards a new existence; and this existence is very much related to her/his will to live and desire to survive. Trying to adapt to a previously non-existent relationality within a new network of bonds (due to personal concerns alone), each contributes to local subjects' actions re-producing the power.

Denizen of the "State of Exception": Subjectification of "Homo Sacer"

Agamben suggests that the most fundamental reality for humans is their various rights and freedoms. They should acquire the status of a norm without an exception. A human as a form is the totality of unchanging principles. S/he is temporally and spatially transcendental with her/his natural rights; and s/he is a political being through the consensus that her/his rights and freedoms are permanent, and they are fully acknowledged. Articulation of their rights and freedoms on a discursive plane is the very source of their political positions (Agamben, 1998, p.76-77).

On the other hand, "if refugees (whose number continuously grow and who represent a considerable segment of humanity today) represent such a disquieting element in the order of the modern nation-state, this is above all because by breaking the continuity between man and citizen, nativity and nationality, they put the original fiction of modern sovereignty in crisis. Bringing to light the difference between birth and nation, the refugee causes the secret presupposition of the political domain -bare life- to appear for an instant within that domain. The refugee is truly the man of rights, the first and only real appearance of rights outside the fiction of the citizen that always cover them over. Defining refugees politically is difficult for this exact reason" (2013, p.158).

Quite normally, the natural transcendence and victimization of the person who is loaded with great rights and freedoms, and named *homo sacer* by Agamben, turn "subjectification" into a key problem for the sovereign. The subjectification level of the "foreign" therefore, stands as an intriguing question, and requires a different strategy.

Foucault (2010) states that free market creates standard forms of life that comply with the organization of life it offers. This is the point where the life of the refugee, as a "foreign subject", is on the verge of acquiring a new meaning. Together with the concept of micro-history as in Foucault's *The Birth of Biopolitics*, historical experiences of a refugee help one better analyze her/his position within a community and relations of power. On a macro level, the refugee is in a discourse construction site which is designated and defined by multiple and random relations from the perspective of political economy; s/he is subjected to various strategies and thus transformed; and finally s/he is allowed entry into a new community based on the forms that comply with relationalities and available discourses. As projected by the political economy, the refugee is allowed entry into pre-defined forms of relations, organizations, and categorizations.

Besides all possible forms of reception, Foucault also warns that the more the power focuses its own national existence, the more it raises *others*' risk of dying by creating the conditions required (Foucault, 2010; Rabinow &Rose, 2006). This is actually what Negri and Agamben indicate, too: Contemporary bio-power points the power which eventually targets exploitation of or the death of others (Agamben, 2000a, 2000b; as cited in Rabinow &Rose, 2006)[12]. Moreover, Agamben enunciates that doctors, lawyers, advocates, philosophers, even families are the representatives of power and they decide who must survive or who must not, on behalf of sovereign authorities (as cited in Hall, 2007, p.36). Today as European societies are investing in health care, we witness at the same time how they are creating tougher laws and financial obligations against refugees. Moreover, thousands of Syrians have been left to die in a very immoral way. [13]

As mentioned before Turkey's humanitarian manner, establishing "cities" to take shelter in, is remarkable, however, some scientific results obtained from these *camps* are worth to be re-questioned: In a research measuring overall satisfaction in camps, more than half of the asylum-seekers (67%) seem to be satisfied with their lives. Syrian refugees living in "tent cities", where the electronic cards that are used in "container cities" do not exist, however, would like to start using electronic cards as they will help them better manage their *culturally accepted* expenditure, especially food expenditure (Yıldız, 2013, p.155). Other demands and comments include the lack of a female doctor (as being examined by a male doctor is *not religiously acceptable*), *Arabic-speaking* teachers and *Arabic books*, not having a TV, thus being unaware of the current situation in their country, the need for improved social conditions and humanitarian treatment in camps, being offered psychological and pedagogical assistance for children to fight war-related traumas, and the desire for long-term stay in Turkey (Yıldız, 2013, p.158-63). All these demands actually might seem natural expectations for an individual who is granted the status of a refugee and, natural rights and their non-transferability in modern politics, regardless of their status, are sacred; and ideally, they should be considered independent from politics and defined without being manipulated by politics.

However, in Agamben's imagination of *camps*, people are neither inside, nor outside of the law. Refugee camps are fields of much debate based on Agamben's camp theorem; surrounded with precautions in a state of exception, camps become ordinary and permanent. Residents of camps are

---

[12] "biopower takes the form of a politics that is fundamentally dependent on the domina-tion, exploitation, expropriation and, in some cases, elimination of the vital existence of some" (Rabinow & Rose, 2006, p.198)

[13] The UNHCR reports that the number of Syrians drowned at the sea, symbolized by baby Aylan Kurdi, is 3.740. http://www.unhcr.org/news/latest/2016/10/580f3e684/mediterra-nean-death-toll-soars-2016-deadliest-year.html.

always known as non-citizens, alienated from socio-political life, reduced to their membership in bare life (Arendt, 1998). To expect being detached from politics, however, contradicts with the fact that (along with the political and legal definition of the concept of a refugee itself) it is the political power which is responsible for the protection of the rights and freedoms. But this is more than a contradiction; it is the place where space, time, and law of the political order are abolished and *bare life* appears (Agamben, 2013). The refugee is there with her/his biological characteristics, rather than her/his socio-political identity; in this place where the law of the political order does not promise complete security, s/he is under the absolute judgment of the sovereign. As natural rights vary and multiply, the projection and protection levels of the power naturally increase. This is the source of that very much needed judgment: this relationship does nothing but re-produce the power and its knowledge, strengthening it even more[14].

Although many refugees intend to "return to their countries" (Yıldız, 2013, p.160), they have already been designated and categorized by the power in Turkey; therefore, the process of subjectification has already started for each and every refugee. Based on Foucault's approach[15] the phases of such subjectification are a) direct targeting, b) penetrating into the all segments of daily life instead of being a structure determining only the limits of a person's political activities, c) manipulating perceptions and interpretations, d) affecting the psychology and decision making processes, and e) proper framing of the whole subjectification. While the presence of "electronic cards" within camps represents an "interpellation", that refugees associate this regulation as "seeing needs in a culturally accepted method" can be the very first political step into the creation of exception. Although the refugee seems to have acquired a space for freedom, in reality s/he is moved into an area of representation by the sovereign through the use of an "electronic card". Is s/he now inside or outside? According to Agamben, modern power functions exactly by designating humans - which is striking. Humans are designated and discursively transformed; this transformation strategy is a

---

[14] Individualism means blessing the biological existence of the human and its uttermost pri-oritization. The power, however, constructs individualism on a discursive level. The Universal Declaration of Human Rights (UDHR) is evidently a fiction of the power aiming subordination through designation; it does nothing but highlights the power's legal and administrative sov-ereignty.

[15] See "Revisiting Foucault through reading Agamben: Implications for workplace subjectifi-cation, desubjectification and the dark side of organizations" by Richard Ek, Martin Fougère and Per Skålén. The study elaborates processes of subjectification and desubjectification in two different philsophers' eyes. For the definition of process of subjectification p. 2-4

representational element of biopolitics (Agamben, 1998, p.72-73). In such a case, they are neither inside nor outside; "the card" describes them, differentiates them and excludes them while it gets them included.

At this point, the concept of "exception" and the phenomenon of "state of exception" should be elaborated: In Agamben's literature on sovereign power in the state of exception is naturally totalitarian and "not only does it hold complete sway over the individual, but, in contemporary societies, the state of exception is permanent, rather than temporary" (Ellermann, 2009, p.4). Thus, according to him, politics and life are variables of a formula; humans experience political life and *bare life* (Agamben, 1998). There are major differences in these two main fields: while living in a community and being an individual are vital in the political life, bare life defines a life outside of politics and laws. The exclusion in bare life determines the borders of city / social life / politics; it still contributes to their construction by being excluded. Exclusion, in other words being pushed outside of the social life, is the first political activity; and bare life is omnipresent in this activity. The key feature of modern politics is the vagueness of the line surrounding the political field and accommodating the bare life, while mechanisms condemning people to uncertainty between their socio-political life and biological existence.

In a way, bare life and political life show a certain resemblance.[16] Sovereignty is constructed by juxtaposing these two different lives on a political plane. The power Agamben (2005) defines is able to penetrate into the bare life, and this ability can be explained by the concept of exception. This concept can be defined as the state of volatility between the law and the power strategy of the sovereign (who politically administers the society) mandating all forms of life to sustain its own existence. The starting point of this biopolitical analysis, for example, is the contemplation on the relation between a war-related refugee influx (regulated by the UN Refugee Agency, and defined in international law as *taking shelter en masse*) and the "efforts to integrate new-comers/sub-population into local/upper-population". In other words, this study deals with the power describing the complete relationship between human and nature, how it re-produces life dominating its own knowledge based on the binary opposition of local and non-local,

---

[16] Agamben, 2001, aktaran Sibel Yardımcı. Kentin Sınırında: Toplumsallaşmanın Yeni Meta-foru Olarak "Kamp". Skop Sanat Tarihi Eleştiri.1/1/2012. Skop Bülten. http://www.e-skop.com/skopbulten/kentin-sinirinda-toplumsallasmanin-yeni-metaforu-olarak-kamp/470. (06.05.2016)

which actually means to decide non-locals' destiny corresponding to national-expedient targets.

The sovereign power is directly governed and shaped by international institutions, the Universal Declaration of Human Rights, and the domestic law. Still, the power claims its independence from the law; and this triggers a contradiction: The power is responsible for the existence and functioning of the law, yet this also elevates it to the position of a "decision-maker". In Foucauldian terms, the power's disciplinary intervention on population goes so far as to re-shaping the most natural forms of human life, including birth and death. Thus, it can define one's both natural and social identity (Foucault, 2013). And this is the source of the mechanism transforming a human into a citizen. It is how the power subordinates an individual with rights and freedoms, and incorporates that individual into its order by categorizing her/him based on citizenship and nationality. Based on his own view on biopolitics, Agamben (1998, p.76-77) defines power as a mechanism assimilating the individual by penetrating into all segments of life, creating "life that does not deserve to live", spying and controlling. According to him, the power creates a representational "camp" in the bare human life with "a constant state of exception or a zone of uncertainty", and this camp is in practice the law of the modern power; camps are able to create and sustain the "state of exception", and individuals are subordinated to this state. Thus, the discourse abolishes normalcy and establishes itself fully authorized (Agamben, 1998, p.79).

Looking at the national newspapers, Turkish government has various methods to keep its authority over refugees and Kurds together by settling Syrian refugees into the villages where Alawite-Kurds live[17]: The newspaper *BirGün* claimed that the next target of the ruling party is to build a new refugee camp for 3 thousand persons in the middle of Mazgirt district of Tunceli (Dersim) province, which has 8 thousand Alawite-Kurdish people reside, with the purpose of changing the cultural and demographic structure in the district, which, inter alia, they have never received vote. There is a rumour in public that in 2019, in 5 years, Syrian refugees probably will have rights for having Turkish citizenships and vote, which means achieving political interest. *Cumhuriyet*, another national newspaper, announces that

---

[17] BirGün Gazetesi, http://www.birgun.net/haber-detay/bir-suriyeli-multeci-kampi-da-der-sim-e-mi-114183.html Date of news: 01.06.2016, 02.07.2016.
http://www.cumhuriyet.com.tr/haber/turkiye/506152/Alevi_koyune_Suriyeli_kampi.html. Date of news: 02.07.2016. 03.07.2016.

the camp in Kahramanmaraş province, in which 27 thousand refugees have been sheltered, will be moved into the Sivrice village[18] -as a container city-where Alawite people belonging to the Bektashi order live as the Turkish-international paper Hürriyet Daily News has affirmed. This paper also mentions local peoples' historical experiences and fears. [19]

Leaving aside the dynamics concerning the current government, political polarization, and othering within the smallest groups such as neighbourhoods and even family houses, one can observe that the integration issue and refugee rights are governed by a set of disconnected regulations - with the exception of the principles of Geneva Convention and the recent judicial implementations for the Syrian refugees. And due to individual preferences and practices, these regulations have little effect on the above mentioned issues. The result is a so-called integration ideal triggering contradictions both in the daily life and politics. As the influx of the refugee population continues en masse and displays regional intensities, if one refers to Agamben's terms, how can the power (which is expected to value the harmony between the daily life and political area) constructs any "integration" within an environment in which the local intersects the non-local?

---

[18] The village of Dulkadiroğlu district.

[19] *The container city being built in Kahramanmaraş has already led to angry protests from local Alevis, who fear that the province's sensitive demography will be unsettled..."We are continuing to build three container cities. These will host 4,000 people in Hatay, in the Dutlu-bahçe neighborhood of the Yayladağı district; and 10,000 people in the Boynuyoğun neighborhood of the Altınözü district. The 25,000-person-capacity container city in Kahramanmaraş, in the Sivricehöyük village of Dulkadiroğlu district, is continuing to be built," said Ergün Turan, the president of TOKİ, a Prime Ministry-affiliated body, on April 17..."When the container city in Kahramanmaraş is completed, a living space much bigger than the facility in Elbeyli, which is the biggest temporary accommodation center in the world, will be constituted," Turan told the state-run Anadolu Agency, referring to the Elbeyli refugee camp in the southern province of Kilis...Earlier in April, locals from Sivricehöyük and other villages nearby rallied against plans to build a container city, with the village head, Mehmet Caner, saying that the refugee population would dwarf the number of local Alevis, who only number around 6,000...Through 1978 and 1980, in the run up to the Sept. 12, 1980 military coup d'état, Alevis were subjected to mass killings not only in Kahramanmaraş, then called Maraş, but also in Sivas and Çorum by ultra-nationalist groups...An appeal by villagers for "urgent stay of execution" in the container city plan has already been filed to an adminis-trative court, with residents citing fears that "Syrian jihadists" would be settled nearby.* http://www.hurriyetdailynews.com/state-housing-agency-toki-building-three-container-cit-ies-for-syrians-in-south-turkey.aspx?pageID=517&nID=97964&NewsCatID=341 Date of news: 18.04.2016, 02.07.2016.

Integration, which is in reality a version of exception, is a key step for employment. Adopting Wallerstein's approach, the anthropologist Özbudun discusses how communification processes provide benefits to the capitalism: There emerges a labor force with few demands, working on little salary, and in unfavorable conditions. Wallerstein underlines how multicultural practices projecting migrants' socialization *to their own cultures and the capitalism creating hierarchies contribute to a decrease in migrants' wages* (as cited in Özbudun, 2010: 60) The refugees in Turkey perfectly represent these economical characteristics. They are subject to a protection regime that reminds them "temporariness" on every step (Yazgan at all., 2015). Not being granted work permits for starting small-scale businesses prevents them from establishing enterprises, and they are deprived of social security. Those starting small-scale businesses (e.g. shop owners) allegedly register their company under a local's name. As this is certainly not something the state cannot foresee, counter-measures rumoured to be in progress. Lack of social aid and deficiencies in medical services, unorganized activities and administrative issues of NGOs constantly disrupt efforts to meet refugees' major expectations. The language barrier hinders communicating and addressing basic demands, let alone the social integration (Çomak, 2016). Currently, the emergence of an exception in which power infiltrates into the multiple layers of life, abolishes distinctive and defining characteristics of those layers or assimilates by transforming them is contentious. Although the concept of exception here is not positive, it is important to note that the conditions in the Turkish refugee camps are not as terrifying as those in the Nazi camps of World War II for which the concept of the state of exception was developed. Turkish refugee camps do not display a state of exception where oppression, coercion, and a state of emergency are present. Here, however, one can just discuss the answer of "why most of the refugees want to leave Turkey and reach Europe?"

According to Ministry of Interior Directorate General of Migration Management and UNHCR Office in Ankara, and academics who are interested in immigration Syrian refugees' integration into the Turkish population is very much related to the government's efforts to meet the accommodation, education, and medical needs, along with other requirements concerning social participation. [20] Besides, political

---

[20] For instance, participation in the labour market or in education are the forms of social participation. However, it is not easy to observe "immigrants' social and political participation in the integration process" immediately, because "it will largely be limited to those forms of social participation that imply involvement in decision-making processes". See Report of

consequences of the interaction between two populations (host/guest or sub-/upper-population) with different historical backgrounds, economic, social and demographic experiences, should be planned ahead because of potential conflicts which are based upon cultural, economic and political matters. In fact Robert Ezra Park does not find such potential conflicts extraordinary; on the contrary they are very normal. They reproduce the point the government needs to be involved in order to reconstruct peaceful environment. Then, at the final stage, full-integration will be possible with structural, "social, economic and political inclusion of newcomers" (as cited in Kaiser and Kaya, 2016, p. 25-26). The legal and controlled integration of all refugees (in and outside of camps, registered and unregistered), that is to say the *normalization* of social participation, requires long-term and well considered government policies. In other words, whereas an exception has emerged in the daily life, the power conceives nothing extraordinary (Baştürk, 2013). From a Foucauldian point of view, one requires a new form of administration to re-produce life (Foucault, 2013). Otherwise and ironically, what is foreseen by politicians is that social, economic, and political chaos that simultaneously offers a critique of the power's administration and triggers the desire for the exception seems inevitable.

Influences of the Culture of Fear

Any discussion on the biopolitics of war refugees would require considering issues such as the reason of war, refugee's intention or reluctance to return, and the duration of her/his stay. Both governments and local populations assume that this period is only "temporary" and will come to an end "when the war ends". Although their desire to return cannot be guaranteed by international bodies, media channels, and the research on the adverse social conditions of refugees, they are still expected to stay until political and social structures of their home countries are recovered.

Refugees in Turkey have been distributed into varying social and economic settings, and their number is constantly increasing. Since their return to Syria is temporarily suspended due to the war and the political crisis, another issue requiring solution is their acceptance by the locals. Regional financial crisis due to increasing illegal work force and decreasing wages, socio-cultural issues of crime and security, growing number of beggars due to lack of accommodation, and disputes driven by distinct socialization practices (Boyraz, 2015:50-57) add up to the alienating, contemptuous, and judging

Council of Europe, 1999. "Political and social participation of immigrants through consulta-tive bodies". Directorate of Social and Economic Affairs.

attitudes of the hosting population towards refugees. Moreover, building suburbs in non-cosmopolite cities[21], the settlement policy recently put into practice by the Directorate General of Migration Management (DGMM) limits refugees' mobility and turns the existing conflicts into discriminations over identities. Different from the "camp policy", "suburb-policy" gives refugees the right of deciding on the provinces in which they would like to reside. This project which is based on so-called "free residence" does not influence inner-city mobility but does intercity-mobility and, refugees must report to the police stations and give autograph "daily, one day or two days in a week" to prove that they are living in the cities that the government send them to. Thus, refugees' inter-city mobility is controlled and they are kept under administrative guard (Başak, 2011, Kahya, 2014).

Collecting sociological and psychological observations from the field, "Syrians in Turkey: Social Acceptance and Integration Research" (Erdoğan, 2015) asks locals whether they agree with the opinion that "refugees should be sent back to their country even if war does not end" to understand locals' reception of Syrians. The results show that 63% disagree with the opinion. Removing "war" from the statement, one observes a decrease in the number of people who disagree to 48%. Although researchers find the initial number "valuable", it does not seem that good based on humanitarian values. The decrease when war is removed from the equation underlines conscientious responsibility and sensitivity towards war. The most important finding of the research is the need to cultivate a *culture of acceptance* for the following reason: 77% of the respondents believe that having Syrians in Turkey on a longer term would lead to issues, whereas this number rises up to 82% in regions where the Syrian population is larger (Erdoğan, 2015, p. 36-37). The research titled "Syrian Refugees and Turkey's Challenges: Going beyond Hospitality" authored by Kemal Kirişçi (2014) reveals that 86% of the respondents believe that the influx of refugees should stop, whereas 30% want them to go back. In his research[22], Kirişçi (2014, p. 28) claims that the local population does not welcome regular migration. When asked how satisfied they are with the camp administration and staff, refugees within Yıldız's (2013, p.157) research report organizational issues, poor

---

[21] The project covers 62 cities except for İstanbul, Ankara, İzmir, Antalya, Bursa. The refugees are not allowed to reside in metropolises.
[22] Find the pdf: https://www.brookings.edu/wp-content/uploads/2016/06/Syrian-Refugees-and-Turkeys-Challenges-May-14-2014.pdf

management, and othering (contemning being "asylum-seekers", not being an Arab; being treated like a beggar) practices.

According to Furedi, such social experiences have their roots in glorifying security and the resulting feelings of reservation and anxiety. Then one can infer that the culture of fear outweighs the culture of acceptance. The fear of foreigners and the feeling of insecurity in relationships affect daily life. Peoples' perception of each other gradually changes, and the dream for a better life puts greater distances between people, and they tend to avoid risks. Weakening traditions and the lack of a relevant social contract trigger all these (Furedi, 2014, p.204). Furedi's *(2014, p.205)* concept of *war of culture* is of utmost importance here, as one witnesses the politicization of morality in Turkey (like in many other countries). In a setting where the borders between right and wrong, free and forbidden, guilt and innocence are vague, people get nervous and reserved, and social solidarity remains unrealized.

Newcomers'/sub-population's integration into locals/upper-population, governments' acts of exception, and cooperation between refugees in their efforts to participate in social and cultural life are closely related to locals' and public's acceptance and support for refugees. Durkheim (1964) underlines the importance of social cooperation and intermediary institutions (religious institutions, associations, etc.) to protect the unity of society and to create collective (rather than individual) benefits to escape from a purely individualist approach. However, his emphasis on the collective consciousness and the feeling of unity confronts with the inconsistent relationality between the power and the subject. Born in such relationality, this cooperation is deeply associated with the humanist re-shaping of the *fear of "other"*, which is the main constituent of fearism - and *fearism* grows out of liberal-humanitarian citizenship discourses and pedagogical discourses (Zembylas, 2010, p.32). *Xenophobia* related categorizations such as exclusion/inclusion, originality/mimicry, us/them might be *potentially* emerging. Tyler (2006) suggests that humanitarian discourses, unlike Xenophobic discourses, want the public to identify 'the human face' of specific asylum seekers/refugees' to make people think that they are "just like us". Such close-up technologies are very beneficial for recognizing 'the victims' of repressive asylum laws; these strategies attempt to reposition asylum-seekers as subjects who matter, 'like us'. Humanitarian 'subjects'...use the frame of their own visibility to make asylum seekers visible..." *(Tyler, 2006, p.194)*. The critical point here is how asylum seekers or refugees are constructed latently as "them" by social institutions, even by humanitarian agencies. Any such critical stance in Turkey can only be achieved through the problematization of the strong nationalist education curricula.

In the meantime, social reflections of the culture of fear are not directly affected by individual feelings or political sensibilities infiltrated into society especially by politicians. On the contrary, fear emerges in individuals and it is directed towards others; and thus, fear turns into a relational mode disciplining bodies based on a special feeling of belonging. This is how fear produces fearful subjects in relation with hellish *others*, and secures the border between us and them the boundary between "what I am" and "which I am not" is the fear itself (Zembylas, 2008, p.70, 2010, p.32-33). Fear helps certain bodies settle into the public space and grants free movement, whereas it restricts others into enclosed areas - just like nation-states. Claiming to sustain the welfare and the character of their country, nation-states develop policies to deny "illegal", unqualified refugees and fake asylum seekers entry. As a nation-state, Turkey is no exception to the abovementioned political attitude. Nevertheless, Turkey shows political support and hospitality towards foreign victims (treating them of their own) with historical sensibilities towards "Islam" and "Turkic origins", and Syrians refugees fall into this category. Domestic polarizations such as othering Kurdish, Alawite, and Armenian populations, however, remain unresolved. Public service announcements and fundraising appeals on the news demand that refugees are granted their basic human rights and treated within moral boundaries, rather than presenting them as a threat against national belonging. On a local level, however, one can observe that the *"we"* who are closely associated with *"others"* are uncomfortable with and prejudiced against them. This reality mimics the Western politics: binary oppositions of bare life/political being and exclusion/inclusion exist despite of all hospitable elements. It reminds one of the pedagogical contradictions in which nationalist education regulations do not have any space for recognition/acceptance/approval of foreigners, whereas it teaches public morality and humanitarian values. As Agamben puts it, politics exists because man lives in language defining who he actually is. "As a living being he separates and opposes himself to his own bare life and, at the same time, maintains himself in relation to bare life in an inclusive exclusion" *(Agamben, 1998, p. 38)*.

Announcing Council of Higer Education's (CoHE) decision to allow Syrian students to study in Turkish universities, Deputy Prime Minister Beşir

Civelek

Atalay[23] said "Humanitarian sensibilities, neighbour relations, and international law commit Turkey to welcome and host Syrian citizens". Ankara University's TÖMER has also announced the opening of additional Turkish classes. The rapid transformation of the refugee population within the camp settings undoubtedly means socio-political cautiousness. Negative reactions (mainly on social media) of university students who have already taken an entrance exam (along with their families), however, prove that the binary opposition between us and them outweighs "peaceful" recognition/acceptance/approval elements, the culture of acceptance actually leads to *deconstruction*, and inclusive exclusion is still valid for the foreigner.

Conclusion

What exactly is the position of the refugee subject (who is allowed a cross-border entry), when the laws defining her/him based on her/his identity and act in contradiction with her/his natural rights and freedoms and thus create a dilemma? How should one "read" his/her future?

Defining the instruments of discursive human rights and freedoms, Foucault tells us that this is how an individual participates into social relations as a subject, and (again on a discursive level) life is organized with those instruments. Here discourses require different institutional creations and norms to subjectify the refugee. Refugee rights are no different than the natural rights of other subjects who are defined as citizens, and refugees cannot be separated from the rule of the power as all subjects gain their rights through the politics. Then one should acknowledge the fact that life is, under all circumstances, surrounded by the power.

Although the main constituents of integration share similarities (employment, education, medical services, life spaces, etc.), geographical and socio-cultural specificities require political, sociological, and anthropological instruments not only for an act of exception, but also for trans-national peace initiatives.

In the anthropological texts, as in Baus's article (2009), "creolization" means "localized". The word refers to a culture which reflects single entity that has pure boundaries; the boundaries that *never cannot be pluralize.* They represent a geographical area which does not open for any possible multicultural structure. The boundaries are defended against outsiders, and identity, language, customs, traditions, even daily practices, all cultural

[23] Press conference. 20 October 2012 cited by Ali Rıza Seydi, 2014. p. 281.

aspects shortly, have to be maintained and transmitted to the next generations (Baus, 2009)[24]. Similarly, culture of war is an important consequence of othering in parts of Anatolia where anthropological fictions are not heterogeneous, especially when the national values are "threatened". One can expect that the power will engage in immediate adaptation efforts to create a culture of acceptance; in other words, prioritize exceptional approximations (prioritize exceptional settings where populations familiarize themselves on the(ir) 'other'). However and remarkably, the news, reviews of research reports and articles reveal the fact that even Islam, which is the most attractive principle for the power today, has nothing to offer for "unity in diversity", when it comes to the ideal/social order.

The analysis of public discourses loaded with anti-other judgments in Turkey is on the power's agenda. The subjective results of the research certainly depend on the historical functioning of the most fundamental principle(s) of the discourse. That is to say, for Syrian refugees in Turkey, integration process will be designed based on the power's projection of social order, the desire to sustain the status quo, nationalistic and homogenizing ideals and surely political interests. Thus, it is possible to observe a manner that is performed by a state of exception while evaluating Turkish government's political approach to Syrian refugees. And if one needs to "read" or "say" something about their future in Turkey, the explanation presents two options for them: first, they can choose to live on an edge that "bare life" and practices of "state of exception" which let them live a life as "included", stigmatized them as "excluded" or they can choose to live in another "modern" country.

References

Agamben, G. (1998). *Homo sacer: Sovereign power and bare life*, Daniel Heller Roazen (trans.), California: Stanford University Press.

Agamben, G. (2005). *State of exception*, Kevin Attell (trans.), Chicago & London: The University of Chicago Press

Agamben, G. (2013). *Kutsal insan. Egemen iktidar ve çıplak hayat,* İsmail Türkmen (çev.) İstanbul: Ayrıntı Yayınları.

Agamben, G. (2000a). *Means without end: Notes on politics.* Minneapolis: University of Minnesota Press.

---

[24] The paragraph is a short summary of certain pages. For detailed anthropological thoughts and examinations, see Daniela Baus's paper titled "Cultural Exchange in a heterogeneous research field approaching scientific culture with Anthropological thought". Pages 96-99.

Civelek

Agamben, G.(2000b). Remnants of Auschwitz: The witness and the archive. New York: Zone Books.

Ahmed, S. (2004). *The cultural politics of emotion*. Edinburg University Press.

Arango, J. «Europa y la inmigración: una relación difícil». Migraciones, nuevas movilidades en un mundo en movimiento. Barcelona: Anthropos, 2006, 91-111.

Arendt H. (1998). *Totalitarizmin kaynakları. Emperyalizm*. Bahadır Sina Şener (çev.), İstanbul: İletişim Yayınları.

Başak, C. (2011). *Mülteciler, sığınmacılar ve yasadışı göçmenler*. Ankara: İç İşleri Bakanlığı Genel Yayını- 686.

Baştürk. E. (2013). Bir kavram iki düşünce: Foucault'dan Agamben'e biyopolitikanın dönüşümü. *Alternatif politika,* 5(3), Aralık, 242-265.

Badiou, A. (2007). *Being and event*. Oliver Feltham (Trans.), New York: Continuum.

Baus, D., (2009). Cultural Exchange in a Heterogeneous Research Field: Approaching Scientific Culture with Anthropological Thought. *Spontaneous Generations: A Journal for the History and Philosophy of Science*, 3(1), 95-104.

Boyraz, Z. (2015). Türkiye'de Göçmen Sorununa Örnek Suriyeli Mülteciler. *Zeitschriftfür Die Welt der Türken*, 7(2) 2015. 35-59.

Butler. J. (2005). *İktidarın psişik yaşamı: Tabiyet üzerine teoriler,* Fatma Tütüncü (çev.), İstanbul: Ayrıntı Yayınları.

Council of Europe. (1999). Political and social participation of immigrants through consultative bodies. *Directorate of Social and Economic Affairs*, Strasbourg, Cedex: Council of Europe Publishing.

Çiçekli B.(2009).Uluslararası hukukta mülteciler ve sığınmacılar, Ankara, Seçkin Yayınevi.

Çomak, H. (2015). Mülteci sorunu ve Türkiye. Seminer. Bilge Adamlar Stratejik Araştırmalar Merkezi (BİLGESAM). http://www.bilgesam.org/incele/2204/-seminer--multeci-sorunu-ve-turkiye/#.VyxxVYSyOkp available on: 06.05.2016.

Durkheim, E. (1964). *The division of labour in society*. New York, Free Press.

Ek R., Fougère M. & Per Skålén (2007) Revisiting Foucault through Reading Agamben: Implications for Workplace Subjectification, Desubjectification and the Dark Side of Organizations. Paper presented at the Fifth International Critical Management Studies Conference (the Open Stream) 11-13 July. Manchester.

Ellermann, A.(2009). Undocumented migrants and resistance in the state of exception. Presentation at the *European Union Studies Association Meeting*, April, Los Angeles, CA.

Erdoğan, M. M. (2015).Türkiye'de Suriyeliler, toplumsal kabul ve uyum: İstanbul: İstanbul Bilgi Üniversitesi Yayınları.

Foucault, M. (2010).*The birth of biopolitics: Lectures at the College de France 1978-1979*, Michael Senellart (ed.), Graham Burchell (trans.), New York: Palgrave Macmillan.

Foucault M. (2013). *Güvenlik, toprak, nüfus,* Ferhat Taylan (çev.), İstanbul. İstanbul Bilgi Üniversitesi Yayınları,

Furedi F. (2014). *Korku kültürü,* Barış Yıldırım (çev.), İstanbul: Ayrıntı Yayınları.

Hall, L. A. (2007). Death, power, and the body: A bio-political analysis of death and dying, Thesis submitted to the faculty of the Virginia Polytechnic Institute and State University. Master of Arts In Political Science, Blacksburg, VA.

Judge, R. (2010). Refugee advocacy and the biopolitics of asylum in Britain. The precarious position of young male asylum seekers and refugees. May. Working Paper Series 60. Refugee Studies Centre Oxford Department of International Development University of Oxford.

Kahya, Ö. (2014). *Türkiye'de sığınmacılık ve uydukent deneyimi. Küresel sorunlar ve çözüm arayışları.* Isparta: Süleyman Demirel Üniversitesi Sosyal Bilimler Dergisi, 4081-4114.

Kaiser B. & Kaya A., (2016). Chapter 1: Transformation and Europeanization of migration policy in Turkey: multiculturalism, republicanism and alignment. Introduction. In Turkish Migration Poliscy. (Eds.) İbrahim Sirkeci and Barbara Push. Migration Series. London: Transnational Press London.

Kirişçi, K. (2014). *Misafirliğin ötesine geçerken: Türkiye'nin "Suriyeli mülteciler" sınavı,* Booking Enstitüsü & Uluslararası Stratejik Araştırmalar Kurumu (USAK), Haziran, Ankara.

Lechte, J.(2008). Fifty key contemporary thinkers. From structuralism to post-humanism. Second Edition. London & New York: Routledge.

Meyer-Emerick, N.(2004). Biopolitics, dominance and critical theory. *Administrative Theory & Practice,* 26(1), 1-15.

Murtola, A. M. (2014). *Experience, commodification, biopolitics.* Critical Sociology. 40(6). 835-854. DOI: 10.1177/0896920513494230

Oksala, J. (2013). *Neoliberalism and biopolitical governmentality.* In Foucault, biopolitics and governmentality. Södertörn Philosophical Studies, (eds.) Jacob Nilsson and Sven-Olov Wallenstein. Stockholm: E-print.

Rabinow P. & Rose N. (2006). Biopower today. Biosocieties. London School of Economics and Political Science, 1, 195–217. Doi:10.1017/S1745855206040014

Sharp, L. A. (2000). *The commodification of the body and its parts.* Annual Review of Anthropology. 29. 297-328.

Sirkeci, I. (2017). Turkey's refugees, Syrians and refugees from Turkey: a country of insecurity. *Migration Letters,* 14(1): 127-144.

Wallenstein, S.O. (2013). *Introduction: The idea of biopolitics. In Foucault, biopolitics and governmentality.* Södertörn Philosophical Studies, (eds.) Jacob Nilsson and Sven-Olov Wallenstein. Stockholm: E-print.

Yazgan, P., Eroğlu-Utku, D., & Sirkeci İ. (2015). Syrian crisis and migration. *Migration Letters,* 12(3), 181-192.

Yıldız, Ö. (2013).Türkiye kamplarında Suriyeli sığınmacılar: Sorunlar, beklentiler, Türkiye ve gelecek algısı. *Sosyoloji Araştırmaları Dergisi,* Sosyoloji Derneği, 16(1), Bahar, 141-168.

Zembylas, M. (2008). *The politics of trauma in education.* New York: Palgrave Macmillan.

Zembylas, M. (2010). Agamben's theory of biopower and immigrants/refugees/assylum seekers: Discources of citizenship and the implications for curriculum theorizing". *Journal of Curriculum Theorizing,* 26(2), 31-45.

Chapter Three

Deserving Refugee or Undeserving Migrant? The Politics of the Refugee Category in Turkey

Funda Ustek Spilda*

Introduction

According to the most recent UNICEF Turkey Report, "In 2015, Turkey became the largest refugee-hosting country in the world with approximately 2.5 million Syrians living under a temporary protection regime (UNICEF, 2015, p. 2) [stress added]. The terminology used in this excerpt from the report shows the duality of the categories used for Syrians in Turkey, utilised not only by Turkey itself, but also international bodies. What is striking is that the term 'refugee' has come to be almost equivocally used for Syrians who fled the war and sought refuge in Turkey, and not so much for any other groups. However despite the widespread use of the term, Syrians are - legally-speaking- not refugees in Turkey, as will be demonstrated later in this chapter. Depending on how they are portrayed, it is possible that the labels used for Syrians range from typical "economic migrants" to "asylum seekers", from "guests" to those "over-stayed their welcome". In all of these categories, there are what Cornelius Castoriadis (1997) calls 'social imaginaries' attached to how Syrians as a group are situated and portrayed in Turkey. These different ways of referring to Syrians, however, are not just semantic differences. Neither are these definitional issues, which could be 'corrected' or 'solved' once a decision is made on which definition to use for administrative, management as well as humanitarian reasons. But these are

* Post-doctoral researcher on ARITHMUS: Peopling Europe: How data make a people, Department of Sociology, Goldsmiths, University of London, United Kingdom. E-mail: f.ustek-spilda@gold.ac.uk.

Acknowledgement: The research leading to this publication has received funding from the European Research Council under the European Union's Seventh Framework Programme (FP/2007-2013) / ERC Grant Agreement no. 615588. Principal Investigator, Evelyn Ruppert, Goldsmiths, University of London.

complex ontological issues that will pose an enormous amount of influence on the lives of refugees as well as how overall social and ethnic diversity is imagined and accounted for in the country. Against this background, I will look at how refugee categories are *made* in Turkey.

Politics of Refugee Categories

In June 2016, Müge Anlı, a TV presenter on a national channel in Turkey connected to a human trafficker on live TV (Diken, 2016). The fact that she provided a platform for a human trafficker on her show might have created a brief outcry but in fact this was just another example of how much refugees and traffickers have become normalised in Turkish TV and news. William Walters has referred to this situation as the "birth of the humanitarian border" (Walters, 2011). The humanitarian border is less concerned with military or political security concerns, and it rather situates refugees as victims to be rescued and cared for (Casas-Cortes et al., 2015, p. 68). This contrasts with the other portrayals of refugees in Turkey (as threats to security) which rest on state management and securitisation apparatuses. However, these seeming contradictions of the ways refugees are portrayed in Turkish news and TV in fact resonate with their contradictory situation vis-à-vis their official status.

Appearances of refugees have indeed become part of the daily routine in Turkish news and TV since 2012, with varying episodes of high or low visibility. As Nicholas De Genova highlighted, the border procedures often entail "the enactment of exclusion through their enforcement", and thus make some migration streams and bodies allowable, legal, while imprinting illegality on others (cited in Casas-Cortes et al., 2015, p. 67). Illegality might entail crossing international borders without paperwork, missing interviews for visa or asylum applications, not renewing visas and permits or not abiding by the rules specified in the permits (ibid). In attempting to understand how the lines are drawn between the legal and illegal categories of migration, the aim in this chapter is to go beyond simple dichotomies and instead look at the category of the "refugee" in Turkey as it constitutes a source of constant contestation.

That the main issue at hand is not there are refugees, but those trying to take their places wrongfully has added a new dimension to the debate over Syrians in Turkey over who deserves to be a "refugee" and who does not. The problem was framed in such a way that if the categories were set up to be able to distinguish those "deserving refugees" from "undeserving migrants", the so-called crisis would come to an end, and it would become a 'mere' distribution and management of a humanitarian issue. Such remarks calling for the need to toughen the criteria to be able to sift rightful claims from wrongful ones are neither unheard of, nor unprecedented (El-Enany, 2013), in fact they are highly publicised and taken up by populist discourses. This is why the image of the ashore body of Aylan Kurdi, the Syrian child who was drowned while trying to cross the Mediterranean, triggered an international sensation (for an extensive report, see Vis & Goriunova, 2015), but not the thousands of other images that circulated in international and national media preceding it. This is also why during the peak of the citizenship debates to Syrian refugees in Turkey in July 2016, those with higher education credentials or sought after occupations (e.g. medical doctors, teachers) were blatantly favoured, whereas others triggered a public outburst on their "un-deservingness" of Turkish citizenship (Sabah, 2016). Against this background, in this study, I propose to attend to the politics of the category of "refugee" in Turkey. I argue that category-making is a political practice and it builds upon several imaginaries, which themselves rest on various value-laden rationalisations. While there is already a hierarchical organisation of 'deservingness' between asylum seekers coming from European and non-European countries in the Turkish context due to the current legal system administering asylum applications, I argue that new invented labels such as 'guests' or "special temporary protection status" introduce new and even more distinct hierarchical differences between the *deserving* Syrians and other non-deserving non-European asylum seekers in the country. The aim of the study is not to provide a technical and legal comparison of various refugee definitions, but rather examine how these categories are taken up and enacted through various moments of official classification practices.

The empirical material for this paper comes from the European Research Council project called ARITHMUS (Peopling Europe: How data make a people), which investigates census practices across 5 countries (Estonia, Finland, the Netherlands, the UK and Turkey) and 2 supranational organisations (Eurostat and UNECE). ARITHMUS is a collaborative research project involving a team of post-doctoral and doctoral researchers[1]. It is concerned with the practical and political problem of assembling multiple national populations into a European population and people. By following working practices in five EU national statistical institutes and two international organisations, the ARITHMUS team is investigating how new

[1] ARITHMUS team members are Evelyn Ruppert (PI), Baki Cakici, Francisca Grommé, Stephan Scheel, Ville Takala and Funda Ustek-Spilda.

digital technologies and forms of data are stimulating methodological diversification and innovations in the classification and enumeration of populations; and the consequences this has for the constitution of who the European people are. The research materials used for this particular paper range from fieldwork observations with national statistical institutes, textual analysis of government documentation on migration statistics, and interviews with national and international bureaucrats working on migration issues in Turkey and the EU. Due to confidentiality reasons, the names of the specific organisations and persons are not disclosed in this paper[2].

Just Who Is A Refugee?

The multiplicity of asylum categories has been widely mentioned, but rarely constituted a source of separate inquiry. In comparison to the legal complexities around the allocation of refugee status, ever more tightly controlled border regimes (see Sales, 2002) and the highly labyrinthine international agreements on the resettlement and relocation of refugees, who ends up being categorised as "refugee" might even appear as a simple undertaking. This is not to say that categorisation is an avoidable exercise, nor it is futile. The criteria for allocating asylum categories, which labels are given to each category (e.g. applicant or seeker, economic or humanitarian) and their subsequent definitions, however, entail important political decisions with important implications. Hence, the lines drawn between different categories to refer to different groups or situations are not arbitrary, and deserve scholarly attention.

As Starr (1992) rightly notes, "Understanding official social classification requires an analysis that takes into account historical context, collective action, and political choice. Historical context is essential because we never start with a bare slate" (p. 264). A brief overview of Turkey's refugee policy demonstrates the importance of historical context to being granted the 'refugee status'. Two main legal frameworks (1934 Law on Settlement (2510) and 1951 Geneva Convention) set the framework for governing the flows of foreigners entering and seeking asylum in Turkey (İçduygu, 2015). The 1934 Law on Settlement was designed in a way to extend Turkish citizenship to the people of Turkish descent and culture living outside of the legal borders of the Republic of Turkey that were drawn in the aftermath of the 1st World War, Balkan Wars and the War of Independence. While the law has since been replaced with many newer legislations, the preference remained for

---

[2] Further details on the ARITHMUS project can be found at www.arithmus.eu

immigrants of "Turkish descent" or moral propinquity to Turkish "culture" (İçduygu, 2015, p. 4).

A continuation of this way of thinking can be observed also in Turkey's controversial position vis-à-vis the 1951 Geneva Convention and the subsequent 1967 New York Protocol. The Geneva Convention was signed in the aftermath of World War II and the main aim was to settle the refugees uprooted by the war in the countries of their preference. Accordingly, it had a clause geographically limiting the right to receive refugee status only to asylum seekers fleeing the "events from Europe" (Kirişci, 2014, p. 8). The 1967 Protocol eliminated this geographical limitation and expanded the right to seek asylum to anyone who needs protection as a result of fleeing from persecution or danger in her native country. Although Turkey signed both agreements, the geographical limitation of refugees from Europe was kept, as a result of which asylum seekers from anywhere but Europe could only be granted temporary protection in Turkey until they were resettled to a third country (Ibid). The geographical limitation was exercised to the extent that even when an asylum seeker's refugee status was recognised through the United Nations High Commissioner for Refugees (UNHCR) procedures, this status was not always recognised in Turkey (Icduygu 2015, p. 5).

Etienne Balibar has noted that, during moments of international crisis, responses inevitably tended to be acted out at a national level (cited in Dines, Montagna, & Ruggiero, 2015, p. 434). Amidst the so-called Syrian crisis, the first Syrian refugees began to enter into Turkey in April 2011. According to Kirişci (2014), the initial migrations took place at a time when the Turkish government still carried considerable goodwill with the regime in Damascus and had hopes for persuading Bashar al-Assad to avoid harsh measures against the protests that began in March 2011. By the end of the same year, however, the story became entirely different, the Turkish government recognised the then Syrian National Council as the representative of the Syrian people, calling for a future of Syria without Assad (ibid). Turkey's expectation, which arguably was also in similar lines with that of the international community in the Western world, was that the Assad regime would not last long (ibid). It was against such a background that Turkey declared an "open door policy" toward refugees fleeing Syria, and created for them a legal framework known as "temporary protection", promising no forced exits (İçduygu, 2015; Kirişci, 2014).

Although Turkey's open-door policy toward Syrian refugees has been considered to be welcoming, ambiguities regarding refugees' possibility to remain in the country and benefit from public services (e.g. education, employment, health, shelter) make this generosity uncertain. One such challenge was that initially Syrians were given a special status called the "guest status". This was an interim status, as they were not able to apply for asylum in Turkey and were also not expected to stay for long to necessitate longer-term arrangements. Although the guest status was subsequently retracted and replaced by the "Temporary Protection Regulation" in 2014, this interim arrangement (and its successive version) had two important implications. First, the guest status meant that refugees were left in a legal limbo with limited rights to access the labour market and the education system. The Temporary Protection Regulation, though opened the legal path to gainful employment and enrolment in the education system and provided important access to the health system, introduced important limitations to how and where these rights could be exercised. One such example is the rule that refugees could be relocated by the Turkish government without any legal process and could only access the health system in their allocated cities of residence (Akgündüz, Van den Berg, & Hassink, 2015, p. 4). Second, these interim arrangements meant that unlike other cases of asylum applications to UNHCR made within Turkey, Syrians were unable to make asylum applications in the same way, as technically speaking, they were provided with a place of residence where they could escape persecution.

It remains a political question why Turkey does not lift the geographical limitation of Geneva Convention, and allows applications to be made by asylum seekers coming from the country's eastern borders. This is especially an important question to bear in mind, when the different statuses Syrians have held in the country are considered, along with the recent debates on allocating citizenship to them. Turkish government's stance toward refugees and who has been given a refugee status since the foundation of the Turkish Republic give us important clues to also interpret the case of Syrians.

According to Starr (1992), official classifications pose two kinds of political choices for governments: first is that they decide what categories they will use or allow to be used, which she calls the problem of *legitimate classification* (p. 265). For the concerns of this paper, this entails that by adhering to the geographical limitation, the Turkish state indirectly ranks asylum applications, ranging from those *deserving* the refugee status (i.e. coming from Europe— legitimate claim) and those *undeserving* (i.e. not fitting the Turkish culture or ancestry and not coming from Europe). With the introduction of the 'guest status', or the temporary protection status, there has been another ranking among those asylum seekers coming from the

Eastern borders, Syrians – *deserving* and the rest – *undeserving* of any protection.

The second problem is of legitimate inference – that is, whether and how governments use classifications, and specifically statistical information based on this inference (Starr, 1992, p. 265). In Turkey, refugee statistics are not part of the official population statistics announced by the Turkish Statistical Institute, and are collected, administered and processed by the Directorate General of Migration Management (DGMM). A brief look at the migration statistics on the DGMM website indicates that it is possible to find information on migration numbers 'to the last digit', however how the data is collected, cleaned, analysed or produced is not provided.[3] The constant stress on the number of Syrians which is claimed to be "almost", "exactly" or "more than" 3 million in Turkey, but less attention paid to their composition (i.e. gender distribution, educational attainment or labour market skills) can be interpreted as the legitimacy of the inference being based on their numbers, rather than their claim on humanitarian protection.

One important point here is the asymmetric power relations in the registration of refugees and their subsequent assignment into different categories (Griffiths 2012). Usually done by 'street-level' bureaucrats and other intermediary agents, such as the border police or local staff, registration of asylum-seekers by migration management agencies does not only include registration of names and other basic demographic details, but also 'on-the-spot' assessments of eligibility for asylum applications, temporary protection and other benefits. While these bureaucrats might have different levels of authority in the final decisions, their involvement in the process is far from mere routinized and administrative work (Ibid). Melanie Griffiths (2012), on her work with the asylum seekers and refused refugees in the UK, stresses that refugees' claims are so mistrusted that the "'truth value' of UKBA [United Kingdom Border Agency] representatives is considered far greater than those subject to the asylum and detention systems, allowing the former to insist on particular versions of the 'truth'" (p. 12). Similarly, Nicholas de Genova (2013) argues that the criteria for granting asylum tend to be so stringent and predicated upon suspicion that, "what asylum regimes really produce is a mass of purportedly 'bogus' asylum seekers" (pp. 1180-1181). In the case of Turkey, truth claims particularly become an issue when there is a heightened likelihood for being granted temporary protection as a Syrian and not for other refugees coming from

---

[3] http://www.goc.gov.tr/icerik/migration-statistics_915_1024, Accessed on 10 Oct 2016.

Turkey's eastern borders. Not only those without official documents but also those with papers need to prove the authenticity of their claims to protection. As Griffiths notes, the issue at hand is not that asylum seekers do not 'lie' (as problematic as this expression is), but that they have to prove their claims, even when they may be uncertain about the details themselves (ibid). Interviews with international organisations reveal that it is difficult to access information about in-camp and outside-of-camp information on Syrians in Turkey; and it is difficult to independently verify the available information from local and governmental agencies. While it is difficult to make assertive claims such as Griffith's without extensive fieldwork on the matter, it is possible to extend her argument to the Turkish context that the truth values of those involved with the enumeration and registration of people and providing them the temporary protection status may not always be the same with those making the applications and the claims.

In addition, the asymmetric power relations exacerbate when higher level bureaucrats and governments also start categorising asylum seekers into 'unique' invented classifications, as in the case of Syrians. Given the historical pre-occupation with the imaginary of refugees only coming from Turkish ancestry or culture, the initial 'guest' category, and the subsequent special temporary protection status, might not be a surprising one. However, with constant stresses on Turkish culture being renowned for its hospitality and its welcoming of guests (see Efe, 2015 for an extensive account) the room to critically debate these policies have been limited. Moreover, even after the "guest status" was technically replaced by temporary protection, the labelling of Syrians as guests continued in media and government discourses (Haberler.com, 2016; Presidency of the Republic of Turkey, 2016) entailing an imaginary for Syrians that is different than past asylum applications made to the country. The category then enacts various liminalities between those with official documents and those *sans papier,* those deserving to be Turkey's *guests*, those deserving the refugee status, and those deserving none.

Scheel and Ratfisch have argued that such hierarchical ordering of refugees is an inevitable consequence of the refugee protection regime which is based on a binary distinction between forced (political) and voluntary (economic) migrants (Scheel and Ratfisch, 2013). They argue that the criminalising effect of this binary logic becomes particularly apparent in the refugee status determination procedures, which 'certify' some claimants into "genuine" refugees, and turn refused applicants into "illegal migrants" (cited in Casas-Cortes et al., 2015, pp. 71–72). Their point is a general criticism of the international refugee protection regime, and it can be argued that, with added categories to this dichotomy, the lines between 'genuine'/ 'deserving' refugees and others become ever more blurred in the case of Turkey.

Consequently, refugee categories are based on moral and political decisions/judgements, and these decisions are evaluated and exercised not only at the macro-level when there is a governmental decision to distinguish them from other applicants for protection, but also at the street-level bureaucracy, when the administrators who are involved in the registration of asylum seekers are given the authority to examine, accept or decline the self-assessments of asylum seekers. Hence, neither the 'guest' category nor the temporary protection provided to Syrians should be read as a mere exercise for 'labelling' Syrians differently so as to respond to their unique status in Turkey. These special statuses should also not be dismissed as a one-off arrangement in the midst of dealing with heightened numbers and unexpectedly long duration of political volatility in Syria. As Starr (1992) puts it, "[B]ureaucracy and law press toward formal definitions, but categories coded by prototypes are undoubtedly important in political thinking" (p.280). For the concerns of this paper, this political thinking differentiates Syrians who deserve a 'welcome' in Turkey, and non-guest non-Syrian asylum seekers from the Eastern borders who do not deserve such welcome.

Deserving Refugee vs. Undeserving Migrant

Turkey began keeping regular statistics on asylum only after the adoption of the 1994 Regulation (Kirişci, 2014, p. 8). The 1994 Regulation on the "Procedures and Principles related to Possible Population Movements and Aliens arriving in Turkey either as individuals or in groups wishing to seek asylum from Turkey or requesting residence permission in order to seek asylum from another country regulation no. 1994/6169" maintained the same geographic limitation on asylum, despite growing domestic and international criticisms on Turkey's uncompromising attitude (ibid). Subsequently, despite being the first detailed legal regulation regarding asylum seekers and refugees in Turkey, categorical ambiguities over who counts as a refugee in Turkey remained, as the Regulation did not clearly differentiate the "stocks vs. flows" of asylum seekers, nor those making individual claims vs. in groups (ibid).

When Syrians began to enter Turkey through the 'open door policy', the legal and administrative system were still laden with ambiguities. The administrative system of refugees were recently transferred from the Border Police in 2012 to the newly founded Directorate General of Migration

Management (DGMM). DGMM was given the authority of 'management' of migration to Turkey, but the migration categories and their individual needs would be settled as an ongoing process, given the changing categories.

However the system was already under strain dealing with the heightened number of applications over the years, and the influx of Syrian refugees further aggravated this strain. DGMM was established in such a context. The Turkish government issued a Temporary Protection (TP) Regulation in October 2014 which granted refugees with biometric identity cards (issued by DGMM), access to social benefits and services such as health, education and entry to the labour market. However, registration of Syrians who are not living in camps and have not resorted to public agencies for any public benefits has been a challenging undertaking. Thus, today there is a necessary line to be drawn between "economic migrant", "asylum seeker" and "person under temporary protection" all by the same agency; as well as between those with and without papers. This formalisation of separate identities, however as Casas-Cortes et al. (2015) put it, are plagued by ever greater incoherence (pp. 57-58).

As mentioned above, due to the Open Door Policy implemented by the Turkish government, the exact numbers of those who crossed the border were unknown in the beginning. The registration procedures were *a posteriori* implemented, with the refugees needing to register with the DGMM if they wished to benefit from social services. Currently, it is assumed that about 10 per cent of Syrians are residing in camps, and the rest are outside of camps but registered – so as to be able to access services[4]. However, this perspective makes two important assumptions. The first one is that Syrians living outside of camps would register. So far most technical and financial capacity has been devoted to establishing new institutions and issuing legal frameworks for the handling of Syrian refugees already in the country, and prevention measures for those willing to enter the country (İçduygu, 2015, p. 9) and there has been a time gap in implementing these laws and facing the sheer volume of refugees. Hence, at least some Syrians living outside of camps may not have registered, and their economic and social livelihoods are managed through informal practices (Milliyet, 2014; SGK, 2015). Although the assumption that these people living on informal

---

[4] Most recent UNHCR data could be found here http://data.unhcr.org/syrianrefugees/country.php?id=224. Last update on 16 February 2017 states the number of Syrians in Turkey to be 2,910, 281. The data notes that as of 6 March 2015, there has not been any new registration appointments by Syrians in Turkey.

arrangements should have registered by now with the Turkish authorities is a plausible one, it nevertheless would require further data.

The second one is that although there has been a significant fall in the numbers of Syrians attempting to enter Europe either by sea or land routes and make their asylum applications there since the EU-Turkey Action Plan (European Commission, 2015), it is nevertheless plausible to assume that there are still Syrians residing in Turkey who are refraining from being registered with the authorities so as to be able to make asylum applications in European countries (see Spijkerboer, 2016 for the effectiveness of EU-Turkey Action Plan). In any case, it is important to underscore that refugee data in Turkey relies on important assumptions, approximations and generalisations.

The registration of Syrian migrants in official statistics through DGMM has important implications for the future projections of population in Turkey, and its ethnic and social diversity. However, in which category they will be counted and whether after a certain point they will be granted citizenship status still remain unclear. Currently the number of Syrian refugees is based on estimations and there seems to be a large gap between registered and estimated number of refugees, and this is often reflected in the numbers presented by international organisations and Turkey's own figures. In the Supporting Syria Conference held in London, on 4 February 2016, these numbers ranged from 2 to 3 million[5], indicating the enormity of the uncertainty of numbers, keeping in mind that the refugee numbers reflect the aims and aspirations of those who state them (Bakewell, 1999).[6] It is also important to reiterate that these numbers largely reflect the number of Syrians in Turkey – despite the fact that they do not legally hold the Convention refugee status.

Here, it is important to re-iterate how the current temporary protection provided to Syrians is different than the "convention refugee status" as it is indicated in the Geneva Convention. The convention refugee status is a legal status recognised by all UN member states that are a party to the 1951 Geneva Convention. It provides long term security for those whose asylum

---

[5] A brief look into the tweets sent by Turkish delegates and international parties that attended the meeting would indicate the big difference and confusion about the actual number and details of Syrians in Turkey.
[6] https://www.supportingsyria2016.com/about/, the official website for the Supporting Syria Conference, includes important information about the funding pledges made during the conference and outcomes.

applications have been accepted, and it is a legal binding agreement, rather than an act of benevolence: such as the past "guest status" given to Syrians or the current temporary protection arrangements. The temporary protection for Syrians rules that they would not be registered by UNHCR and their applications would not be processed for refugee status determination.[7] This means that opportunities for access to social services for Syrians will be limited in comparison to those with the convention refugee status, and also they have limited, if any, opportunities for applying asylum elsewhere than Turkey (see Ekmekci, 2016, for access to health services of Syrians in Turkey). The current situation regarding the access to education and labour market of Syrians and their children further resonate Ekmekci's point that temporary protection provides only limited solutions to the current situation of Syrians.

To elaborate on this further, the different situation of Syrians in comparison to other non-EU persons applying for humanitarian protection and those eligible to make applications for Convention Refugee Status through 1951 Geneva Convention can be considered. Kirişci (2014) notes until very recently, Turkey has been a transit country for refugees, rather than a host country. As mentioned earlier, the 1934 Law on Settlement (2510) was designed in a way to extent citizenship to the people of Turkish descent and culture. While this principle allowed room for interpretation of asylum claims, it also assumed that less number of refugee claims would be made from Turkey's European borders than its borders in the east where subsequent periods of political turmoil have taken place (Tarımcı, 2005). This cultural propinquity v. security approach in fact had already been creating several hierarchies in Turkey's approach to those seeking humanitarian protection. What has been introduced with the separate status provided to Syrians is that, now there is a further level of hierarchical differentiation of categories among those coming from Turkey's eastern borders as well.

Conclusion

This chapter into the making of refugee categories used for production of refugee numbers in Turkey highlighted the inherent politics in these categories. While refugees in general are considered a "deserving" group of migrants, their deservingness is also further established within and through the categories. There is a clear ambiguity about the categories of Syrians in Turkey. They are referred to as 'refugees', 'guests', 'under temporary protection' depending on the circumstances and reasons for referring to

---

[7] UNHCR processes only a small number of cases in Turkey (see the report by Aida: Asylum Information Database, 2015).

them. This categorical confusion, however, is not simply a semantic one, and has important consequences for the livelihoods of Syrians and others seeking humanitarian protection in the country. With no rights to claim refugee status, given that Turkey has not lifted the geographical limitation clause of the 1951 Geneva Convention, despite being party to the subsequent 1967 New York Protocol, the ambiguous categories push them into precarious livelihoods.

The large numbers of displaced Syrians to cross the border into Turkey were clearly not expected; equally unexpected were the numbers who would live outside the camps, owing to the fact that initially only Syrians with valid travel documents (i.e. passports) were allowed to move outside camps and apply for residence permits. Family ties and financial independence enabled some refugees to make their way outside of camps, and Syrians whose entry is considered illegal (often owing to their criminal record in their native country) slowly moved away from the registered zones to invisible livelihoods in bigger cities.

The urgency of hosting a large displaced population might not have allowed room to come up with structured responses to deal with the situation, given that there were also significant administrative and structural changes taking place – such as the founding of Directorate General for Migration Management, to govern all migration-related matters. However, the separate statuses given to Syrians ended up creating ever more divisions among asylum seekers (entering Turkey from its Eastern borders), adding to the already clear division between those coming from Europe and those coming from the Eastern Borders (an outcome of the geographical limitation clause of the 1951 Geneva Convention).

REFERENCES

Aida: Asylum Information database. (2015). *2011-2014: Temporary protection based on political discretion and improvisation - Turkey*. Refugee Rights Turkey. Retrieved from http://www.asylumineurope.org/reports/country/turkey/2011-2014-temporary-protection-based-political-discretion-and-improvisation. Accessed 01 March 2017.

Akgündüz, Y., Van den Berg, M., & Hassink, W. H. (2015). The Impact of Refugee Crises on Host Labor Markets: The Case of the Syrian Refugee Crisis in Turkey. Retrieved from http://papers.ssrn.com/sol3/Papers.cfm?abstract_id=2564974. Accessed 01 March 2017.

Bakewell, O. (1999). Can we ever rely on refugee statistics? *Radical Statistics, 72*, 3–15.

Ustek Spilda

Balibar, E. (2013). On the politics of human rights. *Constellations*, *20*(1), 18-26.

Casas-Cortes, M., Cobarrubias, S., Genova, N. D., Garelli, G., Grappi, G., Heller, C., Tazzioli, M. (2015). New Keywords: Migration and Borders. *Cultural Studies*, *29*(1), 55–87.

Castoriadis, C. (1997). *The imaginary institution of society*. Cambridge, M.A.: MIT Press.

de Genova, N. P. (2013). Spectacles of migrant "illegality": the scene of exclusion, the obscene of inclusion. *Ethnic and Racial Studies*, *36*(7), 1180–1198.

Diken. (2016, June 3). Bu da oldu: İnsan kaçakçısı canlı yayında alkışlatıldı [Eng. trans. This happened: A human trafficker was applauded on air". *Diken*. Istanbul. Retrieved from http://www.diken.com.tr/bu-da-oldu-insan-kacakcisi-canli-yayinda-alkislatildi. Accessed on 01 March 2017.

Dines, N., Montagna, N., & Ruggiero, V. (2015). Thinking Lampedusa: border construction, the spectacle of bare life and the productivity of migrants. *Ethnic and Racial Studies*, *38*(3), 430–445.

Efe, I. (2015). *Türk Basınında Suriyeli Sığınmacılar [Eng. trans. Syrian Refugees in Turkish Media]* (No. 57). Istanbul: SETA: Siyaset, Ekonomi ve Toplum Araştırmaları Vakfı [SETA: Foundation for Political, Economic and Social Research].

Ekmekci, P. E. (2016). Syrian Refugees, Health and Migration Legislation in Turkey. *Journal of Immigrant and Minority Health*, 1–8.

El-Enany, N. (2013). EU Asylum, Immigration and Border Control Regimes: Including and excluding the Deserving Migrant, The. *Eur. J. Soc. Sec.*, *15*, 171.

European Commission. (2015, October 15). European Commission - Press release - EU-Turkey joint action plan. Retrieved January 29, 2017, from http://europa. eu/rapid/press-release_MEMO-15-5860_en.htm. Accessed 01 March 2017.

Griffiths, M. (2012). "Vile liars and truth distorters"; Truth, trust and the asylum system. *Anthropology Today*, *28*(5), 8–12.

Haberler.com. (2016, January 15). Bakan Bozkir: "Türkiye AB"den Suriyeli Misafirlerimiz İçin Herhangi Bir Para Talebinde bulunmamıştır" ("MP Bozkir: 'Turkey has not made any requests for funds from the EU for our Syrian guests". Retrieved March 7, 2017, from http://www.haberler.com/bakan-bozkir-turkiye-ab-den-suriyeli-8066862-haberi/?utm_source=facebook&utm_campaign= tavsiye_et&utm_medium=detay. Accessed 01 March 2017.

İçduygu, A. (2015). Syrian refugees in Turkey. Retrieved from http://labs. ozyegin.edu.tr/ozumigs/files/2015/05/TCM-Protection-Syria.compressed.pdf. Accessed 01 March 2017.

Kirişci, K. (2014). *Syrian Refugees and Turkey's Challenges: Beyond the Limits of Hospitality*. Brookings. Retrieved from http://www.alnap.org/pool/files/syrian-refugees-and-turkeys-challenges-kkirisci-may-12-2014.pdf. Accessed 01 March 2017.

Milliyet. (2014, September 29). Suriyeliler bu illerde kiralık bırakmadı! http://www.milliyet.com.tr/suriyeliler-bu-illerde-kiralik-konut-1947505/. Accessed 01 March 2017.

Presidency of the Republic of Turkey. (2016, July 2). "Suriyeli Kardeşlerimize Vatandaşlık İmkânı Vereceğiz" ("We will provide opportunities for citizenship to our Syrian brothers" Author's own translation). http://www.tccb.gov.tr/ haberler/410/45574/suriyeli-kardeslerimize-vatandaslik-imkni-verecegiz.html Accessed on 01 March 2017.

Sabah. (2016, July 9). Kaç Suriyeli vatandaşlık alacak? ("How many Syrians will receive citizenship?" Author's own translation). *Sabah*. İstanbul. Retrieved from http://www.sabah.com.tr/gundem/2016/07/09/kac-suriyeli-vatandaslik-alacak-iste-detaylar. Accessed on 01 March 2017.

Sales, R. (2002). The deserving and the undeserving? Refugees, asylum seekers and welfare in Britain. *Critical Social Policy*, *22*(3), 456–478.

Scheel, S., & Ratfisch, P. (2013). Refugee Protection Meets Migration Management: UNHCR as a Global Police of Populations. *Journal of Ethnic and Migration Studies*, 1–18.

SGK. (2015, September 1). Kayıtdışı İstihdam Patladı. ("Informal Employment Boomed" Author's own translation). http://www.sgk.com.tr/1812-Haber1-kayit-disi-istihdam-patladi.html. Accessed on 01 March 2017.

Spijkerboer, T. (2016, September 28). Fact Check: Did the EU-Turkey Deal Bring Down the Number of Migrants and of Border Deaths? *Oxford Law Faculty*. Academic post. https://www.law.ox.ac.uk/research-subject-groups/centre-criminology/centreborder-criminologies/blog/2016/09/fact-check-did-eu. Accessed on 01 March 2017.

Starr, P. (1992). Social Categories and Claims in the Liberal State. *Social Research*, *59*(2), 263–295.

Tarımcı, A. (2005). The role of geographical limitation with respect to asylum and refugee policies within the context of Turkey's EU harmonization process (Master's Thesis). Middle East Technical University. https://etd.lib.metu.edu.tr/ upload/3/12606825/index.pdf. Accessed on 01 March 2017.

UNICEF. (2015). UNICEF Annual Report 2015 - Turkey. Paris: UNICEF.

Vis, F., & Goriunova, O. (2015). *The Iconic Image on Social Media: A Rapid Research Response to the Death of Aylan Kurdi* (Visual Social Media Lab No. This report is part of the "Picturing the Social: Transforming our Understanding of Images in Social Media and Big Data Research" project, funded by the Economic and Social Research Council (ESRC). Grant reference: ES/M000648/1).

Walters, W. (2011). Foucault and frontiers: notes on the birth of the humanitarian border. *Governmentality: Current Issues and Future Challenges*, 138–164.

Ustek Spilda

PART 2

CASE STUDIES

Chapter Four

Civil Society and Syrian Refugees in Turkey: a Human Security Perspective

Helen Macreath[±], M. Utku Güngör[¥], S. Gülfer Sağnıç[μ]

Introduction

Turkey adopted an open door policy soon after the arrival of the first Syrian refugees in spring 2011, which made it easy for them to enter the country. But having fled threats of violence and persecution in their own country, Syrians were quickly faced with new security threats in their host countries, with basic humanitarian needs such as food, shelter, healthcare services, and education being major issues. Despite the establishment of camps by the Turkish government, which numbered 26 by 2016 (Pinna, 2016), which provide multiple services, an estimated 90 percent of the Syrian population are living outside these for various reasons (Erdoğan and Ünver 2015: 22). It is international and local non-governmental organisations (NGOs), and civic initiatives who are trying to respond to the needs of these non-camp refugees, filling the vacuum left by the government in the process. The role of civil society actors is critical in the manner in which refugees are hosted, and accepted, at local levels, which in turn may impact the national and international response to protracted refugee situations. Far too often refugee assistance is approached and examined in a top-down manner that renders the agency of civil society invisible. Clearly the legal framework of refugee policy making, organization of large humanitarian assistance, and lobbying for funding from the donor community is conducted at national and

± Researcher at Citizens' Assembly, Istanbul, Turkey. Email: hmackreath@gmail.com.
¥ Researcher and director at Citizens' Assembly, M.A. student at Bogazici University, Istanbul, Turkey. Email: utku@hyd.org.tr.
μ Researcher at Citizens' Assembly and M.A. student at the Bogazici University, Istanbul, Turkey. Email: gssagnic@gmail.com.
Acknowledgement: We are sincerely thankful to Citizens' Assembly (Ca) for providing us with the opportunity to conduct this research and to the Turkish-Swedish Development Cooperation Grant for funding it.

international levels. However the enactment of small-scale humanitarian assistance and local social initiatives depends on the interactions of civil society with refugees. How civil society actors respond to, assist in some cases, and in other cases contest, the presence of refugees within their society are important factors for the ability of refugees to secure assistance and reach a dignified standard of living. This chapter asks the question "What is the role of civil society in terms of providing human security to Syrian refugees in Turkey?"

This chapter examines the impact of civil society organizations' assistance to Syrians in terms of how closely it is aligned down principles of human security. A human security perspective provides a useful frame through which to analyze the response of civil society, and the extent to which the changes and reconfigurations it has undergone in direct or indirect response to Syrians have impacted on its provision of assistance to Syrians. The research contained within the chapter is part of a broader project[1], which covers different aspects of civil society and Syrian refugees in Turkey, including relationships between the state and civil society; relations between different segments of civil society; changes in civil society; and the potential impacts of civil society assistance on future inclusion of Syrians in Turkey. The subsequent sections will explain the methods used in this research, followed by a brief discussion of the concepts of civil society in the theoretical framework, and an elaboration of the principles of human security and the framework employed throughout the chapter. The third section will focus on the activities of civil society towards Syrians, and discuss these within the context of human security.

The Context of Insecurities

Legal ambiguities over the status of Syrians in Turkey have increased their insecurities and the role of civil actors. Syrians are typically referred to as "guests" by Turkish media and government officials. The Turkish geographical limitation on the refugee definition of the 1951 United Nations Convention and its 1967 Protocol, prevents their application to acquire the status of refugee. As part of Turkey's renewal of its legislation under the framework of the ongoing EU accession process, asylum and migration laws and regulations have also been updated. The Law on Foreigners and International Protection (*Yabancılar ve Uluslararası Koruma Kanunu*) was issued in April 2013 and came into force in 2014. This law created a new,

---

[1] "Civil Society and Syrian Refugees in Turkey", Helen Mackreath and Şevin Gülfer Sağnıç, Citizens' Assembly, 2017.

unique, status – that of temporary protection - and Syrians were specified as coming under this status with the 2014 Regulation on Temporary Protection, (LFIP, 2014, art.91).

Until recently, all Syrians were eligible for such "temporary protection" in Turkey on prima facie basis, which means that any Syrian nationals seeking international protection are already admitted to Turkish territory and would not be sent back to Syria against their will (Relief Web, 2013). However, dealing with the presence of Syrians is occurring in an increasingly complex political environment, both domestically and internationally. The question of Syrians' long-term presence is also extremely sensitive, with disagreement about whether to aim for 'integration' – which is by some actors perceived negatively as 'assimilation' – or 'harmonization', which is the preferred term of the Directorate General of Migration Management (DGMM). 'Harmonization' here means a form of integration, where the migrant group can keep its cultural identity but live in 'harmony' with the host society (Hoffman & Samuk, 2016). The government had signaled mixed messages over its intention to grant Syrians living in Turkey citizenship, with President Erdogan's initial announcement on the issue in July 2016 being followed by government officials making public statements about their intention to offer citizenship only to certain groups of Syrians (BBC, 2016). This plan created discomfort in different segments of society. In the period of authority vacuum after the failed coup attempt on 15 July 2016 Syrians have faced increasing insecurities, ranging from being directly targeted in post-coup violence (Cupolo, 22 July 2016), to refugee support systems being weakened by post-coup purges.

Methodology

Two strands of research were used in this study – primary and secondary data. Desk based research was conducted as a means to select interview subjects, to provide background context on how Syrian refugees have been previously dealt with in Turkey, and as evidence of which strategies CSOs are employing to assist them. Within this data set was included journalistic accounts, INGO and CSO reports, and policy reports written by both international and domestic think-tanks.

The primary research was conducted through a mix of interviews and focus groups. Interview subjects were found through a combination of desk based research and snowball sampling. Many CSOs were accessed via journalist reports documenting their work. Another important source of information for CSOs and informal volunteer groups was social media, particularly

Facebook, where many of these groups coordinate and connect with each other. Facebook groups such as 'Volunteer in Istanbul' and 'Syrian Refugee Helpers in Istanbul' are frequently used means by which individuals wishing to volunteer with Syrian refugees find information about opportunities. The method of snowball sampling was also used, particularly among more informal and smaller groups of volunteers, who did not have a large online presence and could only be accessed through word of mouth.

The research was conducted in five cities - Istanbul, Ankara, Izmir, Şanlıurfa, and Gaziantep - and 77 actors participated in total, including government officials. Interviews were semi-structured and face-to-face based on open-ended questions. Interviews were largely conducted in the offices of participants or in locations arranged by interviewees – this also allowed for ethnographic observations of human interaction in the context of the specific social setting. The nature of open-ended questioning allowed the interviewees to bring up topics which they believed to be relevant, and the interview focus to more thoroughly engage in the particularity of the subject. It therefore produced a more incisive and rich data set than could be gained from rigid interview structures. Focus groups were held in four locations – in Istanbul, Ankara, Izmir and Gaziantep – with 12-15 participants attending each and 44 participants in total including a mix of academics and CSO workers. The focus groups were broadly structured around the questions of the moderator and themes devised by the researchers, and the conversations were fluid. Focus groups were also useful to observe and analyze the interaction between participants with different agendas and different experiences, a critical part of the research, and to understand why a particular issue is salient. Our analysis, methods, and data were discussed in an international round-table meeting, held in June 2016, and we benefited from the feedback provided here. As part of our research we also participated in conferences, workshops and meetings organized by CSOs, INGOs, or state institutions in order to observe interactions between the actors, and compare their agendas[2]. We also used questionnaires - 15 in total

---

[2] Including Conference on Work Permits for Foreigners Under Temporary Protection in Turkey (Participant observation and Questionnaires), Ministry of Labor and Social Security, UNHCR and IMPR Humanitarian March 2016; The Situation of Syrians in Turkey: from Temporariness to Permanence, GAR (Migration Researchers' Platform) April 2016; Workshop on the Identification of the Areas for the Empowerment of the Syrian Youth and Children, UNICEF and GAP (Southeastern Anatolia Project Regional Development Administration) May 2016; ICRC Conference 'International Society and Refugees: Responsibilities, Opportunities and Violations of Human Rights', May 2016; World Humanitarian Summit, May 2016.

- to reach a wider sample, including CSOs from different cities, to understand whether it's possible to generalize our findings.

Data analysis was conducted using a combination of the three forms of content analysis outlined by Hsieh and Shannon (2005, p.1277) - conventional (in which "coding categories are derived directly from the text data"), directed (in which "analysis starts with a theory or relevant research findings as guidance for initial codes"), and summative content analysis (which "involves counting and comparisons, usually of keywords or content, followed by the interpretation of the underlying context"). A set of directed codes were devised prior to data analysis, and these were supplemented with conventional codes that emerged from the text. During the coding process these codes then evolved into a mix of 'Categories' and 'Codes'. Due to the length of transcripts a form of simultaneous coding was used – this applies two or more codes within a single datum (Saldana, 2008). Simultaneous coding therefore allowed us a more nuanced and in-depth analysis of the data.

There are a number of methodological limits as a result of the immediacy of the research. Firstly the situation is constantly changing, which means that the data produced will inevitably be quickly outdated. It also leads to an absence of precise information about numbers of individuals involved. Finally, some of the participants may have suffered from research fatigue as a result of a number of similar oriented pieces of research being carried out.

Literature Review

According to former High Commissioner of Refugees, Sadako Ogata, "[R]efugees and internally displaced people are a significant symptom of human insecurity crises" (Ogata, 1999). As such, it is increasingly relevant to discuss the human security of Syrian refugees within Turkey. Since they are not citizens of their host country, refugees are deprived of a series of rights, which renders them precarious politically and economically. Citizens' Assembly-Turkey's (Ca) (formerly Helsinki Citizens' Assembly) report on human security in Turkey indicates that problems associated with Syrians are the primary issues of human security in the country (Akay, 2015). Under these circumstances, the response of the civil society sector towards the refugee flow has a direct effect both on enabling conditions of human security for refugees, and for the host community.

In order to operationalize research on civil society sector, human security, and refugees, these ambiguous concepts must be clearly defined. Since the scope of this paper is too narrow to fully accomplish such an attempt, we will briefly summarize how we defined these concepts for the purpose of this study as well as the terms 'service' and 'aid provision' which are used frequently throughout. According to the 2006 World Bank report, civil society is the "arena of un-coerced collective action around shared interests, purposes and values" (World Bank, 2006). For the purpose of this research, we define civil society as all non-state actors working with Syrian refugees. These include non-state groups operating along various political ideological lines, rights-based associations, humanitarian service providers, faith-based associations, foundations, labor unions, solidarity groups, volunteer initiatives, Syrian initiatives, expat collectives, and individuals. We acknowledge that these groups do not constitute the entirety of what might be considered to be civil society, and which might include groups such as associations (particularly Bar Associations and Teachers Associations), foundations, trade unions, chambers, cooperatives and federations and confederations. Throughout this report we use the term Civil Society Organizations (CSOs) to indicate all formal and informal groups which we have interviewed. These may refer to non-governmental organizations (NGOs), but they also include groups, such as solidarity groups, volunteer collectives, activist groups and religious groups, which do not necessarily identify as NGOs. By 'service' and 'aid provision' we mean material help – such as food, clothes, or coal - and the provision of assistance to overcome daily life problems. 'Right-based' activities terms, on the other hand, are employed to explain activities that aim to impact policy-making processes and policy-makers. Throughout our research it became apparent that many actors conduct these activities concomitantly and sometimes is very hard to classify an activity as service provision or right-based, and they should therefore not be taken as mutually exclusive.

In the context of Turkey, civil society initiatives have, in general, increased quantitatively. Keeping in mind that number of CSOs is only one of many quantitative indicator s of civil society activity official reports in 2011 indicate that in the previous decade there had been a 44 percent increase in the number of CSOs in Turkey. Such developments are explained as a result of the improved ease in founding a CSO and an increase in public awareness. However, it is debatable whether this increase constitutes wider civil intervention in the political decision making procedures. Although the 1999 earthquake was a peak point for the civil society sector in Turkey (Jalali, 2002), until the recent refugee flow there had been no evidence regarding a significant increase in the capacity of CSOs. It is possible to conclude that there is neither an absence nor presence of a civil society in Turkey, but only some of its characteristics. The civil society sector in Turkey is highly populated by ideology-based organizations, rather than issue based ones – such as Kemalism, a modern Turkey, a secular-democratic Turkey or Islamic order, a socialist Turkey. Moreover, many civil society actors in Turkey are ideologically in conformity with the state, which has strong authoritarian tendencies. These conditions make the establishment of a civil society sector separate from the state more complicated.

Human security as a concept and a set of aims for policy making was proposed and promoted by the United Nations (UN), first mentioned by the United Nations Development Program (UNDP) in Human Development Report of 1994. It was proposed as a cure to the shortcomings of conventional understandings of security, typically understood as border security, military security, and state security. Although there are separate derivations of human security in distinct policy making processes, human security is taken here as more of a developmental perspective: economic security, food security, health security, personal security, community security, and political security. The Commission for Human Security (CHS) was formed in 2000 to prepare a comprehensive report on human security. This report discussed the main pillars of human security to be used as a handbook for policy makers and advocacy. They framed human security as shown in Table 1.

Human security is **people-centered** because it defines the needs of security collectively for the community itself. The conventional state security paradigm defines the unit of analysis and counter-measures in accordance with the needs of states, thus ignoring the safety and security of individuals. Rather than focusing on overall threats merely to states, human security proposes the interdependence between human security of individuals and state security, prioritizing the former (Human Security Unit, 2009: 6). Human security is **multi-sectoral** because without interdependence among sectors in policy making processes negative and positive externalities may cause grievances (Ibid). Multi-sectorality is also related to the **comprehensive** characteristic of the concept (Human Security Unit, 2009: 7). Insecurities in separate areas of life are subjects of human security. However, comprehensiveness does not prevent the **context-specific** method of analyzing insecurities (Ibid). Human security perspective takes into account a community's needs, grievances, and capacities. Additionally policy making processes and civil actors designate measures against insecurities at local, national, regional and global level.

Table 1. Human Security Principles (Human Security Unit, 2003)

People-centered	<ul><li>Inclusive and participatory.</li><li>Considers individuals and communities in defining their needs/vulnerabilities and in acting as active agents of change.</li><li>Collectively determines which insecurities to address and identifies the available resources including local assets and indigenous coping</li><li>Mechanisms</li></ul>
Multi-sectoral	<ul><li>Addresses multi-sectorality by promoting dialogue among key actors from different sectors/fields.</li><li>Helps to ensure coherence and coordination across traditionally separate sectors/fields.</li><li>Assesses positive and negative externalities of each response on the overall human security situation of the affected community(ies).</li></ul>
Comprehensive	<ul><li>Holistic analysis: the seven security components of human security.</li><li>Addresses the wide spectrum of threats, vulnerabilities and capacities.</li><li>Analysis of actors and sectors not previously considered relevant to the success of a policy/programmme/project.</li><li>Develop multi-sectoral/multi-actor responses.</li></ul>
Context-specific	<ul><li>Requires in-depth analysis of the targeted situation.</li><li>Focuses on a core set of freedoms and rights under threat in a given situation.</li><li>Identifies the concrete needs of the affected community(ies) and enables the development of more appropriate solutions that are embedded in local realities, capacities and coping mechanisms.</li><li>Takes into account local, national, regional and global dimensions and their impact on the targeted situation.</li></ul>
Prevention-Oriented	<ul><li>Identifies risks, threats and hazards, and addresses their root causes.</li><li>Focuses on preventative responses through a protection and empowerment framework.</li></ul>

Finally, **prevention-oriented** approach is central to human security. Potential insecurities are attempted to be prevented by identifying risks and threats, and specifically addressing the root causes (Ibid). The above-listed characteristics of human security helps to develop more inclusive security policies whose focus is well-being of the individuals and the communities, in general.

A human security criteria provides a useful frame through which to analyze the response of civil society, and the extent to which the changes and reconfigurations it has undergone in direct or indirect response to Syrians have impacted on its provision of assistance to Syrians. Such an ambition for securing the rights of Syrians and their hosts can only be achieved through the coalition between civil society, and the embedded institutions of the state and local authorities – the extent to which this is being realized will also be analyzed briefly here.

Activities of Civil Society Organizations

The CSO response to Syrians in Turkey has been multi-faceted. In responding to the large scale presence of Syrians in the country, the highly fragmented and complex CSO sector in Turkey has both operated along existing trends, whilst also responding in ways which highlight changes in capacity and relations amongst CSOs and between CSOs and the state. The response to Syrians cannot be understood outside the context of the existing domestic socio-political situation in Turkey – this is also true for the civil society sector. Syrians are becoming absorbed into existing struggles within the country, and the ways in which they are being assisted also reflects these struggles. Broadly, the government is taking a very active charity-oriented approach to Syrians – mainly concentrated in the camps, but also through their policies towards refugees; Islamic CSOs, as with the Turkish government, are following the line of Islamic fraternity between the "*ansar* and *muhajir*"[3] as mentioned in the Quran. In contrast, blurred lines between rights-based and needs-based provision and organizational and community-based protection has permeated other, largely secular, CSOS working on the issue. This lack of clarity is particularly prevalent between the many CSOs who had previously had poor relations with each other owing to operational or ideological differences. There are also issues with visibility and coordination of CSOs, with a general lack of information about what roles CSOs are performing – a

---

[3] The word 'ansar' (Arabic الأنصار), or 'the helpers', refers to the local inhabitants of Medina who took the Islamic Prophet Muhammad and his followers (the Muhajirun) into their homes when they escaped from Mecca (hijra).

government official said he *"assumed CSOs were doing a good job because the government is not active outside camps [therefore it is only CSOs working with refugees]"* (Güneş, 2016). Many, particularly Islamic-based organizations, cite the 'invisibility' of the CSO sector in Turkey, caused by humility, as a reason for lack of knowledge of their work and suggest there needs to be greater pride in advertising themselves. There are also differences in opinion in the terms of how successful civil society has been in responding to Syrians, and particularly the role that it should be fulfilling.

Many of the CSOs which have been founded since the influx of Syrians are focusing on social services. In our research 49 CSOs in a sample of 65 institutions were established after 2011 and 40 of them are conducting aid and service provision activities, while some of them are combining these activities with right-based activities. This is also the target area for existing CSOs who have shifted or expanded their operational focus in response to Syrians being in the country, and for the number of Syrian civic initiatives that have been set up (see below for a more detailed discussion). Our research showed that social services provided by CSOs include language classes, psycho-social counselling, information sharing about access to services, women's groups, information about how to find employment and legal aid. From our research, a sizeable number of CSOs, such as Izmir Müzik Derneği (IMD), Anadolu Platform and Minber Sam in Gaziantep, Ad.Dar and Hamiş cultural centers in Istanbul, are focused on cultural and art projects, which have the dual purpose of being a form of psycho-social relief for Syrians, as well as a platform for mutual cultural exchange and creative production between Syrians and Turkish individuals. There are a range of civil society groups which are operational in direct response to Syrians – these include solidarity groups which used to be focused on other issues but shifted to include Syrians; individual volunteers working in small groups or through online based platforms; and small community centers, which have been set up by volunteer individuals or are offshoots of more established CSOs. Solidarity groups do not make up a significant proportion of those CSOs assisting Syrians in our sample but nevertheless represent a notable trend; they are largely reactive in the manner in which they respond to Syrians. They are often more embedded within the localized geographical area in which they are working.

A people-centered response is inclusive and participatory, it considers individuals and communities in defining their needs and vulnerabilities, and in acting as active agents of change, meaning that their own coping mechanisms are identified and enhanced. If a people-centered response to refugees is to be fully inclusive, it should also question which 'people' are being defined as vulnerable – this is not necessarily restricted to refugees, but other members of host communities, whose own vulnerabilities are exacerbated by the presence of refugees. In general, across Turkey, a lack of coordination between different CSOs, or awareness about the existence of CSOs, is creating gaps in information for refugees about what services are available and where to access them. This is impinging upon refugees' self-securing mechanisms, and increasing their level of general insecurity.

Many of the volunteers who are helping Syrians choose basic service assistance as the easiest and most direct way to engage with Syrians, and because they perceive there to be a gap in this provision. Many of these volunteer groups connect via social media, particularly on Facebook where there is a plethora of groups designed to coordinate volunteer activities. Despite the protracted nature of the Syrian presence, their assistance is still taking the form of an emergency situation, being reactive and fragmented in scope, with few resources and no long term sustainability. As a result of this character, it does not provide recipients with the stability of regulated and regular provision.

The extent to which community centers and volunteer groups are operating along people-centered lines is ambiguous – this is often a result of practical obstacles, and inexperience of the individuals who found them rather than active decisions. In some cases aid is irregular and not specific to direct contexts. For instance, one recently founded community centre provided language classes for female refugees, but no space for their children to play, resulting in many young mothers opting to stay at home with their children rather than leaving their children behind. Another community centre, which was set up explicitly to provide assistance specific to the context of Syrian women's lives, had one half of its space inoperable after receiving a large amount of donated clothes which were unwanted by Syrian women. The activities provided by some of these centers may not be in the best interests of the people they are trying to help – one volunteer teaches Syrian women how to make earrings to be sold in America. But, as another volunteer at a different community centre criticized, this does not equip the women with the tools of how to market themselves or set up their own business. It also may not address the specific concerns or desires of the women in the community. Such operational problems are often a reflection of these groups attempting to do too much, with limited resources and experience.

Many faith-based organizations, of different religions, are providing assistance with conditions attached, which may go against the basic rights of aid recipients. Sometimes the conditions or biases within these organizations are not explicitly advocated in their official agenda. Despite one faith-based CSO advocating equal and inclusive assistance to members of all faiths, ethnicities and cultural backgrounds, an interviewed employer said that, in practice, aid was being given preferentially to members of the Christian faith in the case of that specific CSO. Other conditions are more obvious. One Christian social centre in Istanbul provides education only to members of that faith, and the manager of the centre described how *"the Christian community reached an agreement with [a Christian CSO] which says – these people can receive food vouchers from [the CSO], but they must go to Church every week. If they do not go to church for three weeks in a row their financial assistance will be stopped,"* (Aktuğ, 2016). An employee of one large Islamic pro-government CSO said *"we give financial assistance to Syrians with the condition that they stay here in Turkey,"* (Çalar, 2016).

A multi-sectoral response promotes dialogue among key actors from different fields, ensuring coordination across traditionally separate fields. Far from being multi-sectoral there is a trend among civil society in Turkey of either CSOs from different fields not cooperating; or individual CSOs trying to address issues from traditionally separate sectors, such as research and humanitarian work. In some instances the divisions between CSOs in Turkey with clear ideologies and agendas are sharp, and partially reflected in the 'needs' versus 'rights based' discourse. Simultaneously, however, there is a blurring of the division between these two discourses within and between CSOs as many are responding in a reactive manner to the influx of Syrians, or expanding their existing remits in new, and often unforeseen, ways. Coordination between CSOs is variable, with contradicting trends. On the one hand, the potential power and capacity of a fruitful cooperation among CSOs is acknowledged and praised by actors in the field. On the other hand, almost all stake-holders identify problems with cooperation.

Some NGOs which were formally solely research-based have extended into humanitarian work – one representative from a faith-based CSO based in Izmir said *"actually we were only reporting, but then we thought that this was both a humanitarian and Islamic situation and we wanted to help,"* (Aktay and Sağlam, 2016). Another member of a solidarity group based in Izmir described how their group had changed in response to Syrians – *"We established our organization to monitor the [Kurdish] peace process. However when refugees arrive to Izmir we could not close our eyes, and we* started to work on this topic," (Şahin, 2016). Another research organization described how they had shifted their work as a result of the Syrian influx - *"In 2010 our foundation was established by academics in order to make academic research. When we saw the lack of humanitarian help we established a charity for providing humanitarian aid and entered the field."*(Tok, 2016). One human rights organization is providing a range of services - following cases and helping Syrians when they go to state offices, informing them the related articles, laws and rights, releasing reports and conducting press meetings with other organizations. Individual volunteers are also attempting more sustained social service provision which blurs the lines between service provision and rights provision, providing both access to information and language classes.

Cynicism between CSOs working in different sectors is prevalent, particularly from humanitarian organizations who perceive research-oriented organizations as being 'ineffective'— one large faith-based CSO described how *"These other CSOs write reports... but they are absent in the field. There are many cases like this. No one helps, they just run after cases for advertisement,"* (Çalar, 2016). Another faith-based CSO criticized those CSOs who wrote reports but were absent in the field. Such resentments have direct ramifications in the working relationships between these CSOs.

The coalition between civil society and the embedded institutions of the state and local authorities is also fragmented, with coordination being partial and location-specific. At the international level, Turkey has had a hesitant relationship with INGOs, which continued throughout the initial years of the Syrian influx into the country. At the national level, the Disaster and Emergency Management Presidency (AFAD), which is the face of the state in humanitarian assistance, plays a significant role in creating connections and increasing communication between CSOs, hosting monthly meetings within governorates. It is also setting up the Electronic Aid Distribution System (EYDAS) as a means to centralize information about what aid is needed and being given.

At the local governance level, municipalities in Istanbul vary in the levels of support they provide, depending on the actors involved. According to a representative from one newly established community centre in Fatih, set up by a group of expats from different parts of the world including India, Australia, Canada and Europe, *"We tried to reach out to the municipality. But Fatih Municipality didn't respond — they're trying to discourage refugees from coming to Fatih and didn't want to support initiatives,"* (Kay, 2016).

However, another interviewee, a representative of a CSO run by and for Syrian-women, mentioned that they had received help from the same municipality. A solidarity group from Istanbul – which had originally been formed to resist urban transformation projects - explained its reason for not cooperating with a municipality - *"They can defame us. Why? When we resisted urban transformation they can go to people in the neighborhoods and say 'you trust these people, but we gave money to them to create centers, they are with us but now they're exploiting you,"* (Mülteciyim Hemşerim Collective, 2016). There are also cases where municipalities are choosing not to cooperate with CSOs in order to avoid turning their regions into "attraction centers" for refugees. A member of an organization from Izmir gives an example: *"The main concern is keeping these people out of Izmir and not presenting Izmir as a place where refugees feel comfortable,"* (Şahin, 2016). They underline the political motivations behind these actions - municipalities do not want to alienate their voters by spending money on refugees.

A **comprehensive** response addresses the wide spectrum of threats, vulnerabilities and capacities, including actors and sectors not previously considered relevant to any given response. There are differences in the way civil society in Turkey has understood and contextualized the Syrian presence, and our research indicates that charity and right discourses stand as the signifier of bifurcation in the CSO response – *"There are two types of CSOs – charity oriented, which has this mercy logic; and rights-oriented who claim to be human rights oriented, but always sees people as needy and acts with this logic"; There are divisions between rights-based, humanitarian-based, faith-based organizations...Bridging these differences in CSO society is a big issue,"* (Vural, 2016). Many of the CSOs working along a more charity-oriented approach are addressing Syrians in isolation of the embedded context in which many are living in host communities. There has hitherto been a reluctance to address human security threats, which may be considered to have a 'longer term' nature – such as access to education, healthcare and the labour market. While the government passed a new regulation, the "Regulation on Work Permit of Refugees Under Temporary Protection", (2016/8375) on 15 January 2016, which officially allowed the granting of work permits to all Syrians who completed their registration in the country, the percentage of Syrians who have the right to work under the new labour law is negligible owing to factors such as a lack of incentives for Turkish employers to legally hire Syrians staff on the minimum wage. Delays in registering for temporary protection, as well as the language barrier still pose major problems (Human Rights Watch 2016) – while healthcare is technically free for registered Syrians, many are unable to understand their Turkish doctors, and accessing hospitals remains difficult. In September 2014, the Ministry of National Education issued a circular on foreigners' access to education (Yabancılara Yönelik Eğitim Öğretim Hizmetleri, 2014/21, 2014) which lifted restrictions requiring Syrians to produce a Turkish residency permit in order to enrol in public schools, instead making the public school system, and temporary education centers overseen by the provincial education directorate in each province, available to all Syrian children with a government-issued ID. But unregistered asylum seekers are still prevented from getting access to education services.

A context-specific response requires in-depth analysis of the targeted situation. It identifies the concrete needs of the affected communities and enables the development of more appropriate solutions that are embedded in local realities, capacities, and coping mechanisms. In this sense, a critical aspect of rights provision understands how social and economic entitlements of refugees are embedded within the host community in which they live – and the social and economic entitlements of that community. Very few CSOs are providing services which incorporate both Syrian and Turkish, or Kurdish, citizens – this is largely owing to the practical difficulties created by the language barriers between these different groups. Those coexistence activities which do exist are largely targeting children. But some solidarity groups and CSOs of different background are attempting co-existence and integration-targeted relief. One large faith-based CSO, IHH, has a 'sibling families' program in Izmir in which a local Turkish family is responsible for a Syrian family, helping them with their problems and encouraging them to socialize. In Istanbul Turkish individuals, who speak Kurdish or Arabic, from a solidarity group connected to neighbourhood associations make home visits to Syrians, wanting to show they are friendly and also to determine the needs of Syrians. They also volunteer to go to schools with children to help with their registration process, and teach basic health care to both Syrians and local people to encourage them to help each other. Another group of Turkish volunteers in Izmir discussed the importance of activities which involved direct exchange between them and Syrians.

Prevention-oriented responses address the root causes of issues, focusing on protection and empowerment frameworks. It is difficult to align civil society responses to Syrians in Turkey along this criterion owing to the ongoing conflict in Syria, which is continuing to force individuals to seek refuge. But while CSOs may not be in a position to address the root cause of refugee-producing insecurities, they can have a role in establishing processes which "build on people's strengths and aspirations [...]" (Human Security Now, 2003) which recognizes the self-securing capacity of individuals, as well as the importance of the embedded social, economic and cultural networks in which they live in host communities, and exercise their daily rights. In general founders of Syrian institutions cite a lack of recognition, by both government and fellow CSOs, as a major obstacle to their ability to operate in Turkey - slow and bureaucratic relations between Turkish and Syrian institutions which are often interpreted by Syrians as indicating a lack of desire by Turkish officials to interact with them. One Syrian CSO based in Gaziantep described creating an intensive and fast learning program for Syrian children who had lost school years. But the Ministry of National Education did not recognize it. *"The governorate makes meetings about Syrians, but there is not a single Syrian institution there. I attended once accidentally by luck."* (Mustafa, 2016). Despite the large number of Syrian civic institutes being established, equality and cooperation problems are undermining the empowerment of Syrians. *"They [CSOs in Turkey] are making decisions about Syrians, but they don't ask Syrians...Our expectation from Turkish CSOs is to support Syrian institutions. Instead of working for Syrians, its better if they support Syrian foundations, because there is a huge cultural difference between us"* (Mustafa, 2016). Inequalities and hierarchical relations are perceived to be induced by language barriers and cultural differences. Considering the fact that these civil society actors, both Syrians and locals, are a microcosm of society in general, these problems are likely to be a barrier to future inclusion in wider contexts as well.

Conclusion

Attaining the standards outlined in the concept of "human security" is difficult for citizens in many countries, including Turkey. Being a refugee, holding an "aberrant form of citizenship" (Soguk, 1999), makes it even harder. Considering that Syrians in Turkey do not hold an official refugee status and the millions living outside camps have no access to state-sponsored aid, "human security" seems utopian. However, an unexpected and often underestimated actor, civil society, is playing a far-reaching role in terms of assisting Syrians and providing them with human security. Civil society organizations are working as bridges between official institutions and Syrians, and between local populations and refugees, by creating indirect channels of communication. These organizations provide expertise needed by public officials, and local knowledge to international actors. It is clear that the confusion created by the rapid expansion of CSOs, the initially reactive policies necessitated by the emergency nature of the Syrian influx and mixed agendas of different actors over the best medium to long term response to their presence, is impacting the type of support being provided. This is occurring in the context of entrenched confusion across the refugee-oriented world about the placement of protection in humanitarian responses to refugees, the shift from short term emergency provision to long term welfare needs of refugees and the self-securing potential of refugees and their position as 'subject' or 'actor' in their own future. However, despite the fact that there are many problems and gaps in activities within the civil society sector, it is also apparent that it remains a crucial actor in terms of providing human security to Syrian refugee population and that the role it plays has the potential to improve the possible future harmonization of Syrians in Turkey.

REFERENCES

3RP. (2016) Regional Refugee & Resilience Plan 2016-2017 In Response to the Syria Crisis: Turkey. 3RP.

Akay. (2015). *Türkiye'de İnsani Güven(siz)lik.* Istanbul: Helsinki Yurttaşlar Derneği.

BBC Türkçe, Erdoğan'dan Türkiye'deki Suriyelilere vatandaşlık açıklaması, 3 July 2016, Retrieved 27 March 2017 from http://www.bbc.com/turkce/haberler/2016/07/160703_erdogan_suriyeliler.

Commission on Human Security. (2003). *Human Security Now.* New York: UNHCR.

Cupolo, D. (22 July 2016). Syrian shops in Ankara hit in post-coup riots. DW.

Erdoğan, M and Ünver, C. (2015) *Türk iş dünyasının Suriyelilere bakışı.* HÜGO.

Ferris, E., & Kirisci, K. (2015). Not Likely to Go Home: Syrian Refugees and the Challenges to Turkey- and the International Community. Brookings Institute.

Hoffman, S., & Samuk, S. (2016). *Turkish Immigration Politics and the Syrian Refugee Crisis.* Stiftung Wissenschaft und Politik German Institute for International and Security Affairs.

Hsieh, H., & Shannon, S. (2005). Three approaches to qualitative content analysis. *Qualitative Health Research , 15* (9), 1277-88.

Human Rights Watch. (2016, June 20). *EU: Don't Send Syrians Back to Turkey.* Retrieved September 29, 2016, from Human Rights Watch: https://www.hrw.org/ news/2016/06/20/eu-dont-send-syrians-back-turkey

Human Rights Watch. (2015). *Turkey: Syrians Pushed Back at the Border.* Human Rights Watch.

Interior, M. o. (2013). *Patent No. 6458.* Turkey.

Human Security Now: Commission on Human Security, New York 2003, 4.

Jalali, R. (2002). Civil Society and the State: Turkey after the Earthquake. *Disasters, 26* (2), 120-139.

Macreath, Güngör, Sağnıç

Ogata, S. (1999). "Human Security: A Refugee Perspective". Keynote Speech by Mrs. Sadako Ogata, United Nations High Commissioner for Refugees, at the Ministerial Meeting on Human Security Issues of the "Lysoen Process" Group of Governments, Bergen, Norway, 19 May 1999. Bergen.

Pinna, M. Dünyaya Örnek Olarak Gösterilen Türkiye'deki Mülteci Kempları, 28 April 2016, *Euronews*. Retrieved 27 March 2017 from http://tr.euronews. com/2016/04/28/dunyaya-ornek-olarak-gosterilen-turkiye-deki-multeci-kamplari.

Relief Web. (2013). Legal status of individuals fleeing Syria: Syria Needs Analysis Project. Relief Web.

Şahin, Yıldırım (2016). Halkların Köprüsü. Izmir Focus Group with Citizens' Assembly, 22 April 2016.

Saldana, J. (2008). *Coding manual for qualitative researchers.* Los Angeles: Sage P.

Soguk, N. (1999). States and Strangers: Refugees and Displacements of Statecraft. Minneapolis: University of Minnesota Press

The Handbook on application of Work Permit, The Ministry of Labor and Social Security, Retrieved on 27 March, 2017 from http://www.calismaizni.gov.tr/media/1035/gkkuygulama.pdfhttp://www.calismaizni.gov.tr/media/1035/gkkuygulama.pdf.

UNHCR (2016). Global Trends: Forced Displacement in 2015. UNHCR.

UN Human Security Unit (2009). *Human Security in Theory and Practice*, Retrieved on 28 March 2017 from http://www.un.org/humansecurity/ sites/www. un.org. humansecurity/files/human_security_in_theory_and_practice_english.pdf

World Bank (2006). Civil Society and Peacebuilding: Potential, Limitations and Critical Factor. Report No. 36445-GLB.

Yabancılara Yönelik Eğitim- Öğretim Hizmetlerine Dair Genelge, No 2014/21, 23 September 2014.

Interviews:

Aktay, Birgül and Sağlam, Nursen, Mazlum Der. Izmir Focus Group with Citizens' Assembly, 22 April 2016.

Aktuğ, Yakup, Quomsho Centre. Interview with Citizens' Assembly, 6 March 2016.

Çalar, Rasim, IHH Izmir. Interview with Citizens' Assembly, 21 April 2016.

Güneş, Ali, The General Counsel of the Migration and Humanitarian Help Administration of the Prime Ministry. Interview with Citizens' Assembly, 23 March 2016.

Kay, Shannon, Small Projects Istanbul. Interview with Citizens' Assembly, 14 January 2016.

Mülteciyim Hemşerim Collective. Interview with Citizens' Assembly, 8 April 2016.

Mustafa, Cemal, Minber Sam. Gaziantep Focus Group with Citizens' Assembly, 7 May 2016.

Tok, Serhat, International Middle East Peace Research Center (IMPR). Gaziantep Focus Group with Citizens' Assembly, 7 May 2016.

Vural, Kemal (2016). Kırkayak Kültür Derneği. Gaziantep Focus Group with Citizens' Assembly, 7 May 2016.

Chapter Five

Contesting Refugees in Turkey: Political Parties and the Syrian Refugees[1]

Aslı Ilgıt*, Fulya Memişoğlu±

Introduction

Over the course of five years from 2011 to 2016, Syria has turned into the world's leading country of forced displacement, with more than eleven million people, and still counting, had to flee their homes internally and externally (UNHCR, 2015). Turkey has become the largest host country for the Syrian refugees in the region, hosting, as of September 2016, more than 2.7 million Syrian refugees (UNHCR, 2016), around 10 per cent of which reside in 26 'temporary protection centres' (TPCs) in ten cities.[2] This figure is reportedly equal to the total number of immigrants Turkey received between 1923 and 2011 (TIHK, 2014).

Turkey has been in the centre of international attention, initially for its generous humanitarian response to the refugees, and later for its position as refugees' irregular gateway to Europe given the highly limited alternatives for safe and legal access to European countries. Earlier praise from its international partners for its 'open door policy', however, has soon been confronted by increasing criticism for Turkey's alleged support toward the

[1] We thank the discussant and participants of the 2015 Turkish Migration Conference for their helpful feedback.

*Associate Professor in Political Science and International Relations Department, Çukurova University, Adana, Turkey. E-mail: ailgit@cu.edu.tr.

± Assistant Professor in Political Science and International Relations Department, Çukurova University, Adana, Turkey, and Research Officer in Refugee Studies Centre, Department of International Development, University of Oxford, United Kingdom. E-mail: fulya.memiso-glu@qeh.ox.ac.uk.

[2] The Disaster and Emergency Management Authority (AFAD, in Turkish acronym), the main governmental agency responsible for refugee crisis management, updates this information on a regular basis. Received from https://www.afad.gov.tr/en/2602/Current-Status-in-AFAD-Temporary-Protection-Centres, available on: 27.09.2016.

radical groups in the Syrian conflict. In this context, the ongoing Syrian conflict and subsequent refugee crisis has become a major foreign policy instrument for the Justice and Development Party (AKP, in Turkish acronym) government to legitimise its involvement in the Syrian conflict. Meanwhile, the Syrian refugees have also turned into a domestic policy concern and a high-priority topic in political debates, as the country has experienced two national elections, one local election and one presidential election since 2011. In such an environment, the Turkish public's initial welcoming hospitality has later been diversified with both positive and negative domestic perceptions of and attitudes towards Syrian refugees (see, Erdoğan 2015; Kaya, 2016; Özden, 2013). Moreover, the official refugee policies and discourses of the Turkish state have fluctuated over the course of five years since the arrival of the first Syrians in March 2011 due to external and internal changing dynamics.

While there emerged abundant information about the incumbent government's main stance and policies concerning the refugee issue mainly based on regular press releases and government officials' statements (see also, Gökalp Aras and Şahin Mencütek, 2015; Memisoglu and Ilgit, 2016; Sirkeci and Pusch, 2016; Şirin Öner and Genç, 2015), a systematic understanding of where the opposition parties stand in Turkey's refugee debate and how they shape responses to the challenges the country has been facing does not get sufficient attention from the academic or political circles. In this chapter, thus, after providing a brief overview of Turkey's evolving migration/refugee policy, we focus on the discursive continuities and shifts of three major opposition political parties, the centre-left Republican People's Party (CHP), the far-right Nationalist Movement Party (MHP), and the left-wing People's Democratic Party (HDP), that are represented in the Turkish Parliament. Our analysis involves carefully reading specific texts, such as speeches, party manifestos, published interviews, op-ed articles, news reports as well as employing a series of analytical questions. In examining the parties' discourses on Syrian refugees and its implications for their refugee policy, we developed a three-tier framework where we examined the categorisation of refugees, the language of political reasoning and the proposed or preferred refugee policy.[3]

---

[3] This framework is drawn from one of the authors' previous work on discourse analysis. See, Ilgit, A. (2010).

Global refugee regime, domestic politics and refugees

Turkey's refugee and asylum policy within the global refugee regime

Global refugee regime comprises a set of rules, norms, and procedures that are primarily rooted in the 1951 UN Convention Relating to the Status of the Refugees (commonly referred as the Geneva Convention) that govern states' responses to refugees (Betts, 2015). Recent studies point to the converging trends in global migration management and refugee regimes, in which diverse actors justify their increasing interventions in the migration field with an increasing range of practices and new discourses about the definition of migration and responses to it (Geiger & Pécoud, 2010; Joly, 2002). In Turkey, recently we can see these tendencies playing out with the growing interrelationship between asylum and migration through the discourse of 'migration management' as well as with the dominant role of the Turkish state being contested by the rising number of national and international non-state actors in the process (Memisoglu and Ilgit, 2016).

Part of this global trend on migration and refugees is, however, the extent to which the refugee and asylum issues have become a major domestic policy concern in, especially, the Western world. Xenophobic sentiments, anti-immigrant discourses, unwelcoming attitudes are all too common to be witnessed in many countries regardless of the number of the immigrants or refugees that cross over their borders. Hungary's recently built border fence on the Serbian border; the growing popularity of far right parties with anti-immigrant discourse in the Netherlands, Germany, and France; the rise of PEGIDA movement with its protests against refugees and immigrants in Germany; immigration being at the core of the 'Brexit debate' in the United Kingdom; increasing violence and attacks against foreigners in many European countries are recent examples of how immigration and refugee issues have deeply polarized the society and domestic politics. In these countries, anti-immigrant sentiments are instigated and further aggravated by domestic political actors for either personal or political gains. Hungary's President's harsh rhetoric and stand on migration, for instance, is partly arguably to divert the attention from the corruption scandals and to compete with the popular far-right Jobbik party (Juhasz and Hunyadi, 2016). In the United States, the newly-elected president Donald Trump's promises of building a wall along the Mexican border and deportation of all migrants have been part of his election campaign. In Australia, the seemingly domestic consensus on its refugee policy has been replaced by increasing partisan competition since the mid-1990s, when far-right party members with hostile discourses towards immigrants started to gain votes in local and national elections (Maley, 2016).

Similarly, while Turkey has gradually taken part in the global refugee regime, the refugee and asylum issue has also become a major domestic policy concern in the current Syrian refugee influx. To briefly contextualise, Turkey's evolving migration profile over the last three decades has already been a critical issue due to its geostrategic location on the East Mediterranean route, one of the five major global routes of mixed migration flows, transiting the Middle East towards Europe (ICMPD et al., 2007). In 2000, Turkey made the transition from a country of negative net migration to a country of positive net migration (İçduygu *et al.*, 2013). The country's relatively prosperous and stable profile in contrast to continuing political and social upheavals in neighbouring countries and the application of liberal and flexible visa policies towards the neighbouring countries shifted its predominantly migrant-sending status towards a country of transit and destination. Furthermore, increasing immigration controls and restrictive entry measures implemented by the European Union (EU) countries combined with the difficulties associated with establishing effective controls at Turkey's eastern and south-eastern borders are often considered among factors directing mixed migration movements towards Turkey (İçduygu, 2004). While irregular migratory flows via the Eastern Mediterranean route have fluctuated over time before hitting a record number in 2015, the Frontex figures demonstrate that they have already accounted for around 40 per cent of all migrants arriving in the EU as early as 2008-2009 (Frontex, 2017).

Against this background, after decades of developing migration strategies through provisional measures, mounting pressures of mixed migration flows has led Turkey to embark on a substantial overhaul of its migration system since the early 2000s (Kilberg, 2014). Reforming migration and asylum policy also gained precedence as part of the country's accession process to the EU and the requirements to align with the EU *acquis* in this field. Following the establishment of the Bureau for the Development and Implementation of Asylum and Migration Legislation and Strengthening the Administrative Capacity under the Ministry of Interior in 2008, Turkey's two-tier asylum regime has undergone a restructuring process. After a period of legislative drafting that involved consultations with relevant state and non-state stakeholders, the Law on Foreigners and International Protection was submitted to the Turkish Parliament in May 2012 (Memisoglu, 2014). The parliament adopted the law in April 2013, which came into effect a year later.[4] The country's first comprehensive migration and asylum law also established the civil authority, Directorate General of Migration Management (DGMM) under the Ministry of Interior, to be in charge of the management of all issues concerning foreigners, such as entry rules, visa regulations, work and residence permits as well as those in need of international protection. Its local units in all 81 provinces became fully operational in May 2015, taking over all responsibilities related to foreigners from the provincial police departments. Thus, a new institutional, legislative, and administrative framework at central and local levels has been set up, and this policy shift in migration management was supported by civil society organisations and the opposition parties (Memisoglu, 2014). In a parliamentary session on the passing of the law, a member of the MHP, for example, suggested that 'compiling various arrangements under secondary legislation under one bill is a valid decision' and that 'the establishment of the Directorate ends the chaos of managing migration through separate institutions that have no experts in this field'. The MHP, thus, 'supports the law' as it is 'in Turkey's national interests'.[5]

And yet, policy dynamics that characterise Turkey's migration and asylum regime are simultaneously progressive and restrictive (Memisoglu and Ilgit, 2016). An overarching issue is Turkey's application of geographical limitation to the 1951 UN Convention Relating to the Status of the Refugees. Although Turkey has ratified both the Convention and its 1967 Protocol, it grants refugee status only to 'persons who have become refugees as a result of events occurring in Europe'.[6] While geographical limitation is Turkey's distinct rigidity within the global refugee regime, the protracted refugee situation due to the Syrian war and its unprecedented nature in scale has posed multiple challenges, testing the flexibility of its newly established migration system along these parameters.

More specifically, Turkey declared an open-border policy for those fleeing war in Syria as early as June 2011, but this humanitarian response did not bring Syrians a legal refugee status in Turkey, as defined in the 1951 UN Convention. As the numbers nearly reached 10,000 by the end of 2011, the Turkish government announced temporary protection regime (UNHCR,

---

[4] Law on Foreigners and International Protection, No. 6458/2013.
[5] Parliamentary Proceedings 24/3/80, 20 March 2013. Received from http://www.tbmm. gov.tr/develop/owa/tutanak_g_sd.birlesim_baslangic?P4=21915&P5=B&page1=34&page2 =34 , available on: 10.10.2016
[6]'Declarations and Reservations Chapter 5: 1967 Protocol relating to the status of refugees', United Nations Treaty Collection.

2011), an alternative international protection scheme in line with the EU's 2001 Directive on Temporary Protection.[7] This meant protection against forced returns and assistance for all Syrians (both camp and non-camp refugees, with or without identification documents), Palestinians from Syria and stateless people from Syria. While these measures are both parallel to the provisions of the EU's directive, there is no set limit of stay for the temporary protection status in the Turkish context, unlike the EU Directive, which sets a maximum duration of three years. Furthermore, it does not come jointly with a residency permit and it does not allow individuals to lodge individual asylum applications during the length of temporary protection – two major differences with the EU directive that leave Turkey's temporary protection status in flux and make future international protection options uncertain.[8] More to the point, while providing the legal basis for temporary protection, the Law on Foreigners and International Protection leaves its management to the Council of Ministers. This underlines that the future status of Syrians in Turkey under temporary protection is highly dependent on political will rather than Turkey's legal obligations under international refugee law.[9] Thus, the possibility that the Syrians may permanently stay in Turkey based on a firm legal status was largely absent from the public and political debates, reflected by the persistent use of 'guests' when referring to Syrian refugees, which has no equivalence in international law.

This extended ambiguity over the legal status of Syrians has also been subject to criticism from opposition parties, moving the refugee issue into a broader political debate from 2014 onwards. Pointing out that the required regulation on temporary protection has still not been prepared after sixteen months at the time, a parliamentary member of the CHP urged the government to take action in light of increasing number of refugees settling in border regions and the potential social tension this may cause unless new

---

[7] 'On minimum standards for giving temporary protection in the event of a mass influx of displaced persons and on measures promoting a balance of efforts between Member States in receiving such persons and bearing the consequences of thereof', EU Council Directive 2001/55/EC.

[8] This possibility was outlawed later in the Temporary Protection Regulation, as stated in Article 16: 'Individual international protection applications filed by foreigners under this regulation shall not be processed in order to ensure the effective implementation of temporary protection measures during the period of the implementation of temporary protection'.

[9] Article 91 of Law on Foreigners and International Protection.

camps were built to accommodate them.[10] The language of political reasoning on clarifying the legal status of Syrians, however, did not address Turkey's legal obligation to protect refugees as an actor in the global refugee regime. Instead, refugees were framed as victims, yet also a burden caused by the government's open door policy: *'these people are desperate, you brought them to this country but we cannot toss them out of the door in this situation'*.[11]

The long awaited Regulation on Temporary Protection came into effect in October 2014, strengthening the legal framework for Syrians' access to social services, including education and medical care, financial assistance, interpretation services and access to the labour market. Since then, Turkish institutional and policy frameworks have had to adjust to the changing dynamics of the refugee situation, leading the government to shift its emergency response to a long-term planning for refugees living outside the camps. The government's rhetoric also became more reassuring over time in terms of taking into account the long term prospects of refugees in Turkey.[12]

However, a series of elections in 2014 and 2015 have created even less convenient circumstances for an elaborate discussion of the status of Syrian refugees, overshadowed by mounting electoral concerns. As will be discussed in the following section, the Syrian refugee issue has become deeply politicised along party politics, in which opposition parties often instrumentialise the issue for political purposes rather than pursuing an effective and comprehensive agenda for the protection of refugees.

---

[10] Parliamentary Proceedings 24/4/125, 24 July 2014. Received from https://www.tbmm. gov.tr/develop/owa/tutanak_sd.birlesim_baslangic?P4=22219& P5=H&page1=72&page2 =72&web_user_id=15010474 available on: 10.10.2016.

[11] Ibid.

[12] In November 2014, the Deputy Prime Minister Numan Kurtulmuş stated that 'Syrians are here to stay and that the refugees are permanent', signalling a shift in the government's political discourse. More affirmative remarks came later from leading AKP figures, such as the Deputy Prime Minister Mehmet Şimşek: *'First we need to acknowledge that (Syrian) refugees are not here temporarily. We have to be aware of this... In my opinion, we should give them access to education, a good vocational training, and treat them with respect. Perhaps in the short term, they may be a burden, but we should not see it that way. At the same time, we should consider them as entities with a positive value in the long run'* (T24 News, 2016, April 15).

Ilgıt, Memişoğlu

Politicization of refugees: Syrian refugees in Turkish domestic political debates

While the Turkish government through institutional, legal, and administrative changes makes every effort to control the message about and perception of the Syrian refugees at home and abroad; domestically, the Syrian refugees have become a perceived societal security threat and a political issue in three particular ways: as a 'rival victim' group, as a 'voter or demographic' threat, and as having 'unfair' access to public services (Memisoglu & Ilgit, 2016). The three opposition parties have employed these three representations of the Syrian refugees in various circumstances and contexts, thus delivering the message about the 'Syrian refugee problem' to the public as a 'problem for all of us' (Van Dijk, 2002).

The main opposition party, the CHP, has in general considered the Syrians as a burden to Turkey but at the same time argued that it is Turkey's debt to humanity to take care of the refugees until conditions for them to permanently return to Syria get better. Refugees' return to Syria is a recurring theme in the CHP's discourse, usually suggested in a way that it is for the benefit of the refugees themselves. For example, in April 2015, Kemal Kılıçdaroğlu, the leader of the CHP, stated: *'We are going to send our Syrian brothers back. Excuse us. Every person is happy in their homelands where they were born, happy in their own countries'* (Milliyet, 2015, April 22). Such controversial statements especially prior to the June 7 national elections drew criticism from rights-based groups (TRT News, 2015, May 09). Yet, the return policy remained a key feature of the CHP's response to the Syrian refugee crisis later on with an emphasis on the 'potential dangers' of the Syrians in Turkey in the future. In March 2016, the CHP leader repeated his wish to send Syrians back because *'they would be more troublesome in the future, causing disorder and some becoming important actors of Turkey's underground scene'* (Milliyet, 2016, March 11).

A second trope emerging from the CHP's refugee discourse is the connection of refugee issues with the terrorists/militants who are crossing over the border and who are using Turkey both as a base and a crossing point due to Turkey's open door policy (Milliyet, 2016, April 26). Linking open border policy to the lack of border security can also be traced in CHP's narrative that the refugee inflow has increased smuggling activities in the border regions. In this type of narrative, the incumbent government's overall foreign policy is often the main target of criticism, in which preventive measures, such as building walls along the Syria border, are seen as inadequate in enhancing border security.[13]

Finally, representing Syrian refugees as a demographic threat especially in the form of a 'rival group' to other domestic groups in Turkey has become a significant discursive strategy of the CHP when criticising the government. For example, the Syrians were presented as a rival of the domestic workers by creating 'unfair competition' 'with their access to the labour market without paying taxes or abiding by legal procedures' (CHP Manifesto, 2015). In a party group meeting while addressing security threats posed on the border province Kilis where the Syrian refugees outnumber the local population, the CHP leader recognized this demographic shift as a factor that would potentially cause civil commotion and cultural degeneration. A strong discourse of othering is employed when referring to a range of issues as the causes of discontent among the local population since the arrival of Syrian refugees, including polygamous marriages, domestic violence against women, resurgence of infectious diseases, and asking 'what will happen to our brothers/sisters there' (Milliyet, 2016, April 26).

Despite this predominantly populist and harsh rhetoric on the refugee issues, the CHP advocated what might be called a 'middle-ground refugee policy'. In its election manifesto (Turkey First-*Önce Türkiye*) while emphasising the accommodation of 'our brothers who fled the war in Syria in an orderly manner and providing humane conditions', the CHP demands 'stronger cooperation with international organisations to deal with problems associated with mass migration flows from Syria' and 'more transparent/controllable humanitarian aid for the asylum-seekers' (CHP Manifesto, 2015). Prior to the November 1st, 2015 elections, in particular, the party took some concrete steps to demonstrate that the refugee issue was now a high-priority topic on its political agenda. Following the establishment of the Commission to Monitor Migration and Migrants in September 2015, the members of the commission prepared a comprehensive report tackling a wide range of issues from legal aspects to socio-economic vulnerabilities of refugees (CHP, 2016). Lifting of the geographical limitation and the establishment of a Migration and Harmonization Ministry to facilitate refugees' integration are some of the notable policy recommendations raised in the report. It specifically recommends to show no tolerance and to

---

[13] Parliamentary Proceedings 26/1/18, 23 December 2015. Received from http://www. tbmm.gov.tr/develop/owa/tutanak_g_sd.birlesim_baslangic?P4=21915&P5=B&page1 =34&page2=34 available on: 10.10.2016

take preventive measures against racist, discriminatory, and xenophobic discourses targeting asylum-seekers and refugees in Turkey. Paradoxically though, far from the party's more constructive policy agenda, scapegoating of refugees remained as a key aspect of the CHP leader's discourse. In March 2016, the Turkish officials and their counterparts in the EU agreed on implementing a set of policy measures to curb irregular migration flows to Europe via Turkey, including return of all irregular migrants from Greece to Turkey as of 20 March 2016, 'one for one' resettlement from Turkey to the EU, and the EU's financial assistance to Turkey in providing improved living conditions for Syrian refugees (European Commission, 2016). The UN Refugee Agency and many rights-based NGOs immediately shared concerns that 'blanket return' arrangements between the EU and Turkey of any individuals may violate international refugee law (UNHCR, 2016a). Somehow disregarding such rights-based issues concerning refugee protection, Kılıçdaroğlu stated: *'Let's give them €6 billion, and let them take all Syrians, Afghans, Pakistanis themselves'* (Habertürk, 2016, March 11).[14]

In a somewhat similar way but from another angle, the MHP too continued to securitise the Syrians and take up the refugee issue in connection with the protection of territorial integrity, national unity, and more specifically with the Kurdish issue. While Turkey's 'hospitable' response to the refugee crisis is framed as 'a prerequisite of Turkish culture and civilization', the MHP also considered Syrians a burden as the country 'turned into a refugee camp' and it is questionable 'for how long Turkey can carry this burden'. Syrians' uncertain future in Turkey is also represented as a problem for and threat to national unity as 'this issue will open up new questions based on ethnic identities, collective rights and the Hatay question.'[15] Similar to the CHP's stance, open border policy and its implications on border security were criticised for providing easier access for terrorists, thus *'undermining the peace and security of Turkey's own people.'*[16]

Mirroring the party's ethno-nationalist stance, the MHP also employs a recurring identity-based discourse in its response to the refugee problems, showing selective solidarity toward a specific ethnic group, the Turkomans.

---

[14] MHP vice chairman made a similar remark on EU-Turkey deal (Milliyet, 2016a, March 11). A similar remark has also been raised in Kaya (2016).

[15] Parliamentary Proceedings 1/58, 10 March 2016. Received from https://www.tbmm. gov.tr/develop/owa/genel_kurul.cl_getir?pEid=46308 available on: 10.10.2016

[16] Parliamentary Proceedings 26/1/18, 23 December 2015. Received from https://www. tbmm.gov.tr/develop/owa/Tutanak_B_SD.birlesim_baslangic_yazici?P4=22489&P5=H& page1=23&page2=23 available on: 10.10.2016.

In January 2015, the party members submitted a parliamentary question asking for an in-depth investigation of problems faced by 'cognates' living in the Turkoman refugee camp in the province of Osmaniye. As for political reasoning, shared kinship and the Ottoman heritage with the 'Turkomans from Aleppo and Damascus' were represented as the underlying reasons for the 'Turkish state's obligation to protect these people.'[17]

Meanwhile a harsh-anti Syrian rhetoric surfaced during the electoral campaign when a parliamentary member of the MHP suggested that '500,000 tourists will come to Gaziantep' when 'the 500,000 Syrians will leave' (Dyke and Blaser, 2015, June 9). Adopting a security-based approach, the Syrians were framed as a threat to national security and national identity, and the party advocated 'taking measures to protect national security and interests against uncontrollable migration influxes as outcomes of international and regional crises' (MHP Manifesto, 2015). The MHP manifesto (Societal Reconstruction and Peaceful Future - *Walk with Us Turkey/ Toplumsal Onarım ve Huzurlu Gelecek- Bizimle Yürü Türkiye*) makes this connection very clear:

> *Apart from the high economic cost of hosting a sizeable refugee population, Turkey is confronted with theft, rebels, begging, spread of disease, use of drugs, prostitution, child marriages, informal labour, uncontrollable rent increase. This situation not only leads to unhealthy/difficult living conditions for asylum-seekers, mainly children and women, but also negatively affects Turkish population economically, socially and psychologically. MHP will adopt policies that will attempt to repair this disruption of social cohesion, minimising problems for both asylum-seekers and the local population.*

In stark contrast to both the CHP and MHP, the HDP adopted a more moderate tone blended with pro-refugee statements. Despite the emphasis on returning the Syrians back to Syria, the HDP offered this as an option 'if our Syrian brothers would like to go back. If they want to stay, we will take care of them in any part of Turkey, we would grant them citizenship. Villages beyond borders are also our relatives. Our job is to take care of them. We would not leave Syrian refugees alone' (Cumhuriyet, 2015, May 28). While the HDP leader Selahattin Demirtaş made the boldest remark by promising to grant citizenship to those Syrians who are willing to stay in Turkey, the

---

[17] Parliamentary Proceedings 24/64, 25 February 2015. Received from https://www. tbmm.gov.tr/tutanak/donem24/yil5/ham/b06401h.htm available on: 10.10.2016.

party also proposed an inclusive rights-based refugee/migration policy prior to the June 7 elections. Lifting the geographical limitation to the 1951 Convention and supporting equal rights in work place for migrants were among the policy recommendations addressed in the party's election manifesto (Great Humanity- Büyük İnsanlık). In addition, while creating safe entry routes for migrants, building safe accommodation spaces, and facilitating visa arrangements, the HDP recognised the need to combat racism/hate speech against migrants and asylum seekers (HDP Manifesto, 2015). Concerning the geographical limitation, the HDP members also raised criticisms over the prolonged 'guest' status as an alternative to a solid refugee status during parliamentary debates.18 Leaving the party's inclusive policy approach aside, selective solidarity also appears to be prevalent in HDP's discourse when addressing refugee problems (Tugsuz and Yılmaz, 2015). While, for instance, refugees' access to education at all levels is a major issue regardless of ethnic origin, a parliamentary member of the HDP questioned the lack of efforts for the education of Kurds, Yezidis, Assyrians and Christians living outside the camps and the absence of Kurdish language education, highlighting 'the government's efforts in providing access to education for Sunni-Arab Syrian pupils in refugee camps'.19

The most current political debate indicates that the uncertain legal status of Syrian refugees further politicises the issue and that the Syrian refugees remain at the centre of partisan competition as a major domestic political concern for the foreseeable future. For example, President Recep Tayyip Erdoğan's public announcement in July 2016 of plans to grant citizenship to Syrians to facilitate their integration immediately stirred a strong public reaction, with the hashtag *#ÜlkemdeSuriyeliİstemiyoru*m (I do not want Syrians in my country) hitting the worldwide list of trending topics on Twitter. All the three opposition leaders, including HDP leader Demirtaş, who initially proposed granting citizenship to Syrian refugees himself during the election campaign, were also quick to condemn any citizenship plans for the Syrians and blame the government for seeking out political gains by offering citizenship to Syrian refugees (Al Jazeera, 2016, July 3).

---

18 Parliamentary Proceedings 24/5/43, 15 January 2015. Received from https://www.tbmm. gov.tr/develop/owa/Tutanak_B_SD.birlesim_baslangic? P4=22331&P5=H&page1=54&page2 =54 available on 10.10.2016.

19 Parliamentary Proceedings 82, 24 March 2015. Received from https://www.tbmm.gov.tr/ develop/owa/Tutanak_B_SD.birlesim_baslangic?P4=22401&P5=H&page1=62&page2=62 available on 10.10.2016.

Conclusion

Turkey's migration profile has rapidly changed in recent decades, necessitating an overhaul of its migration and asylum policy in response to the mounting pressures of mixed migration flows. While there have been substantial institutional and legislative reforms, as briefly addressed in this chapter, the arrival of unprecedented numbers of refugees from Syria has stretched the capacity to its limits. As Turkey turned into one of the world's largest refugee hosting countries, the incumbent government has kept adjusting its stance and policies in accordance with the ever-changing dynamics of the protracted refugee crisis. The issues discussed in this chapter highlighted that the Syrian refugee situation has soon become a subject to politicisation across Turkey's political spectrum as the country went through a series of elections in 2014 and 2015. And for all the three opposition parties represented in the parliament, the Syrian refugees have often become a political instrument for criticising the government's domestic and foreign policies.

Considering the ongoing nature of the crisis and the diversity of issues involved, there are limits to the assessment of where the opposition parties stand in Turkey's refugee debate and how they shape their responses. Thus, we focused on the parties' categorisation of refugees, their political reasoning and proposed or preferred refugee policies, emphasizing discursive continuities and shifts in their discourse. In general, in the domestic political debates, the Syrian refugees have been perceived as a societal security threat and the political parties politicized the Syrian refugees by representing them to a great extent as a 'rival victim' group and a 'demographic' threat, thus not only having 'unfair' access to public services but also putting the national unity and societal order in danger. After examining the parties' discourses and proposed refugee policies, we argue that the main opposition party CHP has gradually shifted toward a more receptive approach in formulating policies *vis-à-vis* Turkey's rapidly changing migration profile, whereas the MHP appears to be far from putting forward a constructive refugee policy. For both parties, the refugee crisis has incited anti-refugee rhetoric and securitisation debates, which overall contradict with any positive attempts to align their approach in line with global refugee protection obligations. Meanwhile, the HDP has consistently advocated an inclusive refugee/migration policy blended with a pro-refugee rhetoric especially during the electoral campaign in 2015. On the other hand, both

Ilgıt, Memişoğlu

MHP and HDP, at times show selective solidarity with specific refugee groups reflecting their ethno-nationalist background.

In Turkey, the current political debate over the Syrian refugees includes increasing contestation, posing important domestic dynamics for the fluctuation of the official refugee policies and discourses of the Turkish state for the past of six years. The political contestation also confirmed that the Syrian refugee crisis is a multifaceted phenomenon that raises concerns beyond security. Acknowledging the fact that contestation can take an almost infinite number of forms, among political parties or societal groups, between political and non-political actors, etc., our analysis focused on the main opposition parties represented in the Turkish Parliament. Future analysis would benefit a broader investigation into other political and non-political actors' role in the current refugee debate.

References
Al Jazeera (2016, July 3) Erdogan: Syrian refugees could become Turkish citizens. Received from http://www.aljazeera.com/news/2016/07/erdogan-syrian-refugees-turkish-citizens-160703133739430.html available on:10.10.2016

Betts, A. (2015). The normative terrain of the global refugee regime. *Ethics &International Affairs*, 29(4). Received from https://www. ethicsand internationalaffairs.org/2015/the-normative-terrain-of-the-global-refugee-regime/ available on: 10.10.2016

CHP (2016). CHP göç ve göçmen sorunlarını inceleme komisyonu mülteci raporu: sınırlar arasında insanlık dramından insanlık sınavına. Received from http://www. igamder.org/wp-content/uploads/2016/08/SINIRLAR-ARASINDA-BASKI2.pdf available on: 10.10.2016 (in Turkish)

CHP Manifesto (2015). Önce Türkiye [First Turkey]. Received from https://www. chp.org.tr/Public/0/Folder//52608.pdf available on: 10.10.2016 (in Turkish)

Cumhuriyet (2015, May 28). Demirtaş'tan bomba Suriye iddiası [A shattering claim from Demirtaş]. Received from http://www.cumhuriyet.com.tr/haber/siyaset/287027/Demirtas_tan_bomba_Suriye_iddiasi.html available on: 10.10.2016 (in Turkish)

Dyke, J. & Blaser, N. (2015, June 9). What do Turkish elections mean for Syrian refugees? IRIN News. Received from http://www.irinnews.org/ report/ 101607/ what-do-turkish-elections-mean-syrian-refugees available on: 10.10.2016

Erdogan, M. (2015). *Syrians in Turkey: Social Acceptance and Integration,* Istanbul: Bilgi University Press.

European Commission (2016). EU-Turkey Statement: Questions and Answers, European Commission Fact Sheet. Received from http://europa.eu/rapid/ press-release_MEMO-16-963_en.htm available on: 17.02.2017

Frontex (2017). Eastern Mediterranean Route. Frontex, European Border and Coast Guard Agency. Received from http://frontex.europa.eu/trends-and-routes/eastern-mediterranean-route/ available on: 18.02.2017.

Geiger, M., & Pécoud, A. (2010). *The politics of international migration management.* London: Palgrave Macmillan.

Gökalp Aras, E. & Şahin Mencütek, Z. (2015). The international migration and foreign policy nexus: the case of Syrian refugee crisis and Turkey. *Migration Letters,* 12 (3): 193-208.

Habertürk (2016, March 11). Kemal Kılıçdaroğlu: Suriyeliler bütün düzenimizi bozucak [Kemal Kılıçdaroğlu: Syrians will cause disorder]. Received from http://www.haberturk.com/gundem/haber/1208609-kemal-kilicdaroglu-suriyeliler-butun-duzenimizi-bozacak available on: 10.10.2016 (in Turkish)

HDP Manifesto (2015). Büyük İnsanlık [Great Humanity]. Received from http://www.hdp.org.tr/images/UserFiles/Documents/Editor/HDP   Seçim Bildirgesi Tam Metin.pdf available on: 10.10.2016.

ICMPD, Europol & Frontex (2007). Arab and European Partner States Working Document on the Joint Management of Mixed Migration Flows, Mediterranean Transit Migration (MTM) Dialogue. Received from http://www.icmpd.org/fileadmin/ICMPD-Website/ICMPD-Website_2011/Migration_Dialogues/MTM/Factsheets/FINAL_Working-Doc_Full_EN.pdf available on: 18 February 2017.

İçduygu, A. (2004). Demographic Mobility and Turkey: Migration Experiences and Government Responses. *Mediterranean Quarterly,* 15(4): 8-90.

İçduygu, A., Göker, G. Z., Tokuzlu, L. B. & S. Paçacı Elitok (2013). Turkey Migration Profile, Migration Policy Centre, European University Institute. Received from http://www.migrationpolicycentre.eu/docs/migration_profiles/Turkey.pdf available on: 10.10.2016

Ilgıt, A. (2010). Contesting State Identity and Foreign Policy: German Anti-Militarism in   Shades of Red and Green. Unpublished doctoral dissertation, Syracuse University,   Syracuse, New York.

Joly, D. (Ed.). (2002). *Global changes in asylum regimes.* London: Palgrave Macmillan.

Juhasz, A. & Hunyadi, B. (2016). Driven by domestic politics: anti-immigration policy in Hungary. Received from https://www.boell.de/en/2016/06/13/driven-domestic-politics-ant-immigration-policy-hungary available on: 10.10.2016.

Kaya, A. (2016). Syrian Refugees and Cultural Intimacy in Istanbul: "I feel safe here!", *EUI Working Papers RSCAS,* 2016 (59). Florence: European University Institute.

Kilberg, R. (2014). Turkey's evolving migration identity. Migration Policy Institute. Received   from   http://www.migrationpolicy.org/article/turkeys-evolving-migration-identity available on: 10.10.2016

Maley, W. (2016). Australia's refugee policy: domestic politics and diplomatic consequences. Australian Journal of International Affairs, 70(6): 670-680.

Memisoglu, F. (2014). Between the Legacy of Nation-State and Forces of Globalization: Turkey's Management of Mixed Migration Flows, *EUI Working Papers RSCAS,* 2014 (122). Florence: European University Institute.

Ilgıt, Memişoğlu

Memisoglu, F. & Ilgıt, A. (2016). Syrian Refugees in Turkey: An Analysis of Multifaceted Challenges, Players and Policies. *Mediterranean Politics*. Received from http://www.tandfonline.com/doi/full/10.1080/13629395.2016.1189479 available on: 10.10.2016.

MHP Manifesto (2015). Toplumsal Onarım ve Huzurlu Gelecek- Bizimle Yürü Türkiye [Societal Reconstruction and Peaceful Future - Walk With Us Turkey]. Received from https://www.mhp.org.tr/usr_img/mhpweb/1kasimsecimleri/beyanname _1kasim2015.pdf available on: 10.10.2016 (in Turkish)

Milliyet (2015, April 22). Kılıçdaroğlu: Suriyeli kardeşlerimizi geri göndereceğiz [We are going to send our Syrian brothers back] Received from http://www. milliyet.com.tr/kilicdaroglu-suriyeli-kardeslerimizi-mersin-yerelhaber-744369/ available on: 10.10.2016 (in Turkish)

--- (2016, March 11). Kılıçdaroğlu: Suriyelilerden yeraltı dünyasının aktörleri çıkacak [There will be underground actors among Syrians] Received from http://www. milliyet.com.tr/kilicdaroglu-suriyelilerden-yer-alti-izmir-yerelhaber-1261298/

--- (2016a, March 11). MHP: Türkiye daha fazla para verip göndermeli! [MHP: Turkey should give more money and send!] Received from http://www.milliyet. com.tr/mhp-turkiye-daha-fazla-para-verip/siyaset/detay/2207978/default.htm available on: 10.10.2016 (in Turkish)

--- (2016, April 26). CHP lideri Kılıçdaroğlu'ndan sert Kilis tepkisi [Strong Kilis reaction from the CHP leader Kılıçdaroğlu]. Received from http://www.milliyet.com.tr/ chp-lideri-kilicdaroglu-ndan-sert/siyaset/detay/2234227/default.htm available on: 10.10.2016 (in Turkish)

Özden, Ş. (2013). Syrian Refugees in Turkey, European Univerity Institute, Migration Policy Centre Research Report 2013/05.

Şirin Öner, N.A. & Genç, D. (2015). Vulnerability leading to mobility: Syrians' exodus from Turkey. *Migration Letters,* 12(3): 251-262.

Sirkeci, I. & Pusch, B. (Eds). (2016). *Turkish Migration Policy*. London: Transnational Press.

T24 News (2016, April 15). Başbakan yardımcısı Mehmet Şimşek: Suriyeli sığınmacılar geçici olmayabilir [Deputy Prime Minister Mehmet Şimşek: Syrian asylum-seekers may not be temporary] Received from http://t24.com.tr/ haber/simsek-suriyeli-siginmacilar- gecici- olmayabilir, 336377 available on: 10.10.2016

TIHK (2014). Workshop on Syrian refugees organized by the National Human Rights Institution of Turkey (TIHK). Received from http://www.tihk.gov.tr/tr/Duyuru-ve-Haberler/ArtMID/477/ArticleID/14/T252rkiye-İnsan-Hakları-Kurumu-tarafından-d252zenlenen-"Suriyeli-M252lteciler"-Konulu-199alıştay, available on: 13.10.2016

TRT Haber (2015, May 09). Özgür-Der CHP'yi protesto etti [Özgür-Der protested CHP]. Received from http://www.trthaber.com/haber/turkiye/ozgur-der-chpyi-protesto-etti-183741.html (in Turkish).

Tugsuz, N. & Yılmaz, A. (2015). Siyasi partilerin mülteci politikaları [Refugee policies of political parties], SETA Perspektif No. 106. Received from *http://file.*

setav.org/Files/Pdf/20150703162350_siyasi-partilerin-multeci-politikalari-pdf.pdf available on: 13.10.2016 (in Turkish)

UNHCR (2011). UNHCR Global Report 2011: Turkey. Received from http://www.unhcr.org/4fc880bb0.pdf available on: 19.02.2017

UNHCR (2015). 'More than four million Syrians have now fled war and persecution', the UN Refugee Agency (UNHCR). Received from http://www.unhcr.org/559d648a9.html available on: 27.09.2016

UNHCR (2016). Syrian Regional Refugee Response, Inter-agency Information Sharing Portal. Received from http://data.unhcr.org/syrianrefugees/ regional. php available on: 27.09.2016

UNHCR (2016a). UNHCR expresses concerns over EU-Turkey plan. Received from http://www.unhcr.org/news/latest/2016/3/56dee1546/unhcr-expresses-concern-eu-turkey-plan.html available on: 17.02.2017.

Van Dijk, T. A. (2002). Political Discourse and Ideology. Received from http://www. discourses.org/OldArticles/Political Discourse and Ideology.pdf available on 10.10.2016. available on: 10.10.2016

Ilgıt, Memişoğlu

Chapter Six

Syrian Refugees in a Slum Neighbourhood: Poor Turkish Residents Encountering the Other in Önder Neighbourhood, Altındağ, Ankara

Tahire Erman[*]

Introduction

The significance of space/place in the experiences of people is recognized and theorized in the literature, pioneered by Henri Lefebvre (1991). People not only are affected by the place they live in, but also, as active agents, they can create their own place. In this process, spatial clustering, either voluntary or forced, may have an enabling effect both in economic and cultural terms in the former, or create conditions of exclusion and poverty in the latter (Marcuse, 1997). The clustering of rural-to-urban migrants on the peripheries of big cities as they build their *gecekondus*[1] is well-documented in the Turkish context (e.g. Karpat, 1976; Gökçe, 1993; Erman, 2012), with some attention paid to its gendered outcomes (Erman, 1998). Today we are witnessing a new phenomenon in Turkey, which is about the clustering of people of a different nationality such as Syrian refugees[2] in the slum/gecekondu neighbourhoods of Turkish cities.

This paper makes its contribution by exploring Syrian refugees with a spatial perspective; it aims to discuss the role of spatial clustering in the context of Syrian refugees in Turkey. More specifically, it focuses on a slum neighbourhood in the Altındağ district of Ankara inhabited today both by Turkish and Syrian people (Figure 1), and investigates the relationship of the established local residents with the incoming Syrian refugees. It builds upon

[*] Department of Political Science and Public Administration, Bilkent University, Ankara, 06800 Turkey. E-mail: tahire@bilkent.edu.tr.
[1] *Gecekondu* refers to informal housing in Turkey. It literally means "landed overnight."
[2] I use the term "refugee" as a shorthand for their special status in Turkey as those under temporary protection.

the idea that the encounter of Syrian refugees and Turkish rural-to-urban-migrants in the context of poverty and disadvantages carry the potential of producing both hostility and hospitality, affected by broader external forces, which, as will we see in later sections, leads to more hostility than hospitality in this locality. In the following sections, first the local context is described, demonstrating how the presence of Syrians in the neighbourhood has been transforming the place. This is followed by the experiences and perceptions of the local Turkish citizens about their Syrian neighbours and how this has been affecting Syrians' new lives. The Altındağ Municipality's urban renewal project with respect to its potential impacts on local lives is also addressed.

Photo 1. A slum house.

The article is based on a qualitative research conducted between April and June 2016. Several visits to the neighbourhood[3] were paid during which informal conversations, as well as formal interviews (15) were carried out with Turkish citizens, along with interviews with the neighbourhood's muhtar and the director of the Önder Foundation in the neighbourhood. Informal conversations were also carried out with the student under whose guidance an aid initiative by Bilkent students was formed.[4] The interviewing

---

[3] The first visit was on a Saturday in late December, 2015, to an "informal" school run by a university students' aid initiative during which I helped Syrian girls get accustomed to the classroom atmosphere and start learning the Turkish alphabet.

[4] The aid initiative was sponsored in the Social Responsibility Projects Program of the University.

is accompanied by observations during the field visits organized by this aid initiative as we visited Syrian homes to deliver aid.

The respondents were all tenants except for two men, both early comers to the neighbourhood, one of them determined to stay here for the intimate neighbourly relations of the gecekondu, and the other one had moved to an apartment in Karapürçekler, running his developer business in this area. They migrated to Ankara from Bolu-Gerede (2), from the villages of Çamlıdere (4), Kızılcahamam (2), Yozgat (2), Gümüşhane (1), Kırıkkale (1), Kazan (1), Beypazarı (1), and Adana (1). They migrated in the early 1960s (3), early 1970s (2), 1985-86 (2), 1990s (4), 2000s (2), and 2012 (1); one was a second-generation migrant. Among them, three were men and 12 were women.

Önder Neighborhood (Siteler) in Altındağ, Ankara

I compiled the history of Önder neighbourhood from the conversations with the muhtar and several long-term residents and from the literature on the neighbourhood which is quite limited, and connecting it to my theoretical knowledge about the formation and transformation of gecekondus in Turkey, I came up with a description of the historical development of *Önder mahallesi*, which I present below (Photo 2).

Photo 2. Map of Ankara and Önder Neighbourhood (Source: Google Maps).

The Altındağ district in which this neighbourhood is located was left out of the planned city of Ankara in the early Republican era, making it available to land occupation by migrants coming from the countryside, who built their shanties which turned into gecekondus over the years (Şenyapılı, 2004).

Accordingly, Önder neighbourhood is one of the early gecekondu neighbourhoods of Ankara. As the muhtar said, the early comers to the locality were gypsies from Bolu-Gerede;[5] in 1955, it had the reputation of being the place of the gypsies. The presence of gypsies in the Altındağ district goes back to the 1920s when a tribe from Iran migrated to the region, making it also a temporary settlement for various gypsy groups from Anatolia (Şenyapılı, 2004). When the Siteler Industrial Region was set up in 1959, the areas in its vicinity attracted rural-to-urban migrants as the cheap labour force for the industry; they transformed the uninhabited land into their lower-income neighbourhoods (Üstün, 2016) by buying agricultural fields mostly producing wheat and subdividing them to build their houses. The developer from Gümüşhane said, they bought the land in 1961, built a house and moved in in 1963. The Selçuk Avenue was then a narrow street called 'the coal carriers road,' on which the coal was transferred to the Siteler Industrial Region. He continued, "Now they call it the Halep Avenue." The migrants to the area were from the villages of those cities close to Ankara such as Bolu, Düzce, Çankırı and Yozgat as well as from Ankara's districts such as Kızılcahamam and Çamlıdere (Beyhan, 2011). Today, as the muhtar told, those migrants from the provinces of Central Anatolia such as Çorum, Yozgat, Sivas and Tokat along with those from Gerede-Bolu make up the majority of the local population.

Over the years, as observed also in other gecekondu areas (Şenyapılı, 1982; Keyder, 2000; Erman, 2012), some municipal services and infrastructure were provided, converting it into a low-density neighbourhood. As the developer in the research described, when four or five families clustered in a specific location, they were provided with electricity and running water by the municipality when they asked for them; the closeness of the area to Siteler played a significant role in the provision of municipal services to the area. As observed also in many other gecekondu areas, under the populist politics in the national developmentalist era (1950-1980) (Danielson and Keleş, 1985; Öncü, 1988), land titles were distributed; in this area, many families had titles for agricultural land, and not for urban land on which buildings were permitted. Thus, today the majority have titles to their land, yet the land they own is very small since they have shared titles of many land owners, making it a big challenge for developers to negotiate with the land

---

[5] In fact, when I interviewed the Altındağ mayor in 2008 about urban transformation pro-jects, he had told me about the troubles caused by the gypsies from Bolu who had made it very difficult for him to start his urban renewal project in the area, especially by the *çeribaşı*—the leader of the gypsy community. Interestingly, the mayor was also from Bolu.

owners to be able to build apartment blocks on a particular plot (the developer mentioned sixty people who had shares on the plot on which his construction firm was planning to construct its next project). Moreover, as the land was passed over to new generations, the original land was further divided among the heirs. The early comer resident told that the early residents in Önder were timber workers (*keresteci*) at Siteler, and over the years as they improved their economic conditions, they had moved out to apartment districts, but they kept their gecekondus, renting them to families seeking affordable housing; those who stayed in the neighbourhood added new stories to their gecekondus to accommodate their married children in the same building. Today shanty-like houses who are rented by the poor and apartment buildings of few stories sit next to each other (Photo 3).

Photo 3. An apartment building in the area

As new migrants from the countryside moved in and those who improved their conditions moved out, it produced a kind of rotation among rural migrants, keeping the neighbourhood as the place of those with lower socio-economic positions. Those internal migrants who had some economic resources also moved into the neighbourhood in the 1970s; one of my respondents among them described it in her own words: "We bought land and build our house on it. The land was cheaper here." Just like many other gecekondu areas, the 1970s were the years of violent confrontations between the 'revolutionaries' (*devrimciler*) and ultra-nationalists (*ülkücüler*) in Önder, which were ended by Evren's military coup, mentioned by the developer. Since the 1980s, under the double processes of the expansion of the city towards its peripheries as better-off families moved out to the suburbs (Yaşar, 2010; Balta and Eke, 2011), and the transformation of gecekondu neighbourhoods into apartment districts (Erman, 2011; Aslan and Erman, 2014), which were initiated by the adoption of neoliberal policies that ended the urban populist coalition (Keyder, 2010), this neighbourhood has been altered both physically and socially.

Photo 4. Shops in the neighbourhood

Firstly, the neighbourhood has ended up at a location close to the city centre. Secondly, the neighbourhood has failed to commodify, which was enabled by the gecekondu amnesty law (no. 2981, 1984) and the gecekondu redevelopment law (no. 3194, 1985) that legalized the transformation of gecekondus into apartment buildings of no more than four storeys. This was for several reasons, such as the plots of many shared titles and the absentee landlords who allowed the decay of their gecekondus by not spending money for their maintenance, as well as the fact that those who got better-off by their businesses at Siteler made the strategic decision to keep their plots to increase their bargaining power with developers in the future, causing the slummification of the area to varying degrees. Today private developers have started transforming houses into apartment blocks, concentrating on both sides of the main avenue (Selçuk Avenue) (Photo 4). Thirdly, it has been attracting the poorest among internal migrants who do not have any choice but to live in decaying houses (for example, a Kurdish widow woman from Adana in the field study), and among those who had moved to the neighbourhood earlier, only the poorest ones have remained (widow women, older people, unemployed men). Moreover, the TOKI (*Toplu Konut Idaresi*-Mass Housing Agency of Turkey) project in the neighbouring district (*Doğantepe*) has been pushing those tenants displaced by the project to Önder and Hacılar neighbourhoods. And fourthly, the weak presence of state authorities has created an opportunity structure for those looking for a place out of sight for their illegal activities. Accordingly, Önder neighbourhood has become the place of the very poor; it has also become the habitus of criminal activities, particularly the "drug business," increasingly associated with crime and danger. In the boom of urban transformation projects of the TOKI and municipality partnerships in the 2000s, the neighbourhood is targeted by the Altındağ mayor as one of his urban transformation projects because of its location close to the city centre, making it a profitable area to be transformed into high-rise apartment blocks for the middle-classes.

Syrians, many of them from the city of Aleppo, are the most recent wave of migrants moving into Önder neighbourhood, along with Iraqis, Afghans and Somalis. Their demand of housing in the neighbourhood has caused another wave of exodus out of Önder, many Turkish families renting their houses to Syrians and moving out to other neighbourhoods.

We can identify several factors for the attraction of the neighbourhood for Syrians, along with some challenges the neighbourhood brings to their lives, addressed below.

Syrians in Önder Neighbourhood: Opportunities and Challenges

Firstly, the low rents (200-300 Turkish liras) as well as abandoned houses, which means living in low quality, low cost housing have attracted Syrians. As it has served the interests of Syrians, it has also served the interest of the local community by acting against the presence of drug addicts in the locality: "These houses are old houses; they were built 40, 50 years ago. They would collapse any time. If the Syrians had not moved in, *tiner*[6] addicts would have occupied the houses" (interview with the muhtar, 28.6.2016). Secondly, job opportunities have attracted Syrians: the neighbourhood is close to the Siteler Industrial region, which is the main site of the furniture industry in Ankara; it means getting jobs in the informal market, with wages

---

[6] An easily available chemical substance used to dilute paints.

quite low compared to Turkish citizens.[7] Many young boys also work in Siteler for long hours in return of little money. We met Muhammed (age 12) when he returned from work with his hands all black from the machine oil; he was working in Siteler, in a machine repair shop; he was paid 50 Turkish liras weekly and his working hours were between 8 a.m. and 8 p.m.; he worked every day except for one day in a week. Some Syrian boys (40 to 50 in number) also work in collecting waste material for recycling: they get the push cart from the junk dealer (*hurdacı*) in the morning, returning it in the evening with the waste materials they have collected; they are paid 5-10 liras depending on the amount. On one of our visits to the neighbourhood, we met a boy lying still in a couch; we were told that he was run by a car while collecting recycling materials.

Photo 5. Önder Foundation

Thirdly, Önder Foundation (*Önder İlim, Kültür ve Sosyal Hizmet Vakfı* – The Foundation of Science, Culture and Social Assistance) in the neighbourhood has been acting as a strong source of support for Syrians, distributing aid and coordinating aid activities (Photo 5). Set up in 1988, it was originally a civil society organization that aimed to provide educational support to the poor. It was largely transformed into an aid institution for Syrians upon their clustering in the neighbourhood: today, in addition to the aid they distribute, they organize courses for women to teach them skills (sewing, handicrafts,

---

[7] 50-75 Turkish liras of weekly wage for boys and 200 Turkish liras for adult men.

and computer) that would help them to be placed in jobs as well as Turkish language and Quran courses.

Having an Islamic orientation, it was very easy for the Foundation's leaders to take on the mission of helping their "Muslim brothers." The embracing of Syrian refugees by the Foundation was not approved by the local population at the early stages. The director of the Foundation said, *"Our foundation got the first reaction from the people; they threw stones at our storage depot, it was three years ago. They did not want foreign people in their neighbourhood"*. The Foundation holds a strong political position; it acts as a filtering mechanism, choosing for their aid those Syrians who bring a martyrdom certificate to the Foundation from the *Muhalif* (Opposing) groups fighting in Syria (i.e., the Free Syria Army). Thus, those Syrian refugees who are sympathetic to the AKP government are embraced by the Foundation (Photo 6).

Photo 6. "Hanging the giraffe": The symbolic violence against Esad

"Civil initiatives" organized formally as foundations and associations,[8] or informally as "special formations" in the words of the Foundation's director, are pouring aid to Önder. One "special formation" is about a chain of aid coming from outside individual sources to the local women to be distributed to the Syrians. As I learned from the woman respondent who was at the core

---

[8] As said by the Önder Foundation's director, there are two or three foundations and five or six associations, along with twelve platforms working in the neighborhood.

of such an arrangement, "Ali Aid" or "Ahmet Aid" (she saved their numbers on her mobile phone as "*Ali Yardım*" or "*Ahmet Yardım*" and mentions them as such) collects small amounts of money from his circle of acquaintances, like 100 or 200 liras, and gives the money to a local woman who would use her local knowledge to reach needy Syrian families; her help would range from paying electricity bills to finding homes, from buying/finding furniture to grocery shopping, from paying rents to paying for bottled gas. She would cut the aid if she found out that they were cheating on her or when they improved their economic situation which she would detect by the cars they bought.

To sum up, cheap rents, low-paying jobs and the distribution of aid have attracted to the neighbourhood those Syrians from the lower socio-economic strata; many were small-scale tradesmen such as tailors and grocers when they lived in Syria. Some were guided to the neighbourhood from the bus terminal when they asked for cheap housing; others came to join their relatives living in the neighbourhood.

The opportunities that Önder neighbourhood provide for the Syrian refugees of lower standing, however, are accompanied by serious challenges. Firstly, the criminal activities and groups in the locality render them vulnerable. Especially women and children are risk groups. For example, in 2014, there was an attempt by the local drug dealers to use Syrian children staying in an "orphanage"[9] to sell *bonsai* (a synthetic drug); they put the building on fire when they faced resistance;[10] following the event, the orphanage was moved to Gaziantep. Widows and their grown-up daughters may be facing the risk of being pulled into prostitution: as the student in charge of the university aid initiative told me, "*We rehoused a family with eight children to Pursaklar [a district in Ankara known for its Islamist identity] because of our concern that the beautiful girl Zeynep in the family could be kidnapped.*"

The ordinary Turkish people may also constitute a threat to the local Syrian families. The vulnerability caused by their vaguely defined status has opened the path to easy harassment, especially of young women. As I have observed, some Turkish men who define themselves as the protectors of Syrians tend to transgress the boundary of proper neighbourly relations. As observed in the field research, a Turkish man who helped a Syrian family find an old

---

[9] In Turkish, "*yetimhane*"; it was a building spared for women and children who did not have their husbands or fathers with them.

[10] In the press, it was presented as the reaction of Turkish locals to Syrians in their neighbor-hood, not revealing the real reason behind it.

abandoned house to live in, which was close to his house, would come late in the evenings for the young woman in the family (a widow whose husband had been killed in the civil war); eventually the family had to move away: believing that the police would not take their complaint seriously because of their status in Turkish society, they were intimidated to contact the police. Turkish young men find Syrian women very attractive, and incidents causing serious problems to Syrian women are not few; once a Turkish man driving a car chased a Syrian woman who was going to the health centre where she was employed and he forced her to step on the car which she hardly could avoid. Other times they would face verbal harassments. Syrian men are very suspicious of the presence of Turkish men in their houses, keeping their young wives and grown-up daughters in separate rooms from Turkish male visitors.

Violent encounters between the two groups have been spreading. The security problem caused by the presence of Syrians in the locality and the violence against them demonstrate the paradoxical nature of the issue. On the one hand, as the muhtar complained:

> The Syrians spoiled everything when they started coming here. The security problem got worse; the neighbourliness declined. Before, everybody knew each other; we even kept our doors unlocked. We were together 24 hours, eating together, drinking tea together. We were tied by a strong sense of sharing. But now you know nobody, everybody comes here. They may be from ISIS or PKK, they may be outlaws, you never know. But you cannot stop them in the street and ask for their identity card. Even the police cannot do anything about it.[11]

On the other hand, the local Syrians are under the threat of violence. Fights between the youth of the two groups take place from time to time. The high rates of unemployment among the youth, both Turks and Syrians, have been creating risks of engagement in criminal activities; some Syrian youth have started their own drug business, which may cause outbreaks of violence in the near future.

The biggest violent incident took place in the aftermath of the July 15 coup attempt (2016) during which several stores run by the Syrians were put on fire and the merchandises inside the stores were looted; a couple of Syrians

---

[11] I also heard people complaining about the increasing burglary in the neighborhood, which they said the Syrians themselves or the chaotic environment they created caused it.

were seriously injured. The police did not/could not prevent it. In the aftermath of the event, Syrian men gathered in the neighbourhood's square and tried to retaliate but were not allowed by the police. Today they have become more organized in informal ways: when they hear about any such threat, they inform each other and get ready to confront it. The Turkish flags on the windows or hanging them down the balconies are the signs used by the Turkish families to distinguish themselves from the Syrians, which they felt necessary in the aftermath of the coup attempt (Photo 7).

Photo 7. Turkish flags on Turkish homes

Secondly, the district municipality's urban renewal project, which targets the demolition of hundreds of houses, renders Syrian residents vulnerable along with their Turkish neighbours. The Altındağ Mayor declared the neighbourhood along with the Ulubey and Hacılar neighbourhoods as the site of an urban transformation project. In the summer of 2015, some 1.000 houses were demolished, rendering Syrian refugees homeless for the second time, the first one caused by their fled from their war-torn country. Some families moved into TOKI apartments in Baraj neighbourhood in northern Ankara, i.e., high-rise apartment blocks built by TOKI in its partnership with the Metropolitan Municipality of Ankara in the Northern Ankara Urban Transformation Project; they built once again their habitus in a new location. The fact that Baraj is in a remote location and the TOKI apartments there are facing the risk of remaining uninhabited when they fail to be attractive to prospective tenants, has made it available to Syrians. On the other hand, some other families have remained in Önder, trying to survive, several of them living in the houses around the debris left from the demolitions, creating serious health problems (Photo 8).

Photo 8. Debris from the demolition

The area of demolished houses has turned into a garbage dumping site, smelling very bad, and, with its lack of social control, it has been posing serious danger to the local people especially after dark inviting criminals, bonsai users and homeless people to the area. As the muhtar explained, the legal problems between the municipality and some land owners are causing the delay of the project, and yet the mayor is determined to continue with the demolitions, if not this year, then the next one. This has been causing the local population much stress, Turkish and Syrian residents alike; they are concerned about how they can survive in the neighbourhood after its "regeneration". When apartment buildings replace gecekondus, the rents will go up. Today the lowest apartment rent is around 500 Turkish liras. Moreover, as the muhtar explained, apartment owners do not prefer Syrians because of the fact that they have crowded families with many children; they are also perceived as a threat to their safety. Thus, gecekondus provide temporary shelter to many Syrian families as they try to establish their lives in a foreign country. In the words of the muhtar, gecekondus save Syrians time to get ready to move into "normal housing." But gecekondus will soon be gone. Accordingly, the "Little Aleppo," which is described below, is a quite vulnerable formation.

Transformation of the Neighbourhood by Syrians: The "Little Aleppo"

Syrians have been coming to the neighbourhood since 2012. I was told during the interview with the muhtar that they were almost 70% of the local population in 2015; their number exceeded 4.000 in 2014 (Yıldırım, 2014). Despite the fact that this number decreased following the mass demolition of houses in 2015 in the mayor's urban transformation project, they still make up the largest "foreign" group in the neighbourhood. The other "foreign" groups have been moving out of the neighbourhood: Iraqis have moved out mostly to the 'Star' area (*Kuzey Yıldızı*) into the TOKI blocks because of their dislike of Syrians; as a woman devoted to aid Syrians said, only a few Iraqis were left and they were those "who did not have their men as the head of the family." The number of Somalis has also diminished when the state sent them out to a "concentration camp" in the words of the muhtar in Burdur, a provincial city of Turkey. Thus, as Iraqis and Somalis left Önder, Syrians have become dominating the neighbourhood. It is hard to know the exact number of Syrians because of the lack of recent official statistics, yet as I observed, their number is increasing as Syrian families are bringing their female relatives and children to the neighbourhood to live with them, leaving the men back in Syria to fight. A recent example is a Syrian woman who brought her five married daughters and their children to Önder; they are sharing the same apartment until they are relocated in other apartments, 13 children crowding in the place.

Clustering in the same space, Syrians have created their own habitus and reproduced their culture under precarious conditions. Some houses are surrounded by fences to create privacy for the female members of the families (Photo 9). One can see words in Arabic on store fronts, both of those run by Turkish and Syrian merchants (Photo 10). They have turned deteriorating houses into their homes (Photo 11, 12), as well as into grocery stores (some food is brought from Syria), tailor shops (some sew only black *nimas* -- a long dress for women), small bakeries, restaurants, furniture stores, and fashionable clothing stores (See photo 4). The streets once lined by ruined houses have become revitalized as a result, bringing a lively atmosphere (Photo 13). Moreover, they set up a weekly open market of their own, both in Önder and Hacılar, called "Syrian markets" (*Suriyeli pazarı*) (Photo 14).

Photo 9. Syrians putting up fences for privacy

Yet all this happens in an unregulated way. Since the stores are not inspected by municipal authorities, hygiene problems arise. The "informal" open markets take place in the midst of the debris left from the mass demolition of the houses in the Municipality's urban renewal project (Photo 14); interestingly, they are located in the vicinity of the municipality's stand of free bread for Syrians.

September 2013   April 2016

Photo 10. A street in Önder before and after the Syrians

Photo 11. Outside a Syrian home

Photo 12. Inside a Syrian home

Despite these problems, there are advantages of the "Syrian open markets" both for Syrian and Turkish residents: they have access to cheap products (e.g. potatoes that are produced in a neighbouring village are sold directly by the villages for 50 kuruş per kilo, whereas they are 1.20 liras in the weekly "formal" market). The Turkish merchants, who are very few, are happy with their Syrian customers who buy large amounts of food (sacks of potatoes and onions) for their crowded families. However, the merchants at the weekly market on Wednesdays are against the "Syrian market" because it harms their business. Upon their complaint, there would be raids by the municipality police on the Syrian market on Wednesdays, pulling down the stands.

Photo 13. Arabic language on Syrian stores

Moreover, staying out of the regulation by authorities brings advantages to Syrian storeowners: they can sell goods much cheaper than their Turkish counterparts who are expected to comply with the Municipality's rules and regulations and have to pay taxes. This hurts the feeling of fairness in trade of Turkish local storeowners, often making them position themselves against Syrians. The muhtar expressed his views, supporting the concerns of Turkish locals:

> *Syrians do not pay taxes, this is ridiculous. This brings them advantage in competition. Local tradesmen cannot compete with them. Here lots of storeowners went bankrupt. In the stores of Syrians, no hygiene, nothing; in their restaurants, pastry shops, bakeries, no inspection, everywhere is filthy. The municipal authorities allow anything when it is the Syrians' stores.*

Erman

Photo 14. The Syrian open market

Not only in trade but also in the religious sphere Syrians have been transforming the neighbourhood. Quran courses are delivered by Syrian teachers informally; a *medrese* has been opened in the basement of a building by the help of some *vakıf*s, hidden from outside gaze (Photo 15).

Photo 15. The medrese

Among the local Turkish population, especially some poor women are becoming more engaged in religious practices: for example, a middle-aged woman from Gerede-Bolu, whose husband is unemployed, has started participating in *zikir*[12] meetings of her Syrian neighbours with whom she had close relations. Veiled women and girls dominate the public spaces of the neighbourhood, giving the image that the neighbourhood is not part of the capital of secular Turkey. Since the Turkish citizens in this locality are Sunni Muslims of conservative breeding from the villages of Anatolia, excluding the Roman community, the scene of veiled women, except for a few, do not create local reaction. Local Syrian leaders, such as the Syrian teachers in the locality, are strict on creating the same rules and norms that they had back in Syria. For example, I was surprised during my visit to the "informal school" when I noticed the female university students, mostly exchange students from Western countries, covering their heads upon their arrival to the building. When I asked why, I was told that the Syrian teachers who had contacted the university initiative to offer Turkish courses for Syrian children including girls had insisted that the women in the group should cover their heads while teaching Syrian girls, a rule with which I did not comply. They also had insisted that boys and girls should be given courses in different rooms and boys should be instructed by male teachers and girls by female teachers.[13] As I was told, the Syrian leaders in the locality were holding debates about the assimilation question, mostly agreeing to take a position against it.

Syrians renting houses stand out as an important agent of the locality's cultural transformation: what they eat, the way they eat, when they sleep, the way they talk, the way they walk, as will be detailed in the following section using quotations from respondents, differ from the Turkish culture. These cultural differences, along with the conflicts of interest have created tension in the relationship between the Turkish and Syrian locals.

Apart from cultural differences, the distribution of aid to Syrians has created tension between the two groups. The strong presence of Syrians has attracted various groups to this neighbourhood: civil society organizations, politicians, media people, student groups, all started coming, bringing the neighbourhood into public attention. Önder neighbourhood is not a slum neighbourhood kept out of sight anymore, but a neighbourhood which is home to Syrians—"our Muslim brothers" victimized in their country by their

---

[12] *Zikir* is an act of repeating religious utterances as part of rituals in Islam, moving the body back and forth to go into trance.

[13] When a female teacher had patted on the head of a boy, the boy had reacted, running back to his family and complaining that his "ablution was broken."

own government.[14] Ranging from searching for political gains to helping the war victims with altruistic motives, groups appeared in the locality, pouring in aid of various kinds. A neighbourhood of isolation against the outside world has become a place of outsiders coming under the cloak/motive of good will, as told by the head of the students' aid initiative:

> *The neighbourhood was isolated before. Now everybody is here, the ministers, MPs, Europeans, journalists. The neighbourhood has opened itself out to the outside world. This freed it from the control of some specific groups (i.e., the local gangs), the locality released its stress. Before I would not dare to go there, but now we can go there with our women   friends in cars to distribute aid.*

These changes in the locality have affected local Syrians and Turkish citizens differently, causing tension especially when the latter group is excluded from the incoming aid. The relationship between the two groups full of tension and contradiction, and some sympathy, is detailed below.

Local Turkish Citizens' Perceptions of the Other in Their Locality: Hostility versus Hospitality

The local residents described it as a chaos when Syrians first came to the neighbourhood in large numbers; they were sleeping in the streets and in the parks. In the words of a local woman, *"They disturbed the peace in our neighbourhood. We could not even walk in the streets. I have been living here for 32 years, it is the first time that I witnessed such disarray."* Also the different appearance of Syrians surprised the local people in their first encounter, *"The first Syrian I saw was dressed in white, it seemed odd. We were not familiar with such attire; we have somewhat used to it."* They have got rid of the feeling of intimidation by the strangeness of the newcomers, and in the early presence of Syrians in the neighbourhood, several families tried to provide for them, how modest that might be (e.g. a plate of hot soup, some old carpets and furniture). Yet today they have been experiencing conflicts and confrontations as Syrians have settled in the neighbourhood. The cause is firstly cultural: in the words of the Önder Foundation's director, *"We do not have a sectarian problem, everybody is Sunni Muslim, but a cultural problem has occurred."* This is elaborated in the section below.

---

[14] In the press, this neighborhood is called the "home of Syrian refugees in the Turkish capital."

"We don't want them here": local Turkish people's reactions to local Syrians

Cultural differences

As time has passed, Turkish and Syrian residents have come to know each other more closely; they started noticing their cultural differences, which breed contempt by the former against the latter, expressed in the following quotations:

> We donated the furniture and clothing that we did not use to the Syrians. But we are offended when they throw the bread into the garbage. They do not eat bread, they eat lavaş... They do not know how to walk in the street; they, women and children altogether, walk in the middle of the asphalt road. They do not give way when they see a car coming... Their   children are too many.

> They do not throw the garbage in plastic bags, they directly throw them down the balconies. They throw the macaroni and bread right into the garbage.

> When the carpets get dirty, they do not wash them, they just throw them away. We don't have that habit of throwing things away. Look, I found this cloth at the garbage site, I washed it and now I am using it on my table.

> They stay late at night and make so much noise.

The local Turkish citizens seem to differentiate themselves from their Syrian neighbours by emphasizing their cultural supremacy in terms of some mundane features such as cleanliness as well as their life choices such as having less children, which implies being modern and more advanced. Situating themselves as such, they also display a conceited attitude, together with feelings of pity regarding Syrians' religious practices, for example saying that Syrians' lives are better here away from the enforced very strict religious practices in their own country such as little children's fasting.

The cultural differences discourse takes on an alarming tone regarding the gender issue:

> They are so free in their behaviour, both men and women. They stay out late at night. Women dress up and stay at home, they order their

children to do things for them"; "Some (Turkish men) left their wives for them (Syrian women). This is so gross.

The concern of Turkish women about the possible attraction of their husbands to Syrian women has been confirmed in the words of the Foundation's director, who sees some "positive" outcomes as Turkish women feel the need to be obedient to their husbands in their competition with Syrian women:

Many of our women tend to get jealous of Syrian women. Syrian women pay attention to their looks, but Turkish women neglect themselves once they get married. As our men are attracted to Syrian women, our women have become obedient and respectful of their husbands. Before, they would act like the lion of the family.

I was told that some 100 Syrian young women married Turkish men, creating "Syrian type" of relations between the spouses, which means more subordinated positions for women, sharpening the gender inequality in the family in favour of men.

Moreover, the degree of violent behaviour in the Syrian population, including children due to the trauma they experienced in their lives back in Syria, produces dislike in the Turkish residents:

When they fight with guns in their hands, they are so brutal, they never feel any pity for others. They are not merciful like us, they are so away from feeling pity.

During the field trips, I observed the aggressiveness in children, in boys more than girls, while playing, which created serious concerns for our aid group.

The language is another barrier in the neighborly relations between Syrian and Turkish residents. As I observed, Turkish women would get frustrated when their Syrian neighbors remained behind doors without communicating with them; they blamed Syrians for not socializing with them, not recognizing the fact that they did not speak Turkish. This problem was solved in the case of Turkomans from Syria.

The fact that the two groups, despite their common religion, have differences in the cultural practices of everyday life, undoubtedly, creates some tension in neighbourly relations. In this locality, moreover, this is intensified as conflict over material gains arises, demonstrated below.

Competition and contestation over local power and material gains

The negative perception of the local Turkish residents against their Syrian neighbours arising from cultural differences gains a deeper meaning under the imperatives of contestation for economic opportunities and power in the locality. The concentration of Syrians in this neighbourhood has become overwhelming for the Turkish residents:

> *They do not live among us; we live among them. They have become the majority.*

> *In the beginning, it was not like this. We welcomed them. Now they look down on us. They don't want us here. Even their kids dare to speak against us. It is like Turkey is their own country, not ours. They have no fear whatsoever.*

> *They don't like us. Would they be willing to accept us if we went to their country? Definitely no.*

The muhtar agrees, explaining it by the Turkish state's too permissive attitude towards Syrians: "*They started challenging the Turks. Many fights take place among neighbours because of children. Our state has too much goodwill and extreme tolerance for Syrians. This is not good.*"

The unfair bargaining positions of the two groups emerge as another breaking point in their relationship: the fact that Syrians work at any job for very little money and they sell very cheap goods at their stores is interpreted by the Turkish locals as the source of new difficulties in their already troubled lives: "*They do a job of 350 liras for 100 liras, 10 or 11 year olds work for nothing. They are job stealers*"; "*They get the jobs, our men remain unemployed.*"

The increase in rents in the neighbourhood when Syrians moved into old houses, fixing them, is another issue (Photo 16, 17). Tenants as always are the most vulnerable in the locality: While homeowners are benefitting from rent increase, tenants, who are mostly widows, disabled and old people, and the very poor among whom there are recent comers of Kurdish origin, are much concerned about it.

Photo 16. A house inhabited by a Syrian family

In the words of a widow who lives in the old house of her in-laws free of rent:

> *The rents went up. Nobody from our neighbours remained; they all rented their places and went out. It is only people like us who cannot leave here.*

As important as the competition for jobs and housing is the feeling of unfairness that arises when the aid coming to the neighbourhood for the poor goes solely to Syrians:

> *We are also poor people; we are needier than them. We live in destitute. Why don't they give us aid?*

> *We cannot receive aid, all goes to them. We also need social aid, we are poor and helpless. As a Turkish citizen, I am asking for aid.*

> *All the aid goes to them. We just stay petrified. The Vakıf (Önder Foundation) says, 'Nothing for you.'*

> *All the attention is on the Syrians. They (authorities) have forgotten us.*

Photo 17. Another Syrian home

Here it should be mentioned that the social aid from the state authorities is limited to the Municipality's provision of daily bread, supply of coal during winter months (but some Syrian families do not have stoves) (Photo 18), and the distribution of packages of food and hygienic materials twice a year and the aid in cash of the District Governor Office's Social Aid and Solidarity Fund, to which poor Turkish citizens are also entitled. The source of complaints is about the distribution of various goods by those civil society groups who have entered the neighbourhood upon the accumulation of Syrian refugees here. In the words of the muhtar, "*The Municipality and the District Government provide aid both for Turks and Syrians. But the foundations target Syrians. That's why there are complaints.*" Not only the unfairness in the distribution of aid but its misuse by Syrians is highly criticized by the local Turkish citizens, saying that Syrians sell the bread and tea they get for free from the Municipality; it creates the image of Syrians as abusers of the Turkish system.

Photo 18. Syrian children playing with the coal packages distributed by the Municipality

Despite such negative developments as the perception of Syrians has changed from "victimized Other" to "permanent Other" as neighbours, some residents present their attitudes in a positive discourse yet it is clouded by their own experiences; negative feelings and perceptions are not expressed openly, creating ambivalences, which are exemplified below.

"They are our Muslim brothers, but..." "They are humans too, but..." "I like my Syrian neighbour, but..."

In their empathy for Syrians, a few women in the research did not mention negative attitudes. However, as they visualized their Syrian neighbours living next door, they did not welcome the thought of Syrians sharing their neighbourhood, as expressed in this quotation:

> *We welcome them, they are humans too; they have been going through so much suffering. One feels pity for them. (But) They do not fit with our way of doing things. They throw bread into the garbage. I warn them if I see. They throw the bread together with sanitary pads.*

Common religion was also mentioned as shaping their positive attitude, but again Syrians were not welcomed:

> We do our best because they are our Muslim brothers.[15] But we would like them to go. Let them go. In their country, they say they used to live luxurious lives. They do not like the houses here, but they are desperate.

Even the woman who devoted herself to help Syrians complained:

> They all tend to sell the aid they get. They try to deceive you, hiding what they have got before. When they get more aid, they sell the extra, food, coal, stoves. They eat cheese if it is high quality, if it is not, they sell it to their Turkish neighbours. But this is wrong. They should eat it. Turkish people try to do the best with what they have. But Syrians complain, they say they were used to good lives back in Syria and that it is difficult to live this kind of life here. But they should appreciate what they receive.

Interestingly, several women from the gypsy community with whom I talked on the street expressed positive views; they said that they were happy about their easy going Syrian neighbours and the public attention they brought to the locality. A woman whose husband was in jail said: "*We help Syrians. They do not gossip. They mind their own business. They keep away from trouble.*" Their stigmatization in society and the vulnerability of their families for criminal activities have created some kind of bonding with their Syrian neighbours. Moreover, some widows or those women whose husbands worked out of town seemed to have a quite welcoming attitude towards their Syrians neighbours: some empathised with them ["*I suffered a lot in my life. So I want to help them. They are suffering humble people (gariban)*"]; some others brought forward their being devoted Muslims who tried to be in good relations with their Turkish neighbours. However, when it comes to the question of Syrians staying in the neighbourhood as a community, their attitude turned to negative.

In their attempt to reach new opportunities that would bring them material gains (how limited it might be, for example using her Syrian neighbour's free

---

[15] Syrians emphasize Islam as their claim to belonging to the neighborhood: "*Ezan* (call to prayer) is very important to us. Religion is very important"; "We are both (Turkey and Syria) Muslims."

bread card at the municipality's bread stand), some Turkish residents tried to get along with the Syrians, and as mentioned before, a few of those from the gypsy community have become more involved with religious activities to overcome the social stigma attributed to gypsies as the "undeserving poor" who could make their living with criminal activities, joining *zikir* meetings of the Syrians and frequenting the Quran courses at the local mosque.

"I will help them despite their lying": The zekat culture in the Locality"

As the student in charge of the aid initiative called it, there has emerged a "*zekat* culture"[16] in the neighbourhood by external actors. Although in their access to economic resources, the *zekat* culture is more relevant to the middle and upper classes than the poor, in Önder a few local women have devoted themselves to helping the Syrians in their neighbourhood for reasons of *sevap* (a religious reward in Islam for doing good deeds). One of the respondents was embedded in this *zekat* culture. Despite her devotion to aid Syrians, she criticized them: "*They lie a lot. They buy makeup materials, they smoke nargile* (an instrument for smoking tobacco). *But I help them. They get angry at me when I stop giving them aid, cursing at me. But I don't care. The God will decide.*" The reaction from the local Turkish community to the Syrians rendered her vulnerable: "*The Turks are against my activities helping Syrians. The mosque hoca warned me that they might try to harm me, throwing stones at my house. They accused me of helping Syrians because I was paid; they said I was bad luck for the neighbourhood. But I still continue my aid activities. This gives me so much happiness. I feel at peace.*" The "*zekat* culture" is contested in this locality of the poor: the Önder Foundation was set on fire twice, the windows of the truck bringing aid to the Syrians were broken down, and the house of a Turk helping Syrians was stoned.

Conclusion

When the *Other* appears in the locality of the poor, those at the bottom of society, it embodies the possibility of both bonding and confrontation, i.e., hostility and hospitality. The territorial fight between different migrant groups is vividly demonstrated in the spectacular movie West Side Story about Puerto Ricans and Italians/the Irish in the upper west side neighbourhood of Manhattan, New York City. In the post-war American context, in the struggle to open up space for themselves, competition rather than cooperation shaped their relationship. On the other hand, the

---

[16] *Zekat* is a form of alms-giving treated in Islam as a religious obligation.

challenging conditions of public housing in locations of crime and violence again the USA have created cooperation among residents of diverse ethnic and religious groups, helping each other to survive under very disadvantageous living conditions (Clampet-Lundqyist, 2010; Manzo, Kleit and Couch, 2008). In other societies, we observe similar dynamics of cooperation and competition based on local contexts in specific time and place. This hospitality versus hostility between the established population and newcomers is observed when newcomers spatially cluster, making their presence visible. The migrants from Turkey created their colonies for example in Kreuzberg in Berlin ("Little Istanbul") (Kaya, 2000); in the 1970s, Hamburg's St Pauli neighbourhood was mainly resided by Turkish immigrants along with German workers and political activists (personal interview, 2014). In Denmark, Rinkeby neighbourhood was the ghetto of the immigrants from Turkey (Erder, 2006).

The case of Syrians in Turkey, who are given a special status by the Turkish state as "guests under temporary protection," complicates the issue by creating asymmetrical relations between Syrians and Turkish citizens sharing the same locality. As seen in the article, this asymmetry works in some instances to benefit Syrians by keeping them out of state regulations, for example allowing them not to pay taxes for their unregulated businesses, and in many instances it creates conditions of vulnerability by legally defining them via their temporary presence and hence excluding them from citizenship rights. The largely unregulated presence of Syrians in Turkish society, moreover, brings "informality" in the services provided for them by civil initiatives, opening up a space that can be manipulated easily for political causes; as observed in Önder neighbourhood, "civil initiatives" tended to bring the hidden agenda of the Islamization of society.

The encounter of Turkish citizens with Syrians in Önder neighbourhood repeats itself in some other neighbourhoods of the poor in Turkish metropolises, such as Zafer neighbourhood in Zeytinburnu where Kurds from Syria are clustered, and Mehmet Akif neighbourhood in Sultanbeyli where religious Sunni Arabs are clustered, both in Istanbul (Ok, 2016). These neighbourhoods, like Önder neighbourhood, were once gecekondu settlements built by migrants from the countryside, turning into slums over the years. Different from the European context in which the "Syrian refugee problem" is much regulated, keeping them in camps rather than allowing them into cities as "urban refugees," in the Turkish context such encounters of Syrians with the natives in specific localities are observed.

Erman

In such encounters, empathizing with their experiences of victimization, local residents may embrace their Syrian neighbours; or thinking them as their competitors, they may not welcome them. The broader external forces are important in shaping the direction. The "our Muslim brothers" discourse of the government and the mobilization of civil initiatives, formal and informal alike, in bringing relief to the Syrian war victims, who are Sunni Arabs fighting in the Free Syrian Army against the Esad regime and their families, have created a welcoming atmosphere for Syrians in those groups that support the AKP regime. Since the residents of Önder neighbourhood are also Sunni Muslims, many of whom AKP supporters, this has brought a positive attitude at the discursive level, especially during their early presence in the neighbourhood. However, this political discourse has been challenged in everyday experiences as their "Syrian guests" turned into their "permanent neighbours": the active presence of the Other in the neighbourhood, transforming it both culturally and physically into a Syrian habitus, has alarmed the local Turkish community. The reaction to Syrians of the local Turkish population deepens as they resent the fact that the Turkish government and civil initiatives do not care for them by targeting only the Syrians in their aid distribution. Interestingly, even the threat of mass demolition by the Municipality's urban renewal project could not unite the local population although both the Turkish citizens and the Syrian refugees would be victimized by the forced displacement by the Project. On the contrary, during the demolition of the houses, the tension between the two groups escalated, which was hardly prevented from turning into violent confrontations by the police (Kılıç, Berber and Çetin, 2015).

Here we should recognize that the local community is composed of various groups instead of being a homogenous unit. While the local criminal groups have been the most violent ones against the newcomers, ordinary citizens have been torn between helping their victimized Syrian neighbours and taking a position against them because of the Syrians' posing a threat to the reproduction of their everyday lives, both culturally and economically. While widows and some women of the gypsy community welcome the company of their Syrian neighbours, the male youth of nationalistic tendencies react violently against the presence of Syrians in their neighbourhood. Accordingly, based on the modest field research, it seems that gender and ethnicity make a difference in shaping the attitudes of the local people.

As concluding remarks, the lack of enough regulation in responding to the Syrian refugee problem and the politicization of the issue are causing serious harm both to the social fabric of Turkish society and the Syrian refugees who are left to their own fate in the urban context. Those at the bottom who are already vulnerable are hurt the most, yet their victimization remains largely out of the attention of authorities and the larger society.

References

Aslan, Ş. and Erman, T. (2014). The transformation of the urban periphery: Once upon a time there were gecekondus in Istanbul. D. Ö. Koçak and O. K. Koçak (eds.) *Whose City is That? Culture, Design, Spectacle and Capital in Istanbul*. Cambridge: Cambridge Scholars Publishing. pp. 95-113.

Balta, M. and Eke, F. (2011). Spatial reflection of urban planning in metropolitan areas and urban rent: A case study of Çayyolu, Ankara. *European Planning Studies,* 19 (10): 1817-1838.

Beyhan, B. (2011). Toplumsal-bilişsel yakınlık ve işgücü hareketliliği: Hemşehrilik bağları üzerinden bir irdeleme [Social-cognitive proximity and labour mobility: A study through fellowmenship ties]. *Anadolu University Journal of Social Sciences*, 11 (3): 199-238.

Clampet-Lundquist, S. (2010). "Everyone had your back": Social ties, perceived safety, and public housing relocation. *City & Community*, 9 (1): 87-108.

Danielson, M. N. and Keleş, R. (1985). *The Politics of Rapid Urbanization*. New York and London: Holmes and Meier.

Erder, S. (2006). *Refah Toplumunda Getto* [The Getto in a Welfare Society]. Istanbul: Bilgi University Publications.

Erman, T. (1998). Becoming "urban" or remaining "rural": The views of Turkish rural-to-urban migrants on the "integration" question. *International Journal of Middle East Studies*, 30 (4): 541-561.

Erman, T. (2011). Understanding the experiences of the politics of urbanization in two *gecekondu* (squatter) neighborhoods under two urban regimes: Ethnography in the urban periphery of Ankara, Turkey. *Urban Anthropology*, 40 (1,2): 67-108.

Erman, T. (2012). Urbanization and urbanism. M. Heper and S. Sayarı (eds.) *The Routledge Handbook of Modern Turkey*. London and New York: Routledge. pp. 293-302.

Gökçe, B. (ed.). (1993). Geeekondularda Ailelerarası Geleneksel Dayanışmanın Çağdaş Organizasyonlara Dönüşümü [The Transformation of the Interfamilial Traditional Solidarity in Squatter Settlements to Modern Organizations]. Ankara: Undersecretariat of Women and Social Services.

Karpat, K. (1976). The Gecekondu: Rural Migration and Urbanization. Cambridge: Cambridge University Press.

Kaya, A. (2000). 'Sicher in Kreuzberg': Berlin'deki Küçük Istanbul ['Sicher in Kreuzberg': The Little Istanbul in Berlin]. Istanbul: Büke.

Keyder, Ç. (2000). Liberalization from above and the future of the informal sector: Land, shelter, and informality in the periphery. F. Tabak and M. A. Crichlow (eds.)

Informalization: Process and Structure. Baltimore and London: The Johns Hopkins University Press. pp. 119-132.

Keyder, Ç. (2010). Istanbul into the twenty-first century. D. Göktürk, L. Soysal and İ. Türeli (eds.) Orienting Istanbul: Cultural Capital of Europe? Routledge: New York. pp. 25-34.

Kılıç, A., Berber, E., Çetin, S. (2015). Ankara Siteler Bölgesi'nin Önder ve Hacılar *Mahallelerinde Kentsel Dönüşüm Projesi Kapsamında Yapılan Yıkım Faaliyetleri ile İlgili Ön İnceleme Raporu* [The Preliminary Report about the Demolitions Carried out in the Framework of the Urban Transformation Project in the Önder and Hacılar Neighborhoods of the Siteler District in Ankara]. Ankara: Mazlumder.

Lefebvre, H. (1991). *The Production of Space.* Oxford: Blackwell Publishing.

Manzo, L. C., Kleit, R. G. and Couch, D. (2008). "Moving three times is like having your house on fire once": The experience of place and impending displacement among public housing residents. *Urban Studies*, 45 (9): 1855-1878.

Marcuse, P. (1997). The enclave, the citadel, and the ghetto: What has changed in the post-fordist U.S. city. *Urban Affairs Review*, 33: 228-64.

Ok, O. C. (2016). Networks and the sense of belonging: Syrian "refugees" in three localities in Istanbul. Paper presented to the course POLS 568 Urban Politics, Department of Political Science and Public Administration, Bilkent University.

Öncü, A. (1988). The politics of the urban land market in Turkey: 1950-80. *International* Journal of Urban and Regional Research, 12 (1): 38-63.

Şenyapılı, T. (1982). Economic change and the gecekondu family. Ç. Kağıtçıbaşı (ed.) *Sex Roles, Family and Community in Turkey*. Bloomington: Indiana University Turkish Studies 3. pp. 237-248.

Şenyapılı, T. (2004). "Baraka"dan Gecekonduya: Ankara'da Kentsel Mekanın Dönüşümü: 1923-*1960* [From the Shanty to the Gecekondu: The Transformation of Urban Space in Ankara: 1923-1960]. Istanbul: Iletişim.

Ustun, M. T. (2016). Suriyeliler geldiği zaman Ankara örneğinde mekanın yere dönüşüm serüveni [The transformation of space to place when Syrians came in the case of Ankara]. Ş. Geniş and E. Osmanoğlu (eds.) *Küresel ve Yerel Arasında Kentler* [Cities between the Global and the Local]. Proceedings of the Second International Conference of Urban Studies. Ankara: Adamor.

Yaşar, C. G. (2010). Politics of urban sprawl: The case of Ankara. Unpublished Master's Thesis. Ankara: Middle East Technical University.

Yıldırım, U. (2014). Suriyeli mültecilerin başkentteki yuvası [The home of Syrian refugees in the Turkish Capital]. Received from http://www.sabah.com.tr/ ankara.../suriyeli-multecilerin-baskentteki-*yuvası*...Accessed 10 April 2016.

Chapter Seven

Comparative Analysis of Public Attitudes towards Syrian Refugees in Turkish Cities of Ankara and Hatay

Güneş Gökgöz[*], Alexa Arena[±], Cansu Aydın[¥]

Introduction

Out of 2.8 million Syrian refugees in Turkey, about 10% of these people reside in 22 refugee camps situated within Turkish cities (AFAD, 2013; UNHCR, 2016; Sirkeci, 2017). The remainder of the Syrian refugee population in Turkey lives in urban areas amongst the local population. Major cities such as Istanbul, Ankara, and Izmir, as well as the cities located on the Turkish-Syrian border such as Gaziantep and Hatay, host the highest numbers of refugees (Directorate General of Migration Management (DGMM), 2016). Consequently, Syrian refugees are highly visible in most of the Turkish cities where they reside.

Turkey has maintained its ethnically selective immigration policies (i.e. favouring those with Turkish origins) until today, rendering the remainder of arrivals at the mercy of temporary migration schemes. Turkey's relationship to the international refugee regime is indicative of the country's historical response to migration inflows; Turkey maintains a geographical limitation to the 1951 UN Convention Relating to the Status of Refugees and its 1967 Protocol.[1] However, although Turkey is hesitant to grant refugee status

[*] Güneş Gökgöz, Global Migration and Policy Programme, Tel Aviv University, Israel.
E-mail: gunesgokgoz@mail.tau.ac.il
[±] Alexa Arena, Global Migration and Policy Programme, Tel Aviv University, Israel.
E-mail: alexaarena@mail.tau.ac.il
[¥] Cansu Aydın, Public Administration Department, Cornell University, United States.
E-mail: ca376@cornell.edu

[1] As per the original conditions of the Geneva Refugee Convention, Turkey only considers applications for refugee status from citizens of European countries. Most other signatories to the convention expanded their geographic scope to all continents as per the parameters of the 1967 Protocol.

under international law, Turkey granted refugees and those in "refugee like" situations certain rights with the Turkish Law on Foreigners and International Protection and the 2014 temporary protection regulation (For a full account of Turkish Migration Policy see Sirkeci and Pusch, 2016).

Although steps have been taken to incorporate the Syrian refugees, the rapid influx of this foreign population poses both institutional and societal challenges in Turkey. For the first time, Turkey is experiencing unprecedented numbers of urban refugees spread throughout the country who have no ethnic ties to the Turkish majority. Furthermore, the nature of the unending Syrian conflict and the expected permanency of Syrian refugees makes the situation incomparable to previous migration flows. The dual realities of unprecedented levels of immigration into Turkey coupled with the unique characteristics of the influx of Syrian refugees render the issues of integration of Syrians into Turkish society crucial. Consequently, public opinions and attitudes towards the refugees is a topic area that necessitates in-depth analysis.

It has been shown that anti-minority sentiments, hostility, and exclusionary attitudes tend to be higher in areas with greater concentrations of foreigners (Blalock, 1967; Fosset, 1984; Semyonov et al., 2004). In order to examine the relationship between foreign-born population size and exclusionary attitudes held by the majority, this analysis considers two Turkish cities, Ankara and Hatay, with relatively small and large populations of Syrian refugees, respectively.

Ankara, the capital of the Turkish Republic has a population of 5,270,575 people (Sirkeci, 2017). Ankara is host to some 66,998 Syrian refugees, totaling 1.27% of its population (Sirkeci, 2017). Hatay, a city bordering Syria has a population of 1,533,507 people (Sirkeci, 2017). Hatay hosts 379,093 Syrian refugees, constituting 24.732% of its population (Sirkeci, 2017). In Ankara, the refugee population is less visible in daily life, as the city is spread out and the refugee population is scattered around the city. In contrast, in Hatay the refugee population is more visible in the daily life. This is accentuated by the fact that the center of the city is smaller than that of Ankara. It is also relevant to note that the districts in the Hatay city are more dispersed around the city and it is not easy to commute between them. Therefore, interaction between locals and Syrian refugees manifests differently in each district. Regardless of the differing numbers of the refugees, the native populations and refugees do not have a platform to foster positive interactions.[2]

Given the background stated above, the aim of this analysis is twofold. Firstly, it aims to examine whether and to what extent the varying sizes of the Syrian refugee populations in Ankara and Hatay impact exclusionary attitudes held by the locals in Turkey. Secondly, it aims to assess whether and to what extent perceived threat mediates the relationship between exclusionary attitudes and the varying concentrations of refugees in the two cities.

In what follows theories and themes from the literature on public attitudes towards out-group populations are examined. Taking into account the context of the case study and the elaborated theoretical framework, derived hypotheses are presented. The data, variables, and research methodology are then introduced. Findings are represented and discussed in light of the theoretical underpinnings and setting of the research, and final conclusions are drawn.

Theoretical Background: Public Attitudes

Exclusionary attitudes towards ethnic and minority groups pervade all societies. Such attitudes can manifest in the "denial of equal access to political, civic and social or other kinds of rights to foreigners" (Gorodzeisky, 2013, p. 796). Mechanisms generating such attitudes are complex and context-specific.

It has long been theorized that the size of the minority population is relevant to intergroup relations (Blalock, 1967, as cited in Semyonov, 2004). A large body of research has revealed that there are prominent rises in exclusionary attitudes where minority groups are highly concentrated (e.g., Wilcox and Roof, 1978; Taylor, 1998; Semyonov et al., 2004). One of the major explanatory factors linking minority group size and exclusionary attitudes is the concept of perceived threat (Semyonov et al., 2004).

There are multiple types of perceived threat referred to in the literature. Most emphasis has been placed on economic threat. This form of threat is derived from the belief held by members of a receiving society that natives are exclusively entitled to the economic and social resources of the country. Therefore, competition anxiety arises when migrants vie for such sources as

---

[2] Positive interactions are the processes by which people engage in mutually supportive relationships with each other, and lead to a more cohesive society (Orton, 2012).

labour market opportunities and social welfare benefits (Quillian 1995; Scheve & Slaughter, 2001; Facchini & Mayda, 2009; Facchini, Mayda & Puglisi, 2013).

A second form of threat is cultural threat, which has increased in prominence alongside the geographic diversification of immigrant sending countries in recent decades. The shift in the scope of international migration and the consequent introduction of new cultures into receiving countries has rendered cultural concerns as salient factors creating exclusionary attitudes towards newcomers. Cultural threat is traditionally defined as perception of threat to cultural homogeneity and national identity of the receiving society (Semyonov et al., 2004; Gorodzeisky, 2013, Raijman and Semyonov, 2004).

A third type of threat is threat to the safety and security of individuals and groups. Scholars have long studied the link between immigration and crime. There is a popular perception that immigrants are responsible for a large portion of the crime rate in the receiving country, contrary to empirical evidence (Feracutti, 1968, Short 1997, Tonry 1997, Martinez & T. Lee, 2000).

The theoretical underpinnings expounded upon above informed the following four hypotheses. First, it is hypothesized that refugee population size impacts exclusionary attitudes. Second, higher concentrations of refugees in Hatay will lead to greater degrees of exclusionary attitudes held by residents as compared to residents of Ankara. Third, perceived threat plays a mediating role between the concentration of refugees and the exclusionary attitudes. Fourth, in the context of this case study, the greater concentration of refugees in Hatay will lead to higher levels of perceived threat and consequently more exclusionary attitudes as compared to Ankara.

Data, Variables, and Methods

The researchers collected the data for this analysis via structured surveys administered to students on university campuses in the cities of Ankara and Hatay in February and May 2016 respectively. The researchers used convenience sampling to disseminate the surveys to the students in several cafeterias on the campuses where students from a variety of departments and grade levels spend their leisure time.

The questionnaire administered to participants consisted of 28 questions. Related questions were modelled after the European Social Survey and the

Public attitudes towards Syrian refugees

World Values Survey, and were restructured for the context of this study.[3] Initially, pilot surveys were run in Hacettepe University in Ankara during October 2015. The pilot included additional open-ended questions in order to determine whether new themes were required for the final version of the survey.

The universities visited for the data collection are Ankara University, Gazi University, Middle East Technical University, Hacettepe University, and Bilkent University in Ankara, and Mustafa Kemal University in Hatay. Surveys were administered in the Turkish language to 1514 university students, of whom 1014 reside in Ankara and 500 reside in Hatay. In order to avoid any potential influence of immigration background on attitudes towards Syrian refugees, the sample was restricted to native-born Turkish students whose mother and father were also born in Turkey. Therefore, the final sample size employed for the study is 1429 students, of whom 948 reside and study in Ankara and 481 in Hatay.

The focus of this analysis is on exclusionary attitudes towards Syrian refugees. Therefore, the dependent variable is "exclusion from rights". Respondents were asked whether they agree with the following statement: 'The state should give more social and economic rights to Syrian refugees.' (I completely agree = 0, I completely object = 10).

The main independent variable is "city of residence" (Hatay = 1). As mentioned above, Hatay has a significantly larger population of refugees than Ankara. Hence, this variable was used as a proxy for refugee population size. The mediating variable is "perceived threat" which is an index constructed as an average score of responses to the four following questions: 'Is Turkey made a worse or a better place to live by people coming to live here from Syria?' (better place = 0, worse place = 10); 'Would you say it is bad or good for Turkey's economy that Syrian refugees come to live here?' (very good = 0, very bad = 10); 'Do you think the cultural life in Turkey is undermined or enriched by Syrian refugees coming to live here?' (0 = enriched, 10 = undermined); and 'Do you perceive Syrians as a safety/security threat to your well-being and the well-being of the people close to you' (not a security threat = 0, high security threat = 10). A perceived threat index was created by computing the mean values of the four

---

[3] The questionnaire was created as part of a larger research project, as part of the master's thesis of Güneş Gökgöz.

aforementioned variables. The correlation between the variables was confirmed by factor analysis data reduction.

A series of socio-demographic indicators were introduced as control variables. The socio-demographic variables include: gender (female = 1), age (in years), belonging to an ethnic minority (does belong = 1)[4], household income per capita (1 = very low; 2 = lower than average; 3 = average, 4 = higher than average; 5 = very high); religiosity (not religious at all = 0, very religious = 10).

The descriptive statistics depicting the respondents from Hatay and Ankara were compared. In order to test the aforementioned hypotheses, hierarchical linear regression models predicting perceived threat and exclusionary attitudes were estimated. First it was determined whether or not perceived threat is impacted by the relative size of the refugee population.[5] Second, it was tested if exclusionary attitudes are impacted by relative size. The impact of perceived threat on exclusionary attitudes was also examined. Next, the mediating effect of perceived threat on the relationship between relative size and exclusionary attitudes was measured via a mediation analysis. Lastly, in order to determine whether perceived threat is indeed a mediator, a Sobel test was applied. Theoretical framework of our study is depicted in Figure 1.

Figure 1. Analytical model

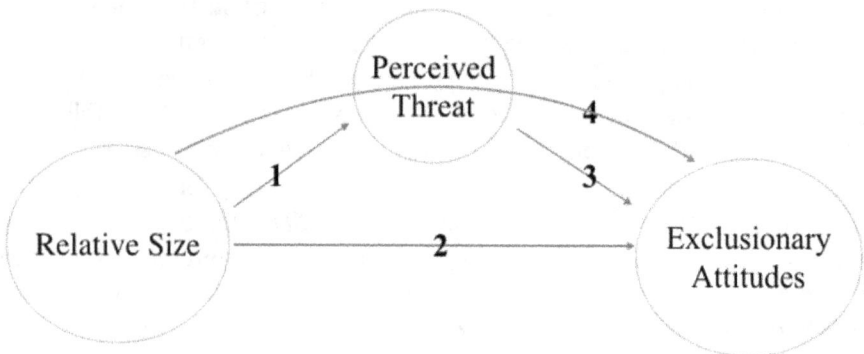

---

[4] The variable 'belong to an ethnic minority' is derived from the survey question "Do you be-long to an ethnic minority group in Turkey or not?" (translated from Turkish to English). Thereby, respondents self-reported ethnic minority membership.

[5] The variable 'city of residence' served as a proxy for the relative size of the refugee popula-tion in Ankara and in Hatay.

Analysis and Findings

Table 1 displays a descriptive overview of the characteristics of the samples from two cities in the study, Ankara and Hatay, as well as the characteristics of the overall sample. The table shows the sample sizes of the respondents from each city and their socio-demographic characteristics including: sex, age, self-reported identification of belonging to an ethnic minority group, religiosity, and self-reported rating of household income per capita. Additionally, values of the support for exclusion from rights and the perceived threat are presented.

Table 1. Descriptive statistics of the study sample

	Ankara	Hatay	Total
Age, mean, (std. d)	22.18 (2.38)	22.26 (2.89)	22.2 (2.55)
Gender, %			
Male	49.5	58.9	52.7
Female	50.5	41.1	47.3
Ethnic minority, %			
No	83	79.4	81.8
Yes	17	20.6	18.2
Income, %			
Very low	12.9	7.2	10.9
Lower than average	39.7	30.5	36.9
Average	30.6	36.9	32.4
Higher than average	11	17.4	13
Very high	5.8	8	6.8
Religiosity, mean, (std. d)	3.83 (2.79)	4.64 (2.97)	4.09 (2.87)
Security, mean, (std. d)	4.57 (3.16)	5.52 (3.45)	4.88 (3.29)
Cultural threat, mean, (std. d)	6.55 (2.97)	6.68 (3.40)	6.59 (3.11)
Better or worse place to live, mean, (std. d)	7.25 (2.39)	7.14 (3.09)	7.21 (2.64)
Economy, mean, (std. d)	7.32 (2.75)	6.91 (3.15)	7.18 (2.90)
Perceived threat index, mean, (std. d)	6.42 (2.05)	6.56 (2.29)	6.46 (2.13)
Exclusionary attitudes, mean, (std. d)	6.53 (3.04)	7.17 (3.37)	6.76 (3.17)

The data show slight cross-city variations in the values of support for exclusion from rights. It was found that respondents pronounced higher levels of exclusionary attitudes in Hatay than in Ankara on average. Similarly, levels of perceived threat in Hatay were respectively higher on average. The four factors included in the perceived threat index are displayed. Findings align with the theoretical framework suggesting that relative size of the out-group population and threat perception are positively correlated with one exception; perceived economic threat is higher in Ankara than in Hatay despite the fact that Syrian refugees are more highly concentrated in Hatay.

One of the most striking findings (not displayed in Table 1) is the frequency of responses to the question regarding exclusionary attitudes: results showed that 57% of all respondents favour severe or total exclusion from social and economic rights.[6]

Table 2. Coefficients of linear regression equations predicting perceived threat, perceived economic threat and exclusionary attitudes

	Perceived threat		Exclusionary attitudes	
	(1)	(2)	(3)	(4)
Age	-0.06***	-0.06***	-0.04	-0.04
Sex	(0.02)	(0.02)	(0.03)	(0.03)
Ethnic minority	0.031	0.05	0.04	0.09
Household Income	(0.11)	0.11	(0.15)	(0.15)
Religiosity	-0.72***	-0.74***	-0.64***	-0.67***
City of residence	(-0.15)	(-0.15)	(0.20)	(0.20)
Perceived threat	-0.014	-0.03	0.01	-0.03
	(0.05)	(0.05)	(0.07)	(0.07)
	-0.04**	-0.05**	0.03	0.2
	(0.02)	(0.02)	(0.03)	(0.03)
	-	0.21*	-	0.68***
	-	(0.12)	-	(0.04)
	-	-	0.68***	0.54***
	-	-	(0.04)	(0.16)
	8.12***	8.10***	3.09***	3.09***
	(0.54)	(0.54)	(0.77)	(0.77)
Adj. R²	0.022	0.023	0.227	0.232
*p ≤ 0.1, **p ≤ 0.05, ***p ≤ 0.01				

Table 2 shows the results of linear regression analyses predicting perceived threat and exclusionary attitudes. In the first model of Table 2, the set of control variables are a function of perceived threat. In Model 2, city of residence is added to the equation. This allowed the impact of relative size of the refugee population on perceived threat to be tested. Both Model 1 and 2 reveal that those who belong to an ethnic minority group in Turkey perceive Syrian refugees as less threatening than those who do not identify as an ethnic minority. Interestingly, in both models the effects of gender and household income per capita are not statistically significant predictors of perceived threat. Also, in both of the models it is found that perceived threat tends to decrease as religiosity and age increase. Lastly, in Model 2, it is found that respondents who reside in Hatay tend to project higher levels of perceived threat compared to their counterparts in Ankara.

The results of the regression analysis for exclusionary attitudes produced a similar result to the modelling of perceived threat. In Table 2 Model 3, the set of control variables are listed as functions of exclusionary attitudes. In addition, perceived

---

[6] Responses in the range of 7 to 10 were considered highly exclusionary.

threat was included in order to examine if perceived threat is a determinant of exclusionary attitudes. In Model 4, city of residence was added to the equation. In both of the models, support for exclusion from rights was less pronounced amongst those who belong to an ethnic minority group in Turkey. The effects of age, gender, household income, and religiosity were not statistically significant predictors of exclusionary attitudes. In both Models 3 and 4 it was found that support for exclusion from rights is likely to increase with perceived threat. Additionally, Model 4 showed that respondents who reside in Hatay assert higher levels of support for exclusion from rights as compared to their counterparts in Ankara.

Table 3. Direct, indirect, and total effect on exclusionary attitudes

	Total effect	Direct effect	Indirect effect (via perceived threat)
City of residence	0.638***	0.543***	0.14*
*$p \leq 0.1$, **$p \leq 0.05$, ***$p \leq 0.01$			

In Table 3 the direct and indirect effects via perceived threat on support for exclusionary attitudes are listed. In order to calculate the total, direct, and indirect effects, Baron and Kenny's method (1986) was utilized. In the regression analysis, it was found that city of residence impacts exclusionary attitudes, as does the perceived threat. Moreover, city of residence was found to be a significant predictor of perceived threat. Therefore, all conditions were met to run a mediation test to determine whether perceived threat plays a mediating role between relative size of the refugee population and exclusionary attitudes. To reiterate, the data listed in Table 3 confirmed that there is a causal relationship between perceived threat and exclusionary attitudes. The result of the mediation test indicated that the effect of the city of residence on exclusionary attitudes is only partially mediated by perceived threat. In order to determine if this finding was significant a Sobel test was conducted. Accordingly, the mediating effect of perceived threat was in fact statistically significant. Moreover, the findings of the total and direct effects were in line with the findings in Table 2.

Discussion

The primary aim of this comparative analysis between two Turkish cities was to examine the theoretical proposition that there exists a positive correlation between out-group size and exclusionary attitudes towards that minority population; and thus, to contribute to a better understanding of the social mechanisms informing Turkish natives' inclination to exclude Syrian refugees from rights in Turkey. Data reveal that over half of the respondents would deny granting more social and economic rights to refugees. This is a topic of increasing importance as Turkey transitions into an immigration country hosting a large number of Syrian refugees, especially in light of the fact that President Recep Tayyip Erdoğan recently discussed the possibility of granting Syrian refugees citizenship (Butler, 2016).

The results of the present research demonstrate that perceived threat and the resulting exclusionary attitudes held by Turkish natives towards Syrian refugees in Turkey are quite substantial. In line with the theoretical explanations, the data show cross-city variations in perceived threat and consequently in levels of support for exclusion from rights. That is to say that respondents who reside in Hatay, where the relative refugee population size is greater, tend to perceive Syrian refugees as a threat to Turkish culture, to safety and security, and to overall life quality (with the exception of economic life) more so than their counterparts do in Ankara; and as a result, they are more prone to prefer exclusion of refugees from rights than those who are in Ankara.

Notably, the findings reveal that respondents who self-reported as members of an ethnic minority group in Turkey feel less threatened by Syrian refugees than those who do not belong to an ethnic minority. These findings are in line with the theoretical underpinnings of cultural threat; it is expected that ethnic minority group members would not be culturally threatened by newcomers because they already fall outside of the country's cultural and national homogeneity. Similarly, members of ethnic minorities in Turkey are more inclined to convey inclusive attitudes towards these refugees than those who do not belong to an ethnic minority. The underlying reason for this could be their capacity to relate to the experience of being an ethnic minority. An alternative explanation could involve more positive and inclusive attitudes based upon shared ethnic ties between Syrian refugees and certain segments of Turkish society, such as Kurdish and Arab ethnic minority members.[7] It is necessary to note that Hatay is an ethnically diverse city whose history is intertwined with that of Syria.[8] This can also explain why the levels of negative attitudes (whether exclusionary attitudes or perceived threat) are only slightly higher in Hatay than in Ankara despite sizable differences in the refugee population sizes in the two cities. In addition to ethnic commonalities, shared religious background can explain the finding

---

[7] Syrian refugees are ethnically diverse, many coming from Sunni-Arab, Kurdish, and Turk-men ethnic backgrounds. Previous research has shown that the refugees prefer to reside in areas where these ethnic minorities are located in Turkey, due to the ease it provides in adaption processes (Apak, 2014; Dinçer, 2013).

[8] The people of Hatay have large ethnic and religious diversity, parallel to that of Syria's composition. Hatay was in fact a Syrian territory until the referendum held in 1939.

that greater religiosity decreases perception of threat. However, this impact is not observed in exclusionary attitudes.

On this point it is necessary to acknowledge one of the limitations of this study; many university students in Hatay and Ankara, the participants in this study, originate from other Turkish cities.[9] Therefore, although it is possible that the explanations above accurately capture the cross-city differences in the influence of cultural and ethnic ties between the natives and the Syrian refugees, conclusions cannot be drawn because most of the students are not native to Hatay or Ankara. Consequently the research did not take into account the ethnic and cultural ties of Hatay with the Syrian communities, as the data was gathered from students many of whom come from other cities.

Other limitations of this study derive from the fact data was collected from only one subgroup of Turkish society, university students, whose education level is above the Turkish societal average. In fact, university students comprise approximately 7% of the Turkish population, and 11% of the Turkish population hold university degrees. Furthermore, the financial situation of respondents was not a factor in shaping attitudes towards refugees, as students are not usually in the labor force and do not compete for jobs. This may explain why contrary to expectations grounded in the theory, economic threat was lower in Hatay than in Ankara. Additionally, the fact that older respondents reported lower levels of perceived threat can be correlated with higher levels of educational attainment. Furthermore, university students are temporary residents who spend a great deal of time on campus; it is possible that students do not hold the same views as all long-term residents. While these limitation must be noted, it cannot be undermined that university students are the researchers, policymakers, politicians, and civil servants of tomorrow. Consequently, while the claim cannot be made that the attitudes and opinions of students are representative of the attitudes of the Turkish society as a whole, they are nonetheless very important to understand.

The findings indicate that the policies of the Turkish government and the efforts of the non-governmental organizations (NGOs) that operate in Turkey are falling short of fostering positive attitudes towards the Syrian refugees.

---

[9] One-fifth of the respondents at the universities in Ankara originate from Ankara, and the remainder of participants come from various parts of the country. Likewise about 35% of respondents at the university in Hatay are originally from Hatay, and while there are students from the other 80 Turkish cities, the majority of respondents come from the proximate cities.

For example there are numerous national and international NGOs operating in Hatay, yet there are no concrete or united efforts aimed at creating an interaction ground between the locals and the refugees. As such, it is recommended that these entities further their efforts to integrate these refugees into the host communities. Particularly, the creation of 'positive interaction' would enable the parties to build relationships, a sense of belonging, and further mutual respect. Positive interaction is claimed to empower migrants, enable host communities to recognize the contributions of migrants, provide grounds to resolve conflicts, and aid in the creation of a cohesive society (Orton, 2012). In this regard a great step would be to support the means of 'positive interaction' and facilitate opportunities for the refugees and host communities to engage in 'positive interaction' with each other.

To conclude, this research illustrates that the varying sizes of Syrian refugee populations in Ankara and Hatay impacts exclusionary attitudes held by natives in Turkey. It was shown that perceived threat shapes exclusionary attitudes towards Syrian refugees, supporting the theoretical tenets outlining the effect of out-group population size and perceived threat on exclusionary attitudes. Further research is necessary to analyze the attitudes of other segments of the Turkish society, as well as other mechanisms that potentially intervene between relative refugee population size and natives' exclusionary attitudes, such as prejudice, stereotypes, social distance, and perceptions of in-group versus out-group based on the commonalities between the Turkish natives and Syrian refugees.

References

Apak, H. (2014). Suriyeli Göçmenlerin Kente Uyumları: Mardin Örneği/Adaptation of the Syrian Immigrants to Urban: A Case Study of Mardin. *MUKADDIME, 5*(2).

Baron, R. M., & Kenny, D. A. (1986). The moderator–mediator variable distinction in social psychological research: Conceptual, strategic, and statistical considerations. *Journal of personality and social psychology, 51*(6), 1173.

Berti, B. (2015). The Syrian refugee crisis: Regional and human security implications. *Strategic Assessment, 17*(4), 41-53.

Blalock, H., 1967. Toward a Theory of Minority-Group Relations. Wiley, New-York.

Butler, D. (2016, July 5). *Turkey's Erdogan moots plan to grant citizenship to Syrians*. (D. Dolan, & R. Boulton, Editors) Retrieved from Reuters: http://www.reuters.com/article/us-mideast-crisis-syria-turkey-idUSKCN0ZL155

Celik S., (2015, May 17). 6 Milyon Öğrenci Üniversite Okuyor/ 6 Million People Study at Universities. *Memurlar.net.* Retrieved from http://www.memurlar.net

Public attitudes towards Syrian refugees

Dinçer, O. B., Federici, V., Ferris, E., Karaca, S., Kirişci, K., & Çarmıklı, E. Ö. (2013). *Turkey and Syrian Refugees: The Limits of Hospitality*. International Strategic Research Organization (USAK).

Düvell, F. (2014). Turkey's Transition to an Immigration Country: A Paradigm Shift. *Insight Turkey, 16*(4), 87.

Facchini, G., & Mayda, A. M. (2009). Does the welfare state affect individual attitudes toward immigrants? Evidence across countries. *The review of economics and statistics, 91*(2), 295-314.

Facchini, G., Mayda, A. M., & Puglisi, R. (2013). 5 Individual Attitudes towards Immigration. *Immigration and Public Opinion in Liberal Democracies, 52*, 129.

Ferracuti, F. (1968). European migration and crime. In *Crime and culture: Essays in honor of Thorsten Sellin*, edited by M.E. Wolfgang. New York: John Wiley & Sons.

Fosset, M.A., 1984. City differences in racial occupational differentiation: a note on the use of ratios. *Demography* 21, 655–666.

Gorodzeisky, A. (2013). Mechanisms of exclusion: Attitudes toward allocation of social rights to out-group population. *Ethnic and Racial Studies, 36*(5), 795-817.

Herda, D. (2015). Innumeracy in Turkey: Misperceptions of an Emerging Immigrant Population. *Insight Turkey, 17*(2), 187.

Kirişci, K. (2007). Turkey: A country of transition from emigration to immigration. *Mediterranean politics, 12*(1), 91-97.

Martinez, R., & Lee, M. (2000). On Immigration and Crime. *Criminal Justice 2000: The Nature of Crime: Continuity and Change , 1*, 485-524.

Orton, A. (2012). Building Migrants' Belonging Through Positive Interaction. Council of Europe Policy Document, p14.

Pettigrew, T.F., 2000 'Systematizing the predictors of prejudice', in David O.Sears, Jim Sidanius and Lawrence Bobo (eds), *Racialized Politics*, Chicago, IL: The University of Chicago Press, pp. 280-301

Quillian, L. (1995). Prejudice as a response to perceived group threat: Population composition and anti-immigrant and racial prejudice in Europe. *American sociological review*, 586-611.

Raijman, R., & Semyonov, M. (2004). Perceived threat and exclusionary attitudes towards foreign workers in Israel. *Ethnic and Racial Studies, 27*(5), 780-799.

Republic of Turkey Ministry Of Interior Directorate General of Migration Management. (2016, June 8). Migration Statistics. Retrieved: http://www.goc.gov.tr/icerik6/temporary-protection_915_1024 _4748_ icerik.

Scheve, K. F., & Slaughter, M. J. (2001). Labor market competition and individual preferences over immigration policy. *Review of Economics and Statistics, 83*(1), 133-145.

Semyonov, M., Raijman, R., Tov, A. Y., & Schmidt, P. (2004). Population size, perceived threat, and exclusion: A multiple-indicators analysis of attitudes toward foreigners in Germany. *Social Science Research, 33*(4), 681-701.

Short, James F. 1997. Poverty, ethnicity, and violent crime. Boulder, Colorado: Westview Press.

Sirkeci, I. (2017). Turkey's refugees, Syrians and refugees from Turkey: a country of insecurity. *Migration Letters, 14*(1), 127-144.

Sirkeci, I., & Pusch, B. (2016). *Turkish Migration Policy.* London: Transnational Press London.

Syrian Refugees in Turkey, 2013 (Rep.). (2013). Turkey: Republic of Turkey Prime Ministry Disaster and Emergency Management Presidency (AFAD).

Taylor, M.C., 1998. How White attitudes vary with the racial composition of local populations: numbers count. *American Sociological Review* 63, 512–535.

The World Bank. (2016). Retrieved from Net Migration: http://data.worldbank. org/indicator/SM.POP.NETMhttp://data.worldbank.org/indicator/SM.POP.NET M

Tonry, M. (1997). Ethnicity, crime, and immigration. *Crime and justice*, 21, 1-29.

UNHCR. (2016, June 2). Retrieved from Syria Regional Refugee Response: Interagency Information Sharing Portal: http://data.unhcr.org/syrianrefugees/ country.php?id=224

Universite Mezunu Oranı: Avrupa %37 - Türkiye %11 / Ratio of University Graduates: Europe 37% - Turkey 11% (2014, April 11), *Akademik Personel.* Retrieved from: http://www.akademikpersonel.org

Wilcox, J., & Roof, W. C. (1978). Percent Black and Black-White Status Inequality: Southern versus Nonsouthern Patterns. Social Science Quarterly, 59(3), 421-434.

Chapter Eight

Temporary Education Centres as a Temporary Solution for Educational Problems of Syrian Refugee Children in Mersin

Bilge Deniz Çatak[Υ]

Introduction

In Syria, anti-regime demonstrations which started in March 2011 turned into violent conflicts and soon after a full-scale civil war broke out. The current situation of armed conflicts across Syria has caused widespread migration which makes Syria the world's largest source country of refugees (UNHCR, 2014, 8). Before the conflict, the population of Syria was 20.7 million people (World Population Policies 2011, 491). Because of warfare in their countries 4.8 million Syrians were forced to leave their homes and sought protection especially in neighbouring countries such as Turkey, Lebanon, Jordan, Iraq and Egypt (UNHCR, 2016).

One of the most significantly affected countries by the Syrian refugee influx is Turkey which has a 911 km land border with Syria. With the arrival of Syrian refugees, for the first time Turkey became the largest refugee hosting country worldwide with 2.8 million Syrian refugees by the end of 2016 (UNHCR, 2014; Sirkeci, 2017, 27). Mass migration of Syrian refugees started with 252 people who had entered Turkey via Cilvegözü border gate on 29 April 2011 (Erdoğan, 2015, 317-320). After Syrians started to come to Turkey, Turkish government referred to Syrian arrivals as 'guests'. Turkey applied an 'open-door policy' for Syrian refugees upholding the 'non-refoulement'[1] principle. In 2014 Turkey declared 'Temporary Protection Regime' which granted Syrians who entered into Turkey without visas, protection from

---

[Υ] Bilge Deniz Catak is a research assistant and PhD student in the Department of Sociology at Mersin University, Turkey. E-mail: bdenizcatak@gmail.com.

[1] Non-refoulement: No contracting state shall expel or return ("refouler") a refugee in any manner whatsoever to the frontiers of territories where his life or freedom would be threatened on account of his race, religion, nationality, membership of a particular social group or political opinion (UNHCR, 1977).

forcible return, and access to humanitarian assistance (Human Rights Watch, 2015, 15). The Turkish government has built 25 camps hosting 255000 Syrians (Erdoğan, 2015, 318). While few people live in camps compared to the overall population, majority of Syrian refugees struggle to live in cities throughout the country.

Figure 1. Population Pyramid of Syrian's in Turkey

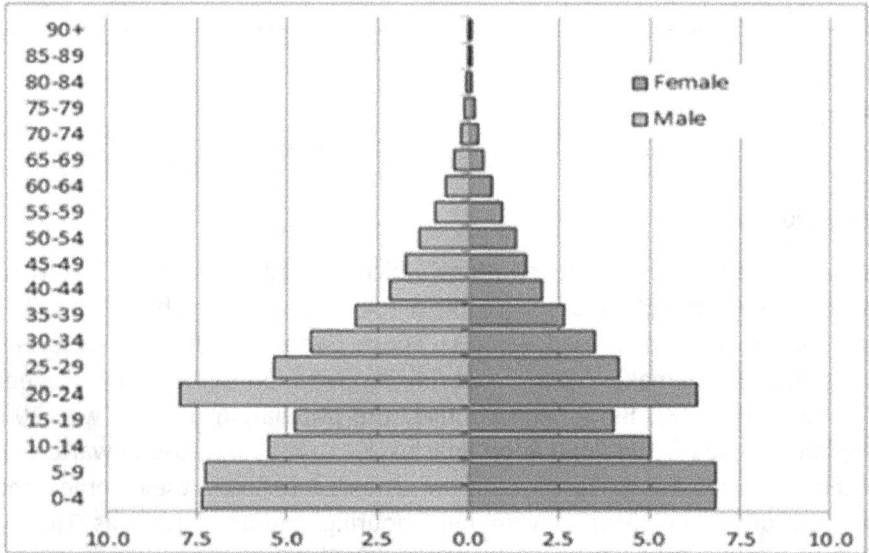

Source: Sirkeci, 2017:133-34

In Turkey, among the 2.8 million Syrians, approximately 1.3 million are children aged between 5-17 years (Directorate General of Migration Management, 2017). (Figure 1). Syrian refugee children's experience of traumatic separation from their homeland and Syria's ongoing conflict has taken a heavy physical and psychological toll on them. Bombs have destroyed their homes and schools; friends and family members were killed (UNHCR, 2013, 9).

The journey into exile and transition into a new life have caused many Syrian refugee children missing years of schooling (UNHCR, 2013, 44-48). With living a long time in other countries, the savings and possessions of most Syrian refugees were lost or destroyed. When the sources are limited, education can be placed at the bottom of the hierarchy of needs and therefore assigned the lowest expenditure. Generally, education ranks lower than a stable income, food, medical care and shelter on families' priority of needs. In this structure, Syrian children's education needs are inextricable from other services and needs (Questscope, 2013, 12).

Temporary education centres

Turkey's policies have evolved over the last five years, shifting from an emergency response to one that takes into consideration longer-term concerns of protracted displacement (Human Rights Watch, 2015, 14). The subsequent Temporary Protection Regulation of October 2014 states that education activities for foreigners shall be conducted inside and outside of camps under the control and responsibility of the Ministry of National Education (MONE) (Temporary Protection Regulation, 2014, 28(1)). In connection with this regulation MONE began registering non-camp 'temporary education centres' (TEC) so that they could be incorporated into the national education framework (Human Rights Watch, 2015, 20). This regulation also lifted restrictions that required Syrian children to produce a Turkish residency permit in order to register to a school (Human Rights Watch, 2015, 7).

Turkish public schools are officially available to all Syrian primary and secondary school-aged students as long as they are registered as beneficiaries of temporary protection with the government (MONE, 2014/21, Article 4). Apart from the public schools, MONE began to accredit a parallel system of private TECs that offer a Syrian curriculum in Arabic (Human Rights Watch, 2015, 6). Despite these regulations, since Syrian refugees began to enter Turkey, less than one-third of the 620.000 Syrian school-aged children are attending school. It means 415.000 children remain unable to access education. In Turkey's 25 government-run refugee camps, approximately 90 percent of school-aged Syrian children regularly attend school. However, these children represent just 15 percent of the Syrian refugee school-aged population in Turkey (Human Rights Watch, 2015, 5-7).

Temporary Education Centres

This study explains educational needs of Syrian refugee children and maps some of the services provided by various organisations as well as the MONE. It tries to outline gaps, challenges and progress on education of Syrian children. To see education and training applications for refugee students in the current situation, interviews were conducted in TECs. In-depth interviews were conducted with 6 teachers (3 Syrian and, 3 Turkish teachers), 2 principals, and 3 officers of relevant foundations to identify problems of Syrian children and also some practises such as curriculum development, literacy courses, teacher training, and hiring practises by the local, regional, and international organisations in Turkey. Officials in Mersin Province Directorate of National Education were also interviewed for this study.

Mersin is currently hosting 144.000 Syrian refugees of which 35.000 are children. According to data released by the MONE, 17.000 Syrian children have enrolled in a school (Mersin Provincial Directorate for National Education, March 2016). There are three options for Syrian refugee children to get education in Mersin. One of these options is private Turkish schools that charge students tuition fees. However, it should be noted that this option is available for very few students. Second option is enrolment to free public schools but bureaucratic affairs and overcrowding make it difficult to enrol in these schools. Also, in public schools teaching is in Turkish and this causes problems for refugee children who do not know Turkish. The third option for refugee children to have education is TECs in which a vast majority of Syrian children have an education in Arabic using Syrian curriculum.

TECs include primary and secondary schools (5-17 ages) and they offer a modified Syrian curriculum in Arabic. Syrian children can enrol in these centres as long as they have a 'Temporary Protection Foreigner ID card'. In these centres Syrian children are also taught Turkish through language courses that are given by Turkish teachers assigned by the MONE.

> *Temporary education centres follow same school calendar with other Turkish schools. The lessons are in Arabic in these centres. And also there are Turkish lessons depending on the grade level. Native citizen Turkish teachers apply to MONE to work in temporary education centres as temporary teacher. Turkish teachers receive a salary from the MONE and get paid different salaries from Syrian teachers (Temporary Education Centre-2, Principal).*

> *In Syria we have a saying that 'Uneducated people make a mistake'. We opened this centre to prevent Syrian children from being ignorant. Our school offers a version of the Syrian education system. We also have Turkish lessons. The rest is unclear, whether we stay or not (Temporary Education Centre- 3, Officer of foundation).*

> *Because of the uncertainty in Syria's situation, there were not any regulations about the education of Syrian children. To prevent them from becoming a lost generation and prevent them from getting involved in crime, some foundations of Syrian donors have established Syrian schools (Temporary Education Centre-1, Principal).*

> *Before the made arrangements, some misconduct and negative situations took place. Some people have taken aids for themselves instead of giving them to children. For this reason, the MONE wanted*

to take control of these education centres. So, principals were assigned by MONE. Presently, two principals are working here, one of them accountable to the MONE, and the other accountable to the foundation. It is like a dual system (Temporary Education Centre-2, Officer of foundation).

The provision of educational services in TECs is the result of a partnership between the MONE, UNICEF, UNHCR and other donors. While the MONE is primarily responsible for the coordination and supervision of these centres, UNICEF and UNHCR provide technical and financial support. Each TEC is managed by the MONE coordinator who functions as a principal or headmaster. UNICEF provides Syrian volunteer teachers working in TECs with financial incentives and training (Human Rights Watch, 2015, 17). While Syrian teachers are regarded as volunteers and receive money from UNICEF, Turkish teachers receive their salaries from the MONE. The other expenses such as electricity, water and the rent of the school building are covered by the Syrian foundations and donors themselves.

We are regarded as volunteers here, like a volunteer at UNICEF. Every month we get paid 900 Turkish Lira for our transport fees, etc. But it is not like a salary. In this school Syrian teachers also have a diploma for teaching. We check diplomas and send them to the MONE. Sometimes teachers don't bring their diplomas with them. In this situation they send their certifications from Syria in any way (Temporary Education Centre-2, Syrian teacher).

Turkish teachers in this school have to be a primary school teacher, a Turkish language teacher or a literature teacher. Every teacher has a certificate for teaching (Temporary Education Centre-2, Turkish teacher).

Salaries of Syrian teachers are paid by UNICEF, but actually it is not a salary, it is more like a scholarship. And it is not enough. Okay, it was based on voluntariness at the beginning, but these people have to continue their lives. Sometimes payments can be delayed for two or three weeks (Temporary Education Centre-1, Principal).

Students do not pay for this school. They pay only for the transportation service and it is like 50-75 Turkish Lira per month. Electricity and water bills are paid by the association (Temporary Education Centre-3, Turkish teacher).

Çatak

There have been several revisions of the official Syrian textbooks that are currently used in TECs. References and photos relating to the current Syrian Government were removed from the books and also several geographical maps were edited (UNICEF, 2015: 10). The curriculum they use is largely the same as the official curriculum used in Syria, with some differences especially concerning the history books (Human Rights Watch, 2015, 19). One of the most emphasised issues throughout the interviews was modifications on Syrian curriculum.

> Books have been coming from Harbiye district of the Hatay province in Turkey. There is a scientific council which consists of Syrian scholars. They organise these books. Books have been distributed for free. Some of the books have been coming from areas in Syria that are controlled by the opposition groups. Some books come from these organisations (Temporary Education Centre-2, Officer of foundation).

> These books are coming from Hatay and Gaziantep. They are for free. But sometimes there are not sufficient number of books for all children. The content of the books is the same with the Syrian curriculum but everything about the Syrian president Assad was removed from the books (Temporary Education Centre-1, Principal)

> Books come from Hatay, Gaziantep, Kilis, and Saudi Arabia. Turkish books are organized by the Turkish teachers who are working in the temporary education centres. We have to take money for Turkish books because we press them (Temporary Education Centre-1, Syrian teacher)

> Someone who has the power, write history in his way. Bashar al-Assad and Hafez al-Assad have dominated for writing history. But we made modifications (Temporary Education Centre-3, Officer of foundation).

Many classes of TECs in Mersin are mixed. But some Syrian families do not want their children to go to school where boys and girls are not separated. In these situations, families may prefer to enrol their children to the schools that separate boys and girls, especially in the secondary grades. Mostly, education of TECs depends on the approach of the foundation that supports the centre financially.

> This school is mixed as the Turkish schools. Some parents have demanded for separating girls and boys, but we have not accepted this (Temporary Education Centre-2, Officer of foundation).

Temporary education centres

> In this school boys and girls have education together until the 4th grade. After that point, girls and boys have education on different floors. Children have a 20 minute break time. In the first break girls go out, and in the second one boys have a break (Temporary Education Centre-1, Turkish teacher).

> There is no school uniform that students have to wear. But association has an impact on this centre. This association has strict rules. For example, they   insist on giving children a religious education. They try to interfere with our clothes. They have warned me about my clothes, my hair and my beard (Temporary Education Centre-2, Syrian teacher).

Because of some social obstacles, the education of many Syrian refugee children is interrupted. During the interviews TECs teachers, principals and persons responsible for the foundations have expressed these obstacles.

> War environment and fighting is normal for these children. Violence they had witnessed in Syria affects their behaviours here (Temporary Education Centre-1, Principal).

> People have fled from the battle, some have found a job, and others could not find a job. They could not take any belongings with them. They spend all the money they have for education (Temporary Education Centre-3, Officer of foundation).

> Relatives of some students still live in Syria. They hear that someone close to them has died because of the bombardment or fighting. Consequently, children are affected (Temporary Education Centre-1, Turkish teacher).

> Students argue about armed groups fighting in Syria. There are a lot of groups who have been fighting in Syria, and families of students usually support one of these armed groups. When they hear something about the fighting groups in their family life, they bring these arguments to the school (Temporary Education Centre-1, Syrian teacher).

> Every month three or four students drop out of school, and three or four new students enrol. Some of them go to Europe, or their father gets a job in a different city and they have to move there. Because of

these reasons they drop out. And also a lot of students have to work (Temporary Education Centre-2, Syrian teacher).

We have difficulty in teaching Turkish, and they have difficulty in understanding. Hence, we have to tell something in English. And also some students have to work. They work in the mornings, and come to school after work. There are students whose families are in Syria, they are alone here, and they live with their friends from Syria. They work and come to school (Temporary Education Centre-2, Turkish teacher).

Some Syrian families go back to Syria, or go abroad especially to Europe. Parents can land a job in a different city and they have to move, some families move to another district and they prefer enrol their children to schools close to their home. Most often boys but also girls have to work, due to this reason they can't continue their education. Some of them work part time, but there are children who find a full time job and then have to choose working (Temporary Education Centre-1, Principal).

Syrians have become the largest immigrant group in Turkey and it is likely that they will be the centre of attention in migration debates for the future (Sirkeci, 2017, 133). The Syria crisis has created also education emergency and the unprecedented exodus of people will resonate beyond the next generation if initiatives fail to address the escalating instability and associated crises of a generation of children and young people with limited literacy, language and formal education (Deane, 2016, 49).

Conclusion

Education is one of the fundamental human rights, but sometimes it is interrupted by extraordinary situations like conflicts. While the civil war is extended in Syria, a generation of refugee children cannot get the education because of prolonged displacement, low financial income, lack of security, and missing the required documentation. Millions of refugee children from Syria are at risk of becoming 'a lost generation'. Even enrolling to school has some challenges and education problems are never-ending for them. To adopt to a new school environment, a new curriculum and sometimes a new language is difficult for children.

Intertwined obstacles prevent Syrian refugee children from accessing education in Turkey and also the other host countries. Some of the factors preventing Syrian refugee children's school enrolment are the time in which they left Syria, the amount of time they were out of school while in Syria, the

Temporary education centres

level of violence they and their families' experienced, language barriers, bureaucratic obstacles, desire to return to Syria or to go another country and protection concerns especially for young girls (Questscope, 2013, 22). Some reasons dissuade families from engaging Turkish school system because children have to work due to financial difficulties experiences by families, school documents could be lost in the migration process and children can have difficulties in keeping up with the Turkish curriculum (UN WOMEN, 2013, 10). In some situations, self- settled refugees could find housing in affordable areas, removed from central city locations where schools are more widely available. This means students have to travel and incur those costs to continue their education (Ahmadzadeh, Çorabatır, Hashem, Al Husseini, & Wahlay, 2014, 4).

Since Syrian refugees arrived to Turkey, education was not considered to be a significant problem compared to shelter, food, and health necessities. Associated with prolonged displacement, access to education in camps and non-camp settings has emerged as another fundamental issue. On the first days of Syrian refugees, they did not attend to public schools because of the lack of regulations and uncertainty about the future.

After realizing that Syrian refugees are not going to leave Turkey soon, some arrangements were made to meet the education needs of Syrian children. With the regulations, the MONE started to control TECs, which were managed by Syrian voluntary agencies before. Syrian foundations still provide financial support while the MONE has control on the education affairs in the schools. But as the name implies, these centres are 'temporary' and Syrian refugee children need permanent solutions about their life including education needs. Whether they plan with their family to go abroad, or stay in Turkey, they have a right to plan their education life. To integrate Syrian refugee children to Turkey's formal schooling, the MONE plans to make all Syrian refugee children enrol in public schools in a rather short period of time. Beginning with the 2016-2017 school year, every Syrian first-year pupil has to enrol in public schools instead of TECs. With this regulation the MONE is planning to integrate Syrian refugee children into the national education system and formal schooling.

Lack of reliable and accurate information regarding the numbers and residential locations of Syrian children make it difficult to identify and resolve some significant problems. The question of why Syrian children miss out on education and what challenges the refugee children face with should be answered properly. After the regulation which ensures all Syrian children to enrol in public schools, problems of exclusion and discrimination can occur.

Çatak

Some arrangements should be made to make sure that Syrian children and local children can have a good quality education together without alienation and humiliation.

References

Ahmadzadeh H., Çorabatır M., Hashem L., Al Husseini J., & Wahlay S. (2014). Ensuring quality education for young refugees from Syria (12-25 Years). Refugee Studies Centre. Oxford University.

Deane, S. (2016). Syria's lost generation: Refugee education provision and societal security in an ongoing conflict emergency. Tadros M. & Selby J. (Eds.). *Ruptures and ripple effects in the Middle East and beyond. 47:3.* IDS Bulletkkin.

Erdoğan, M. (2015). Türkiye'ye kitlesel göçlerde son ve dev dalga: Suriyeliler. Erdogan, M., &Kaya, A. (Eds.). Türkiye'nin Göç Tarihi (p. 317-342). İstanbul: Bilgi Üniversitesi Yayınları.

Human Rights Watch (2015). When I picture my future, I see nothing: Barriers to education for Syrian refugee children in Turkey. USA. Retrieved 10.01.2016 from https://www.hrw.org/report/2015/11/08/when-i-picture-my-future-i-see-nothing/barriers-education-syrian-refugee-children.

Ministry of Interior Directorate General of Migration Management. (2017). 'The distribution of age and gender of registered Syrians under Temporary Protection. Retrieved 21.02.2017 from http://www.goc.gov.tr/icerik6/ temporary-protection_915_1024_4748_icerik

Ministry of National Education. (2014). 'Yabancılara Yönelik Eğitim-Öğretim Hizmetleri Genelge 2014/21. Retrieved from http://mevzuat.meb. gov.tr/html/yabyonegiogr_1/yabyonegiogr_1.html

Questscope (2013). Factors Affecting the Educational Situation of Syrian Refugees in Jordan. Retrieved 08.01.2016 from http://www.questscope.org/blog/ 20130416/participatory-reflection-and-action-pra-study-syrian-refugees-jordan.

Sirkeci, I. (2017). Turkey's refugees, Syrians and refugees from Turkey: a country of insecurity. Migration Letters, 14(1), 127-144. Retrieved from http://www. tplondon.com/journal/index.php/ml/article/view/788

Temporary Protection Regulation. (2014). Retrieved from http://www. goc.gov.tr/files/_dokuman28.pdf

UNHCR (1977). Note on Non-Refoulement. (Submitted by the High Commissioner) EC/SCP/2, Retrieved from http://www.unhcr.org/excom/scip/3ae68ccd10/ note-non-refoulement-submitted-high-commissioner.html

UNHCR (2013). The future of Syria: Refugee children in crisis. Retrieved 10.12.2015 from http://unhcr.org/FutureOfSyria/executive-summary.html.

UNHCR (2014). World at war. Global trends, forced displacement in 2014. Retrieved 27.12.2015 from http://unhcr.org/556725e69.html

UNHCR (2016). Syria regional refugee response. Retrieved 19.1.2016 from http://data.unhcr.org/syrianrefugees/country.php?id=224

Temporary education centres

UNICEF (2015). Curriculum, Accreditation and Certification for Syrian Children in Syria, Turkey, Lebanon, Jordan, Iraq and Egypt. Retrieved 15.01.2016 from http://www.oosci-mena.org/uploads/1/wysiwyg/150527_CAC_for_Syrian_ children _report_final.pdf

UN WOMEN (2013). Gender-based violence and child protection among Syrian refugees in Jordon. With focus on early marriage. Jordon.   Retrieved 25.11.2015 from http://www.unwomen.org/en/digital-library/publications/ 2013/7/syrian-refugees

World Population Policies. (2011). Retrieved from https://esa.un.org/unpd/wpp/ DataQuery/.

Çatak

Chapter Nine

Social Identity Motives, Boundary Definitions, and Attitudes towards Syrian Refugees in Turkey

Nagihan Taşdemir*

Introduction

Research shows that definitions of in-group boundaries play an important role in the prediction of attitudes towards immigrants (Lödén, 2008; Meeus, Duriez, Vanbeselaere & Boen, 2010; Pehrson, Vignoles & Brown, 2009; Verkuyten & Martinoviç, 2015). These definitions in Turkey are conceptualized as national participation and national essentialism (Taşdemir & Öner-Özkan, 2016b; Taşdemir in press) although they have often been dimensioned as civic and ethnic/cultural definitions abroad (Reijerse, Van Acker, Vanbeselaere, Phalet & Duriez, 2013). National participation includes more inclusive criteria but is less likely to be associated with positive inter-group attitudes compared to national essentialism, which includes more exclusive criteria (Taşdemir & Öner-Özkan, 2016b; Taşdemir, in press). However, studies (e.g., Reijerse et al. 2013), conducted mostly in Western countries, show that civic or more inclusive definitions predict more positive attitudes towards the immigrants than ethnic/cultural or more exclusive definitions.

Research also suggests that social identity motives; self-esteem, distinctiveness, belonging, continuity, and efficacy, play important role in the prediction of inter-group attitudes (Brewer, 1991, 1993, 2007; Fritsche, Jonas, Ablasser, Beyer, Kuban, Manger & Schultz, 2013; Pickett & Brewer, 2001; Smeekes & Verkuyten, 2014; Tajfel & Turner, 1979; Vignoles, 2011). A qualitative study in Turkey demonstrates that participants attribute meanings to having a Turkish identity based on these motives (Taşdemir & Öner-Özkan, 2016a). In addition, a study, utilizing the same data set with this study, finds that Turkish identity self-esteem, distinctiveness, and belonging play a more important role in the prediction of attitudes towards Syrian

---
* Assist. Prof. at Anadolu University, Department of Psychology. Eskisehir, Turkey. E-mail: spsynagihantasdemir@gmail.com.

refugees than Turkish identity continuity and efficacy (Taşdemir, under review).

The present study aims to investigate how national participation and national essentialism as well as national identification mediate the relationships between Turkish identity motives and attitudes towards Syrian refugees. Previous research in Turkey has focused on the boundary definitions (Taşdemir, in press) and social identity motives (Taşdemir, under review) separately in the prediction of inter-group attitudes. However, there seems to be no earlier study examining the effects of social identity motives, in-group identification, and boundary definitions together in one study (see Brewer, 2001). Below, firstly, the relationships between social identity motives and inter-group attitudes are presented. Secondly, the relationships between boundary definitions and inter-group attitudes are overviewed. Then, the present study is introduced further.

Social Identity Motives and Inter-group Attitudes

It is now widely accepted that people strive for a positive social identity or to be members of positively evaluated groups, which is proposed by Social Identity Theory (SIT) (Tajfel & Turner, 1979). The main assumption underlying this proposition is that people attempt to maintain or enhance their self-esteem, thus tend to favour their in-groups over the out-groups. To explain this proposition, Abrams and Hogg (1988, p.320) put forth the Self Esteem Hypothesis (SHE), which involves two corollaries: 1) positive differentiation of in-group from the out-group will enhance social identity and thus self-esteem, and 2) low self-esteem will increase in-group favouring tendency due to people's need for self-esteem. However, research indicates inconsistent evidence for SEH. In a review study, Rubin and Hewstone (1998) find empirical support for corollary 1 but not for corollary 2. In another review study, in opposition to Corollary 2, researchers show that people with higher self-esteem are more likely to display in-group favouring tendency (Aberson, Healy, & Romero, 2000). Consistent with this, in the Netherlands among native and immigrant children, Verkuyten (2007) shows that the tendency for in-group favouritism increases with both personal and social self-esteem.

Rubin and Hewstone suggest that it is important to differentiate SIT's social self-esteem (e.g., "my group is valuable") from personal self-esteem (e.g., "I am valuable") in the studies of inter-group attitudes. They explain that in SIT, 'the notion of social self-esteem involves a redefinition of self-esteem at the group level as an attitude concerning a collective self-image' (1998, p. 42). Thus, according to SIT (Tajfel & Turner, 1979), in-group members are motivated to manage their social self-esteem derived from shared self-image of their in-group. In this way, the present study considers social identity motives based on people's perceptions or images of Turkish identity (see also Thomas, Brown, Easterbrook, Vignoles, Manzi, D'Angelo, & Holt, 2017).

In addition to self-esteem, researchers argue that processes of social identity and inter-group relations are guided by motives, such as distinctiveness (Brewer, 1991; 1993; Jetten, Spears, Postmes, 2004), belonging (Baumeister & Leary, 1995; Brewer, 1991), continuity (Sani et al., 2007; Smeekes & Verkuyten, 2013) and efficacy (Breakwell, 1996; Cinnirella, 1996; Fritsche, Jonas, Ablasser, Beyer, Kuban, Manger & Schultz, 2013). SIT, indeed, not only emphasizes people's need for self-esteem but also their need for positive in-group distinctiveness (Tajfel & Turner, 1979). According to this theory, when individuals perceive themselves as in-group members and other group as a relevant (e.g., proximal) comparison group, they try to achieve positive in-group distinctiveness (in order to enhance their self-esteem) (Tajfel & Turner, 1979).

Thus, SIT proposes that more positive evaluation of the in-group is the result of, or reaction to, low in-group distinctiveness, or there is a positive relationship between low in-group distinctiveness and in-group favouritism (Jetten et al., 2004). On the other hand, Self-Categorization Theory (SCT) (Turner et al., 1987) proposes that to the extent inter-group differences are perceived greater than the intragroup differences; people are more likely to differentiate the in-group from the out-group. Accordingly, SCT suggests that the more positive evaluation of the in-group is the reflection of high in-group distinctiveness or there is a positive relationship between high in-group distinctiveness and in-group favouritism (Jetten et al., 2004). Depending on the context of inter-group relations, researchers show that both kinds of relationships may be observed (Jetten, Spears & Manstead, 1997; Jetten, Spears & Postmes, 2004). For example, in the USA, researchers find that individuals, who emphasize the distinction and superiority of national in-group in defining being American, express more negative attitudes towards the immigrants than individuals who emphasize the national welfare and attachment (Li & Brewer, 2004).

Optimal Distinctiveness Theory (ODT) (Brewer, 1991, 1993) proposes that people identify with optimally distinctive groups, which can meet their need not only for distinctiveness (inter-group differentiation) but also for belonging (intragroup inclusion). Pickett and Brewer (2001) show that both threatened in-group distinctiveness and in-group inclusion increase participants' perceptions of in-and out-group homogeneity, which they assume to satisfy their needs for both distinctiveness and belonging. Thus, ODT claims that based on both the need for distinctiveness and belonging people favour their in-group over the out-group.

The need for belonging, indeed, is defined as a fundamental human motivation (Baumeister & Leary, 1995). It refers to people's need to enhance feeling of acceptance by others (Vignoles, 2011). Yzerbyt, Castano, Leyens, and Paladino (2000) report that to the extent people perceive their in-group entitative (i.e., perceiving in-group as homogeneous with common goals and common fate), they are more likely to satisfy their need for belonging. In addition, those individuals, who perceive the in-group more entitative tend to display more in-group favouring tendency (Castano, Yzerbyt, Paladino, & Sacchi, 2002; Effron & Knowles, 2015; Gaertner & Schopler, 1998).

Social continuity motive refers to people's need for a sense of connection across time and space whereby people tend to perceive their national in-group as enduring entity (Reicher & Hopkins, 2001; Sani et al., 2007). Smeekes and Verkuyten (2014) show that when Dutch people perceive higher levels of cultural continuity, they are more concerned about the preservation of their national culture and identity, and thus more likely to perceive continuity threat from the Muslim immigrants. Similarly, Jetten and Hutchison (2011) report that the more people perceive in-group continuity, the more they are likely to be concerned about losing historical continuity. Jetten and Wohl (2012) finds that when presented with discontinuity of English history, participants with higher levels of English identification express more concern for the in-group's future and more opposition to immigration.

Social efficacy motive refers to people's need to enhance feelings of competence, control, or power (Breakwell, 1996). Fritsche et al. (2013) show that those individuals, whose sense of self-efficacy is threatened, express more in-group favouritism. Researchers claim that people may construct their social identities based on this motive. Breakwell (1996), for example, reports that efficacy motive guides participants' constructions of European identity, such as European Community having control of financial markets and attempting to create a Euro-army. According to Lyons (1996), in order to perceive their national in-group efficacious, people tend to remember sporting victories but forget sporting defeats. Cinnirella (1996) suggests that, with motives for power and control, in open-ended responses, British participants display a concern for matters of national independence and having control over the world affairs.

Social identity motives, boundary definitions and attitudes

As reviewed, research demonstrates that each social identity motive plays an important role in the prediction of inter-group attitudes (Fritsche et al., 2013; Pickett & Brewer, 2001; Smeekes & Verkuyten, 2014; Vignoles, Golledge, Regalia, Manzi, & Scabini, 2006). A recent study in Turkey, utilizing the same data set with this study, has examined effects of social identity motives in combination and showed that self-esteem, distinctiveness, and belonging are stronger predictors than continuity and efficacy (Taşdemir, under review). As noted, another study in Turkey has also showed that Turkish identity boundary definitions, particularly, national participation, are an important predictor of attitudes towards Syrian refugees (Taşdemir, in press). The present study aims to examine how motives underlying perceptions of Turkish identity in combination predict national identification and Turkish identity boundary definitions and how these variables, in turn, mediate the relevant relationships.

Definitions of Boundaries and Inter-group Attitudes

Definitions of in-group boundaries refer to the criteria people use to separate "us" (in-group) from "them" (out-group) (Wright, 2011). Researchers focus on definitions of in-group boundaries to explain attitudes towards immigrants or refugees (Ha & Jang, 2015; Heath & Tilley, 2005; Jones & Smith, 2001; Meeus et al., 2010; Pehrson at al., 2009; Pehrson & Green, 2010; Verkuyten & Martinoviç, 2015; Wakefield et al., 2011). In studies conducted mostly in Western countries, these definitions are generally represented by civic, cultural, and/or ethnic criteria (see Reijerse et al., 2013). According to civic definition, people who respect the nation`s political institutions and laws and who are willing to be a member should be national in-group members. According to cultural definition, people who share and enjoy the same culture should be national members. According to ethnic definition, people who share the same ancestry should be in-groupers.

In this way, civic criteria are more voluntariness-based for belonging to national in-group, whereas cultural and/or ethnic criteria are relatively unachievable for immigrants to become a member of national in-group (Reijerse et al., 2013). Consistent with this, in a cross-cultural study, in Belgium, France, Germany, Hungary, the Netherlands, and Sweden, researchers show that people, who endorse higher levels of civic definition, express less negative attitudes towards immigrants. On the other hand, people, who endorse higher levels of cultural and ethnic definitions, which were closely related to each other, express more negative attitudes (Reijerse et al., 2013).

Indeed, studies, in general, conceptualize definitions of national in-group boundaries as two dimensions, one representing civic criteria, the other representing ethnic/cultural criteria (Duriez, Reijerse, Luyckx, Vanbeselaere & Meeus, 2013; Ha & Jang; 2015; Pehrson, Brown & Zagefka, 2009; Pehrson & Green, 2010). Civic or achievable definition involves criteria, such as "respecting the nation`s institutions and laws" and "feeling the nationality" (Wright, 2011). Ethnic/cultural definition involves criteria, such as "to be born in a country", "living most of one's life in a country, "being a follower of the country's religion", "speaking the country's language", and "having citizenship" (Jones & Smith, 2001). Researchers commonly demonstrate that civic definitions are related to more positive attitudes and ethnic/cultural definitions are related to more negative attitudes towards immigrants (Lödén, 2008; Pehrson, Brown & Zagefka, 2009; Reijerse et al., 2013; Verkuyten & Martinoviç, 2015). In an experimental study, for example, those participants, who were reminded of civic criteria ("if you feel Scottish, you are Scottish"), expressed more willingness to help a Chinese immigrant than those participants, who were reminded of ethic criteria ("if your ancestry is Scottish, you are Scottish") (Wakefield et. al., 2011).

It is notable that definitions of national in-group boundaries are not fixed and likely to change across time, region, and socio-political context (Arslan-Akfırat & Öner-Özkan, 2010). For example, researchers in Turkey explored definitions of Turkish identity boundaries in an open ended fashion (Taşdemir & Öner-Özkan, 2016a) and conceptualized these definitions as national participation and national essentialism (Taşdemir & Öner-Özkan, 2016b; Taşdemir, in press). The former represents criteria about being citizen, living in a country, adopting Turkish culture, speaking Turkish, admiring Atatürk's doctrines, and feeling responsibility for the country. The latter represents criteria about having a Turkish mother/father, being a Muslim, and feeling nationality (reverse coded) (Taşdemir & Öner-Özkan, 2016b). Notably, in a later study, criteria about being a Muslim changed a dimension and loaded on national participation (Taşdemir, in press).

However, it is consistently found that in Turkey, national participation, including more inclusive criteria, predicts more negative inter-group attitudes than national essentialism, including more exclusive criteria (Taşdemir & Öner-Özkan, 2016b; Taşdemir, in press), which differs from studies conducted mostly in Western countries (e.g., Reijerse et al., 2013; Verkuyten & Martinoviç, 2015). It is arguable that there has been a difference between Turkey and Western countries in the development of national identity (Ercins & Görüşük, 2016). In Western countries, the immigrants, who came afterwards, have played a role in the emergence of

Social identity motives, boundary definitions and attitudes

civic and ethnic/cultural distinction. In Turkey, already being a multicultural country, however, the War of Independence (1923) and nation building process was influential on the construction of national identity (Ercins & Görüşük, 2016). Turkish identity was constructed as a superordinate identity representing a variety of ethnic and cultural groups altogether (Erkal, 1998; see also Waldzus, Mummendey & Wenzel 2005). Turkish in-group membership was defined as achievable instead of ascribed and citizens of Turkish Republic were considered to be Turkish (Bilgin, 1998). In this context, however, there have been inter-group disagreements, especially with Kurds, which, in turn, increased the emphasis on common territory, citizenship, language, and culture in the definition of Turkish identity (see Waldzus, Mummendey & Wenzel 2005). Accordingly, the inclusiveness of national identity, relative to ethnic identity, have been issued and discussed (Altun, 2011; see also Gaertner, Dovidio, Banker, Houlette, Johnson, & McGlynn, 2000).

Social Identification, Boundary Definitions, Social Identity Motives, and Inter-group Attitudes

According to SIT (Tajfel & Turner, 1979), perceiving themselves as in-group members, individuals come to express in-group favouritism and evaluate their in-groups more positively compared to out-groups. Researchers interpret this proposition in the way that there is a positive relationship between in-group identification and more negative inter-group attitudes (Levin & Sidanius, 1999). However, studies suggest that these variables are not consistently positively correlated with each other (Hinkle & Brown, 1990; Mlicki & Ellemers, 1996). Pehrson, Vignoles and Brown (2009) explain and show that cultures differ in the definitions of national identity, and thus they differ in the relationships between in-group identification and inter-group attitudes. In addition, studies based on Common In-group Identity Model (Gaertner & Dovidio, 2000) show that (more inclusive) superordinate national identification; instead of (more exclusive) subordinate ethnic identification, predict more positive inter-group attitudes (Andrighetto, Mari, Volpato, & Behluli, 2012).

Thus, the relationships between in-group identification and inter-group attitudes are likely to change depending on the kind of in-group (Dovidio, Gaertner, Hodson, Houlette & Johnson, 2005) and the definitions of national identity boundaries (Pehrson, Vignoles & Brown, 2009). The present study investigates how Turkish identification relates to the attitudes towards Syrian refugees as well as how it is predicted by social identity motives.

Recently, researchers examine how a variety of social identity motives has an influence on social identification (Smeekes & Verkuyten, 2014; Thomas et al., 2017). The idea is that individuals' perception of a group satisfying their need(s) may influence their social identification (Thomas et al., 2017). Smeekes and Verkuyten (2014), in the Netherlands, indicate that among other social identity motives, continuity is the strongest predictor of national identification. Thomas et al. (2017) find that team members identify with their group to the extent that they perceive their group as providing a cohesive (belonging), temporally persistent (continuity), and meaningful identity. Notably, there seems to be no agreement with respect to which social identity motives are stronger predictors of social identification (e.g., Jaspal & Breakwell, 2014).

In addition to in-group identification, social identity motives may affect the definitions of in-group boundaries. According to Brewer (2001), for example, groups defined in relatively exclusive ways (e.g., in more ethnic/cultural ways) are more likely to have clear boundaries and thus to satisfy people's need for belonging than groups defined in relatively inclusive ways (e.g., in more civic ways). In a similar way, researchers argue that how nations construct their boundaries are closely related to individuals' sense of belonging and solidarity within a nation (Nieguth, 1999; Shulman 2002). However, there seems to be no previous study considering directly how social identity motives have an influence in the boundary definitions.

The Present Study

Earlier research in Turkey demonstrates that among social identity motives, self-esteem, distinctiveness, and belonging (Taşdemir, under review) and among boundary definitions, national participation is likely to predict the attitudes towards Syrian refugees (Taşdemir, in press). Using the same data set, the present study aims to investigate how national identification and boundary definitions mediate the relationships between social identity motives and attitudes towards Syrian refugees.

The study considers attitudes in terms of in-group favouritism, social distance, and perceptions of cultural and realistic/materialistic threats. Perceptions of threats are particularly crucial in the understanding of attitudes towards immigrants or refugees (Hainmueller & Hopkins, 2014; Wright, 2011). Home country members are likely to perceive both realistic/materialistic (Sherif 1966) and cultural threats (Sears, 1988) from the immigrants (Pehrson & Green, 2010). According to Realistic Conflict Theory (Sherif, 1966), negative inter-group attitudes arise when groups compete for the scarce material resources. Realistic/materialistic threats correspond to the economic, physical or political competition between the groups (Esses, Jackson & Armstrong, 1998). Cultural threats correspond to the culture and worldview differences (Riek, Mania & Gaertner, 2006). Home country residents, who perceive realistic/materialistic and/or cultural threats, tend to express more negative attitudes towards immigrants (Verkuyten, 2009).

Individuals' perception of threat may vary depending on their definitions of in-group boundaries. Research shows that, compared to more inclusive definitions (civic ones), more restrictive and exclusive definitions (ethnic/cultural ones) increase with the perception of threat (Ha & Jang; 2015; Pehrson & Green, 2010; Wright, 2011). A study in Turkey, as mentioned above, finds that national participation is likely to increase with the perception of threat compared to national essentialism (Taşdemir, in press). The study also shows that the more participants perceive the threat, the more they display in-group favouritism and social distance towards Syrian refugees.

The present study examines how national identification, national participation, and national essentialism play a role in the relationships between social identity motives and perception of threat, which predicts in-group favouritism and social distance towards Syrian refugees. Based on the literature review above, this study expects that social identity motives would predict national identification (Smeekes & Verkuyten, 2014) and boundary definitions (Brewer, 2001). Previous research suggests that among social identity motives, continuity is the strongest predictor of (Dutch) national identification (Smeekes & Verkuyten, 2014). It would be exploratory in this study to see, among social identity motives, which is a stronger predictor of national identification in Turkey. It is argued that different social identity motives may underlie different social identifications (Vignoles, 2011).

It would also be exploratory in this study to see how social identity motives predict national participation and national essentialism. Although researchers expect that exclusive or cultural definitions may be more related to the need for belonging than inclusive definitions (Brewer, 2001; Nieguth, 1999; Shulman, 2002), no previous study seems to examine social identity motives in combination in the prediction of civic, ethnic, or cultural criteria based definitions.

Syrian Refugees in Turkey

Fleeing the context of civil war, Syrian refugees started to cross into Turkey in April 2011. Upon arrival, they have been accepted as "guests" by government. As the number of Syrian refugees has risen, each passing day,

Turkish people perceived that refugees were not about to return home in a short time (Ünal, 2014). Meanwhile, the Law on Foreigners and International Protection was introduced in April 2014 and Syrian refugees were provided with the status of *temporary protection*. It is estimated that today over 3 million registered Syrians live in Turkey (Yucesahin and Sirkeci, 2017). According to İçduygu (2015), Turkey's model of a *temporary protection* is a distinct solution in regard to refugee crisis and may result in permanent settlement of Syrians.

Syrian refugees were initially sheltered in tent cities near border. As their number has increased quickly, they started to spread across Turkey and, by late 2014; most of them were living outside camps (Yucesahin and Sirkeci, 2017). Outside camps many Syrians faced difficulties in finding housing, having employment, and accessing education and health services (İçduygu, 2015). Meanwhile, homeless and unemployed refugees participated in the labour market at very low wages, which sparked a reaction among the host population (Tunç, 2015). Erdoğan (2014) reported that Turkish people think that Syrian refuges give harm to the economy (% 70, 8) and they should not be allowed to obtain work permits permanently (47,4 %).

The cultural, lifestyle and language differences with the Syrian refugees have also become an issue among the host population (Oytun & Gündoğar, 2015). Erdoğan (2014) reported that Turkish people tend to perceive a social-cultural distance with Syrians (45,3 %) and believe that Syrians would not be able to adapt to Turkish society (66,9 %). In addition, they think that Syrian refugees constitute a safety risk (62,3 %) and they should not be provided with citizenship in future (84,5 %) (Erdoğan (2014). Accordingly, host population in Turkey tend to perceive economic, material, physical, social, and cultural threats from the Syrian refugees (Özdemir & Öner-Özkan, 2016). Consistent with this, İçduygu (2015, p.3) expects that "...as the Syrian population grows, social tensions and xenophobic reactions against refuges will increase with implications for the political, economic, and social stability of Turkey as a whole".

In such a context, it seems important to unravel the correlates of attitudes towards Syrian refugees, particularly perceptions of threats. The present study has an interest in the individuals' perceptions of national identity. The study investigates how individuals' underlying national identity motives; definitions of boundaries, and level of national identification are related to their perceptions of threats and thus, in-group favouritism and social distance towards Syrian refugees. As reviewed above, these variables may be closely linked with the attitudes towards the refugees.

Social identity motives, boundary definitions and attitudes

Method

Participants

157 university students (109 women, 47 men) in Anadolu University in Turkey participated in the study. Their age range was 18-27 (M = 20.99, SD = 1.66). Participants identified their national in-group identities as citizen of Turkish Republic (82), Turk (60), citizen of the World (4), Laz (2), and Arabic (1). 8 of participants did not respond to the relevant question. Participants scored relatively high in the items asking how they defined themselves in terms of "Turk" (M = 5.71; SD = 2.06) and "citizen of Turkish Republic" (M = 5.78; SD = 1.99). The correlation coefficient between these two identity items was .83. They scored relatively low in terms of European (M = 4.06; SS = 2.00), Kurdish (M = 2.23; SD = 1.84), Arabic (M= 2.23; SD = 1.71) and Laz (M = 2.75; SD = 2.16).

Measures

Social Identity Motives

Social identity motives were measured with the measure of motives attributed to having a Turkish identity. It was developed based on the themes explored by Taşdemir and Öner-Özkan (2016a) using thematic analysis. Social self-esteem included 4-items (e.g., "To have a Turkish identity means to be proud of being Turk"). Social distinctiveness included 3 items (e.g., "Turkish identity is an identity that makes Turks distinctive from others"). Social belonging included 3 items (e.g., "To have a Turkish identity feels oneself a part of a whole"). Social continuity included 2 items (e.g., "Turkish identity is an identity that will exist forever"). Social efficacy included 3 items (e.g., "Turkish identity has power to speak her voice to the World").

5-dimension confirmatory factor analysis was employed allowing latent variables correlated with each other (see Smeekes & Verkuyten, 2013). The model fit with 5 factors was acceptable [$\chi 2$ (80, N = 156) = 131.407, p < .001, GFI = .90, AGFI = .85, NFI = .91, CFI = .96, RMSEA = .06]. The factor loadings changed between .33 and .85 for social self-esteem, between .71 and .81 for social distinctiveness, between .74 and .80 for social belonging, between .80 and .83 for social continuity, and between .63 and .80 for social efficacy. The factor loading for each item was statistically significant. The alpha coefficient scores for reliability were .80, .81, .83 and .78 for social self-esteem, social distinctiveness, social belonging, and social efficacy, respectively. The correlation coefficient between the items for social continuity was .66. All items can be seen in Appendix 1.

Boundary Definitions

Boundary definitions were measured with the measure of definitions of Turkish identity boundaries (12-items) (Taşdemir and Öner-Özkan, 2016b). The measure involved items in the form of "people … can have a Turkish identity". Participants indicated their degree of agreement with items referring "who are citizens of Republic of Turkey", "who protect Turkish culture against change", "who live in Turkey", "who contribute to Turkey", "who speak Turkish", "who adhere to Atatürk's principles, "who are Muslim", "who are willing to feel Turkish", "who have a Turkish father", "who have a Turkish mother", "who come from a Turkish family", and "who have Turkish origin". The first 7 items constituted national participation. The latter 5 items constituted national essentialism (Taşdemir in press). The alpha coefficient scores for reliability were .69 and .80 for national participation and national essentialism, respectively. It is notable that in a previous study (Taşdemir and Öner-Özkan, 2016b) the item referring to being a Muslim loaded on national essentialism but in a later study using the same dataset with this study, it changed a dimension and loaded on national participation.

Perception of Threat

In order to measure perception of threat, the items developed by Stephan, Ybarra and Bachman (1999) and adapted to Turkish by Balaban (2013) were used. Originally, the measure included 20-items but for the present study, 8 of them were selected considering the Syrian refugees in Turkey. It included cultural ("Syrian refugees give harm to Turkish cultural values"), realistic/materialistic ("Syrian refugees decrease job opportunities for Turkish people"), and social threat items ("Syrian refugees increase the crime rates") (see Ha & Jang, 2015).

According to factor analysis results on 2-factor solution (based on cultural and realistic/materialistic treats) only 1 item (Syrian refuges are not as moral as Turkish people in terms of doing work) loaded higher on second factor. 4-items loaded higher on first factor, other 3-items loaded high (.45 and above) on both factors. Thus, perception of threat score was calculated as one dimension with 7-items. The item loaded high on second factor was not used. The alpha coefficient score for reliability was .88.

Social Distance

In order to measure social distance, participants responded to the measure of social distance (Bogardus, 1947). The measure included 7-items (e.g., "I accept to work with a Syrian refugee in the same workplace") and was adapted to Turkish by Bikmen (1999). The alpha coefficient score for reliability was .92.

In-group Favouritism

In order to measure in-group favouritism, participants responded to 2-items referring to Turks and Syrian refugees. Firstly, participants were asked "how positive or negative do you feel toward a (group)" on a 7-point scale ranging from "I feel strongly negative" (1) to "I feel strongly positive" (7) (Esses et al., 2005). Secondly, participants were asked how close they feel toward a (group) on a 7-point scale ranging from "I feel very distant" (1) to "I feel very close" (7) (Li & Brewer, 2004). The correlation coefficients between the items were .58 and .71 for Turks and Syrian refugees, respectively. Scores on these items were averaged to create in-and out-group evaluation scores. In-group favouritism score was calculated by subtracting in-group evaluation score from out-group evaluation one.

In-group Identification

In order to measure national in-group identification, participants indicated their degree of endorsement of identities of "Turk" and "citizen of Turkish Republic" in the form of "I see myself as …" These two identities were highly correlated (r = .83) and they were averaged for creating in-group identification scores. Participants responded each item in the measures on a 7-point scale (1 = strongly disagree, 4 = neither agree nor disagree, 7 = strongly agree).

Results

Mean Scores and Correlations

Descriptive and correlational results are presented in Table 1. As seen, participants scored relatively high in national identification, social identity motives, perception of threat, and in-group favouritism. Perception of threat correlated relatively highly with social identity motives, national participation, social distance, and in-group favouritism. In-group identification correlated relatively high with social identity motives, national participation, and in-group favouritism. One-way ANOVA revealed no gender difference in any of the study variables.

Regression Analyses

As seen in Table 2, multiple regression analyses showed that among social identity motives, belonging emerged as a stronger and significant predictor of national identification. Social self-esteem and social belonging motives emerged as stronger and significant predictors of national participation.

Social efficacy motive emerged as a predictor of national essentialism. As seen in Table 3, in-group identification predicted only in-group favouritism among other manifestations of attitudes towards the refugees.

Structural Equation Modeling

Based on the present results and the results from previous studies (Taşdemir in press, under review), a model was proposed, as seen in Figure 1. The proposed model was tested using the program AMOS 22. Social identity motives were allowed to correlate each other. The proposed model was not fitted the data properly with high RMSEA score (above .10) [$\chi 2$ (29, N = 157) = 90.507, p < .001, NFI = .89, CFI = .92, RMSEA = .12]. The examination of the correlation coefficients suggested that correlation coefficient between in-group favouritism and social distance was relatively high. Thus, as seen in Figure 2, a path from in-group favouritism to social distance was added in the model. The model fit was acceptable [$\chi 2$ (29, N = 157) = 56.567, p < .01, NFI = .93, CFI = .96, RMSEA = .08]. Except for the path from national essentialism to social distance, all the paths in the model were significant.

Mediation Analyses

SPSS PROCESS Macro Model 4 was used to test the indirect effects. Bias-corrected 95% Confidence Interval (CI) was calculated based on 10,000 resamples (Hayes, 2013). The indirect effects for social belonging, b = 0.16, 95% CI [.09; .25], and for social self-esteem, b = 0.16, 95% CI [.08; .26] through national participation on the perception of threat were significant. The indirect effect for social belonging through national identification on in-group favouritism did not differ significantly from zero, b = 0.03, 95% CI [−.04; .12].

Discussion

The present study attempts to understand how in-group identification and boundary definitions mediate the relationships between social identity motives and attitudes towards Syrian refugees. Results indicate that among social identity motives, belonging is a significant predictor of national identification in Turkey. Turkish participants had a tendency to associate national in-group membership with a feeling of belonging compared to feelings of self-esteem, distinctiveness, continuity, and efficacy. The more participants believed that Turkish identity provides the feelings of wholeness, unity, and sharing of sadness and joy, the more they defined themselves in terms of Turkish identity.

Turkey is a multicultural country and after the war of independence, it was aimed to create a unitary nation and citizens of Turkish Republic were considered to be Turkish (Altun, 2011). In this context, it was particularly emphasized that Turkish identity unites and represents everybody living in the country regardless of ethnic group orientation. It was given importance to be in unity and solidarity by sharing both sadness and joy. However, inter-group disagreements occurred in Turkey (Altun, 2011), which resulted in further emphasis on concepts like common culture, common language, common leader (Atatürk), and common territory (as reflected in national participation). Accordingly, it may not be surprising that participants displayed tendency to relate having a Turkish identity with a feeling of belonging, which is likely to be felt in entitative groups (Castano, et al., 2002; Effron & Knowles, 2015; Gaertner & Schopler, 1998; Yzerbyt et al., 2000). It may also be argued that in the relevant context of Turkey, participants perceived more threat to, or were more sensitive with, the feeling of in-group belonging and thus attempted to enhance or maintain this feeling more compared to others (Vignoles, 2011).

Consistent with present results, Optimal Distinctiveness Theory proposes that people tend to identify with optimally distinctive groups, which provide them with a sense of belonging (Brewer, 1991, 1993) and thus with a sense of security (Brewer, 2007). In addition, results seem to confirm the idea that need for belonging is a fundamental human need (Baumeister & Leary, 1995). However, considering Social Identity Theory (Tajfel & Turner, 1979) and Self-Esteem Hypothesis (Abrams & Hogg, 1988), results seem to suggest that at least in the context of Turkey; social belonging is a more important motive underlying national identification than social self-esteem.

On the other hand, in European countries, where immigrants joined afterwards following the establishment of nation-state, social continuity seems to be a more important motive underlying national identification than self-esteem, distinctiveness, belonging and efficacy. This implies that in these countries, people are more likely to perceive threat to, or be sensitive with, the in-group (cultural) continuity (Vignoles, 2011). In the Netherlands, for example, Smeekes and Verkuyten (2013) find that social continuity motive is the strongest predictor of national identification and Smeekes and Verkuyten (2014) demonstrate that Dutch people tend to perceive threat against Dutch cultural continuity from the Muslim immigrants. Accordingly, in order to enhance or maintain the feeling of in-group continuity, in European immigration countries, people may have a tendency to associate national identification with the social continuity motive.

Although the indirect effect for social belonging through national identification was not significant, results show that those participants, who scored high in national identification, displayed more in-group favouritism. This seems consistent with SIT (Tajfel & Turner, 1979), which proposes that people defining themselves in terms of in-group membership tend to evaluate in-group positively compared to the relevant out-group. However, it does not seem that national identification in Turkey is likely to predict more negative attitudes towards Syrian refugees. Results do not suggest national identification as a significant predictor of perceptions of threat and social distance (see Brewer, 1999). It is notable that in the present study, measure of national identification does not involve items about affective and evaluative perceptions of in-group. Rather, it involves the items about perception of self in terms of Turkish in-group membership. However, some researchers report that affective dimension of social identification is more likely to predict more negative attitudes (see Taşdemir, 2011).

Secondly, results show that among social identity motives, self-esteem and belonging are significant predictors of national participation, which, in turn, increase with the perception of threat. National participation conceptualizes Turkish in-group membership in terms of common citizenship, culture, language, religion, leader, territory, and responsibility for the country. In this way, national participation seems to emphasize involvement with Turkish nationality in terms of cultural 'values', 'norms', 'behavioural patterns' and 'institutional arrangements' together (Nieguth, 1999). It views multicultural Turkish nation as a community of people, who not only share the same territory and are the citizens of the same state, but also enjoy the same culture, the same country, religion and the same political leader, Atatürk.

Accordingly, it may not be surprising that those participants, who perceive Turkish identity as favourable and something to be proud of, as well as providing feelings of wholeness, unity, and solidarity, score higher in national participation. Consistent with this, researchers claim that a sense of belonging and solidarity is mostly determined by how nations construct the boundaries of their national identity and relative cultural homogeneity in a nation may function to unite people together and evoke emotional attachment (Nieguth, 1999; Shulman 2002). According to Brewer (2001), groups defined in relatively exclusive ways are more likely to have clear boundaries and thus to satisfy people's need for belonging than groups defined in relatively inclusive ways. In addition, groups, which provide people with a sense of belonging and inclusion, give rise to their sense of self-esteem (Brewer, 2007). Notably, social self-esteem and belonging in this study predict a more inclusive definition, rather than a more exclusive one. However, national essentialism focusing on ethnic homogeneity is not likely to represent the multicultural Turkey (Bilgin, 1998) and thus not likely to

Social identity motives, boundary definitions and attitudes

evoke a sense of belonging and attachment for Turkish participants as evidenced in this study. The results, therefore, seem to suggest that Turkish participants felt more inclusion (belonging) and positive in-group regard (self-esteem) within boundaries defined in national participation rather than within boundaries defined in national essentialism.

National participation, in turn, predicted perceptions of threat with Syrian refugees, which increased with in-group favouritism and social distance towards them (Taşdemir, in press). As noted, national participation includes not only civic elements but also cultural and behavioural elements, which may not be easily achievable for Syrian refugees. For Syrian refugees, who are relatively new in the country, it seems difficult to meet the criteria of national participation. The present results suggest that those participants, who emphasize Turkish identity self-esteem and belonging, score higher in national participation and perceive more realistic/materialistic and cultural threats from Syrian refugees. This may be interpreted in the way that participants perceive these threats against feelings of belonging and self-esteem, which they derive from Turkish in-group membership defined based on national participation.

Participants, who perceive more threats, in turn, evaluate their in-group more positively and express more tendency to distance themselves from Syrian group. As noted, perceptions of treats have a crucial role in the understanding of inter-group attitudes and occur when a group puts the other group's welfare or worldview at risk (Riek, Mania, & Gaertner, 2006). Perceptions of threats are likely to cause individuals to experience inter-group anxiety or uncertainty about how to behave towards the out-group members (Riek, Mania, & Gaertner, 2006), which may explain why participants scoring higher in perception of threat expressed more negative attitudes towards Syrians. People with perceptions of threats indeed do not tend to support the multiculturalism or the recognition of different cultural groups (Verkuyten, 2009). In this way, it seems critical working harder for providing Syrian refugees with better life conditions in Turkey in order to accelerate their adaptation into the society. In a long run, Syrian refugees may be involved with national in-group culturally, officially, socially, and behaviourally, as defined in national participation. It may be also possible that within the process of multifaceted adaptation, Syrian refugees may contribute for the "more diverse", "multicultural", and "democratic" Turkey (Erdoğan, 2014) and may change the definitions of national in-group boundaries in much more inclusive ways.

Thirdly, results show that among social identity motives, efficacy was a significant predictor of national essentialism. The more participants believed that Turkish identity represents power, leadership, and control; the more they defined boundaries in terms of ancestry and ethnic origin. This implies that groups defined in relatively exclusive and restrictive ways may function to satisfy people's need for efficacy. Very recently, researchers propose and show that ethnic in-group identity, compared to common in-group identity, tend to increase disadvantaged group members' group efficacy beliefs (Ufkes, Calcagno, Glasford & Dovidio, 2016). One of their explanations is that it may be more likely for ethnic in-group members to expect each other to take action against their in-group's disadvantaged position. This may suggest that in relatively homogeneous groups people feel more empowered, particularly in contexts of unequal inter-group relations. In this sense, the present results may suggest that those, who focus on ethnic origin and ancestry in the definition of Turkish in-group boundaries, perceive more status differences between the groups. Thus, they may be more in need for maintaining or enhancing the feeling of in-group efficacy. Notably, these interpretations deserve further investigation of the relevant relationships.

In the proposed model, however, the path from national essentialism to social distance was not significant, although they were significantly related in the previous study (Taşdemir, in press). This study utilizes structural equation modeling, which conducts more parsimonious analyses. Accordingly, the present results seem to suggest that national participation, rather than national essentialism, is associated with in-group favouritism and social distance through the perception of threat. National participation, in turn, is predicted by feelings of social self-esteem and belonging. Thus, it seems that among social identity motives, self-esteem and belonging through national participation; and distinctiveness directly (see Figure, 2) are stronger predictors of attitudes towards Syrian refugees than social efficacy (and continuity) (see Taşdemir under review).

The present study extends past work (Taşdemir in press; under review) by examining how in-group identification and boundary definitions play a role in the relationships between social identity motives and attitudes towards Syrian refugees in Turkey. This study is among the first to show that social identity motives are linked with the definitions of national in-group boundaries and thus attitudes towards immigrants. Notably, however, the study has limitations. For example, the items for social identity motives, which were developed based on qualitative findings, are not well distinguished from each other (see also Smeekes & Verkuyten, 2013). Secondly, the extent to which people are in need of social identity motives were not asked openly, they were just assumed based on people' s perceptions of social identity. Future studies should question people's need considering both social and personal motives. Thirdly, there was a gender imbalance in the sample although results did not show any significant gender difference. A previous study in Turkey also found no gender difference considering attitudes towards Syrian refugees (Keleş, Aral, Yıldırım, Kurtoğlu, & Sunata, 2016). Lastly, it is notable that examining social identity motives in combination in relation with national boundary definitions and different manifestations of inter-group attitudes, this study contributes to the relevant literature.

REFERENCES

Aberson, C. L., Healy, M., & Romero, V. (2000). In-group bias and self-esteem: A meta-analysis. *Personality and social psychology review*, 4(2), 157-173.

Abrams, D., & Hogg, M. A. (1988). Comments on the motivational status of self-esteem in social identity and intergroup discrimination. *European journal of social psychology*, 18(4), 317-334.

Altun, N. (2013). Modern Türkiye'de kimlik: Kürt kimliğinden Kürt sorununa. *Akademik İncelemeler Dergisi*, 8 (2), 45-67.

Andrighetto, L., Mari, S., Volpato, C., & Behluli, B. (2012). Reducing competitive victimhood in Kosovo: The role of extended contact and common ingroup identity. *Political Psychology*, 33(4), 513-529.

Arslan-Akfırat, S. & Öner-Özkan, B. (2010). Ulusal/etnik kimliklerin stratejik inşası: Kuzey Kıbrıs örneği, *Bilig* 52, 1-32.

Balaban, Ç.D. (2013). The roles of intergroup threat, social dominance orientation and right-wing authoritarianism in predicting Turks' prejudice toward Kurds. Yayınlanmamış Yüksek Lisans tezi, Orta Doğu Teknik Üniversitesi Sosyal Bilimler Enstitüsü, Anakara.

Baumeister, R. F., & Leary, M. R. (1995). The need to belong: Desire for Interpersonal attachments as a fundamental human motivation. *Psychological Bulletin*, 117, 497–529.

Bikmen, N. (1999). National identity and Ethnic Prejudice in Turkey. Yayınlanmamış Yüksek Lisans tezi, Boğaziçi Üniversitesi Sosyal Bilimler Enstitüsü, İstanbul.

Bilgin, N. (1998). Cumhuriyet fikri ve yurttaş kimliği. A. Ünsal (Ed.), *75 yılda Teba'dan Yurttaş'a içinde* (139-151). İstanbul: Tarih Vakfı Yayınları.

Breakwell, G. (1996). Identity processes and social change. G. M. Breakwell & E. Lyons (Ed.), In *Changing European identities: Social psychological analyses of social changes* (13-30). Oxford: Butterworth-Heinemann.

Brewer, M. B. (1991). The social self: On being the same and different at the same time. *Personality and Social Psychology Bulletin*, 17(5), 475-482.

Brewer, M. B. (1993). The role of distinctiveness in social identity and group behavior. M. Hogg & Abrams (Ed.), In *Group motivation: Social psychological perspectives* (1-16). New York: Har&ster-Wheatsheaf.

Brewer, M. B. (1999). The psychology of prejudice: In-group love or out-group hate? *Journal of Social Issues*, 55, 429–444.

Brewer, M.B. (2001). In-group identification and inter-group conflict: When does in-group lo& become out-group hate?, R. D. Ashmore, L. Jussim, and D. Wilder (Eds.) (17-41). In *Social Identity, Inter-group Conflict, and Conflict Resolution*. New York: Oxford University Press.

Brewer, M. B. (2007). The importance of being we: Human nature and intergroup relations. *American Psychologist*, 62(8), 726-38.

Bogardus, E. S. (1947). Measurement of personal-group relations. *Sociometry*,10 (4), 306–311.

Castano, E., Yzerbyt, V. Y., Paladino, M. P. & Sacchi, S. (2002). I belong, therefore, I exist: In-group identification, in group entitativity, and in group bias. *Personality and Social Psychology Bulletin*, 28, 135-143.

Cinnirella, M. (1996). A social identity perspecti& on European integration. G. M. Breakwell & E. Lyons (Ed.), In *Changing European identities: Social psychological analyses of social change* (253-274). Oxford: Butterworth-Heinemann.

Dovidio, J. F., Gaertner, S. L., Hodson, G., Houlette, M. & Johnson, K. M. (2005). Social Inclusion and exclusion: Re-categorization and the perception of Inter-group boundaries. D. Abrams, J. M. Marques & M. A. Hogg, (Ed.), In *The social psychology of inclusion and exclusion* (246-264). Philadelphia: Psychology Press.

Duriez, B. Reijerse, A. Luyckx, K. Vanbeselaere, N. & Meeus, J. (2013). Which national group will I identify with? The role of preferred and perceived identity representations. *Nations and Nationalism*, 19(3), 456-474.

Effron, D. A. & Knowles, E.D. (2015). Entitativity and intergroup bias: How belonging to a cohesive group allows people to express their prejudices. *Journal of Personality and Social Psychology*, 108 (2), 234-253.

Ercins, G. & Görüşük, L. (2016). Türkiye'de & Batı'da Çok-kültürlülük Gerçeği. *Turkish Studies*, 11(2) 383-401.

Erdoğan, M.M. (2014). Türkiye'deki Suriyeliler: Toplumsal Kabul ve Uyum Araştırması. Hacettepe Üniversitesi Göç ve Siyaset Araştırmaları Merkezi, Ankara.

Erkal, M. E. (1998). *Etnik tuzak* (5. baskı). İstanbul: Der Yayınevi.

Esses, V. M., Jackson, L. M., & Armstrong, T. L. (1998). Intergroup competition and attitudes towards immigrants and immigration: An instrumental model of group conflict. *Journal of Social Issues*, 54, 699-724.

Esses, V. M., Dovidio, J. F., Semenya, A. H. & Jackson, L. M. (2005). Attitudes toward immigrants and immigration: The role of national and international identities. In D. Abrams, J.M. Marques & M.A. Hogg (Ed.), In *The social psychology of inclusion and exclusion* (317-337). Philadelphia: Psychology Press.

Fritsche, I., Jonas, E., Ablasser, C., Beyer, M., Kuban, J., Manger A-M. & Schultz M. (2013). The power of we: Evidence for group-based control. *Journal of Experimental Social Psychology*, 49, 19-32.

Gaertner, S. L., Dovidio, J. F., Banker, B. S., Houlette, M., Johnson, K. M., & McGlynn, E. A. (2000). Reducing intergroup conflict: From superordinate goals to decategorization, recategorization, and mutual differentiation. *Group Dynamics: Theory, Research, and Practice*, 4(1), 98.

Gaertner, L. & Schopler, J. (1998). Perceived in-group entitativity and intergroup bias: An interconnection of self and others. *European Journal of Social Psychology*, 28(6), 963-980.

Ha, S.E. & Jang, S-J. (2015). Immigration, threat perception, and national identity: Evidence from South Korea. *International Journal of Intercultural Relations*, 44 (1), 53-62.

Hainmueller, J. & Hopkins, D.J. (2014). Public attitudes toward immigration. *Annual Review of Political Science*, 17, 225-249.

Hayes (2013). *Introduction to Mediation, Moderation, and Conditional Process Analysis: A Regression-based Approach*. New York, NY: Guilford Press.

Heath, A.F., & Tilley, J. R. (2005). British national identity and attitudes towards immigration. *International Journal on Multicultural Societies*, 7(2), 119-132.

Hinkle, S. & Brown, R. (1990). Inter-group comparisons and social identity: Some links and lacunae. In D. Abrams & M. Hogg (Eds.), *Advances in Social Identity Theory* (pp. 48-70). New York: Harvester Wheatsheaf.

İçduygu A. (2015). Syrian Refugees İn Turkey-The Long Road Ahead. Migration Policy Institute, Washington.

Jaspal, R., & Breakwell, G. M. (Eds.). (2014). *Identity process theory: Identity, social action and social change*. Cambridge University Press.

Jetten, J., Spears, R. & Manstead, A.S.R. (1997). Distinctiveness threat and prototypicality: combined effects on intergroup discrimination and collective self-esteem. *European Journal of Social Psychology*, 27, 635 - 657.

Jetten, J. & Hutchison, P. (2011). When groups ha& a lot to lose: Historical continuity enhances resistance to a merger. *European Journal of Social Psychology*, 41, 335-343.

Jetten, J. Spears, R., & Postmes, T. (2004). Intergroup distinctiveness and differentiation: A meta-analytical investigation. *Journal of Personality and Social Psychology*, 86, 862-879.

Jetten, J. & Wohl, M. J. A. (2012). The past as a determinant of the present: Historical continuity, collective angst, and opposition to immigration. *European Journal of Social Psychology*, 42, 442-450.

Jones, F.L. & Smith, P. (2001). Diversity and commonality in national identities: An exploratory analysis of cross-national patterns. *Journal of Sociology*, 37 (1), 45-63.

Keleş, S. Ç., Aral, T., Yıldırım, M., Kurtoğlu, E., & Sunata, U. (2016). Attitudes of Turkish youth toward Syrian refugees in respect to youths' gender, income, education, and city: A Scale Development Study. In: Eroglu, D., Cohen, J.H., Sirkeci, I. (eds), *Turkish Migration 2016 Selected Papers*, London: Transnational Press London, 155-163.

Levin, S., & Sidanius, J. (1999). Social dominance and social identity in the United States and Israel: In-group favoritism or out group derogation? *Political Psychology*, 20, 99 – 126.

Li, Q. & Brewer, M. B. (2004). What does it mean to be American? Patriotism, nationalism, and American identity after 9/11. *Political Psychology*, 25(5), 727-739.

Taşdemir

Lödén, H. (2008). Swedish: Being or becoming? Immigration, national identity, and the democratic state. *International Journal of Social Sciences*, 3(4), 257-264.

Lyons E. (1996). Coping with social change: Processes of social memory in the reconstruction of identities. G. M. Breakwell & E. Lyons (Ed.), In *Changing European identities: Social psychological analyses of social change* (31-40). Oxford: Butterworth-Heinemann.

Meeus, J., Duriez, B., Vanbeselaere, N. & Boen, F. (2010). The role of national identity representation in the relation between in-group identification and out-group derogation: Ethnic versus civic representation. *British Journal of Social Psychology*, 49, 305-320.

Mlicki, P.P., & Ellemers, N. (1996). Being different or being better? National stereotypes and identifications of Polish and Dutch students. *European Journal of Social Psychology*, 26(1), 97-114.

Nieguth, T. (1999). Beyond dichotomy: concepts of the nation and the distribution of membership. *Nations and Nationalism* 5, 2: 155–73.

Oytun, O. & Gündoğar, S. S. (2015). Suriyeli Sığınmacıların Türkiye'ye Etkileri Raporu. Orsam-Tesev Rapor No: 195, Ankara.

Özdemir, F., & Öner-Özkan, B. Türkiye'de Sosyal Medya Kullanıcılarının Suriyeli Mültecilere İlişkin Sosyal Temsilleri1. *Nesne Psikoloji Dergisi*, 4(8), 227-244.

Pehrson, S., Brown, R. & Zagefka, H. (2009). When does national identification lead to the rejection of immigrants? Cross-sectional and longitudinal evidence for the role of essentialist in-group definitions. *British Journal of Social Psychology*, 48, 61-76.

Pehrson, S. & Green, E.G.T. (2010). Who we are and who can join us: National identity content and entry criteria for new immigrants. *Journal of Social Issues*, 66 (4), 695-716.

Pehrson, S., Vignoles, V. L. & Brown, R. (2009). National identification and anti-immigrant prejudice: Individual and contextual effects of national definitions. *Social Psychology Quarterly*, 72(1), 24-38.

Pickett, C. L., & Brewer, M. B. (2001). Assimilation and Differentiation Needs as Motivational Determinants of Perceived In-group and Out-Group Homogeneity. *Journal of Experimental Social Psychology*, 37(4), 341-348.

Reicher, S. & Hopkins, N. (2001). *Self and nation*. London: Sage.

Reijerse, A., Van Acker, K., Vanbeselaere, N., Phalet, K. & Duriez, B. (2013). Beyond the ethnic-civic dichotomy: Cultural citizenship as a new way of excluding immigrants. *Political Psychology*, 34 (4), 611-629.

Riek, B. M., Mania, E. W. & Gaertner, S. L. (2006). Inter-group threat and out-group attitudes: A meta-analytic review. *Personality and Social Psychology Review*, 10, 336-353.

Rubin, M., & Hewstone, M. (1998). Social identity theory's self-esteem hypothesis: A review and some suggestions for clarification. *Personality and Social Psychology Review*, 2(1), 40-62.

Sani, F., Bowe, M., Herrera, M., Manna, C., Cossa, T., Miao, X., & Zhou, Y. (2007). Perceived collective continuity: seeing groups as entities that move through time. *European Journal of Social Psychology*, 37(6), 1118-1134.

Social identity motives, boundary definitions and attitudes

Sherif, M. (1966). *In common predicament: Social psychology of intergroup conflict and cooperation*. New York: Houghton Mifflin.

Shulman, S. (2002). Challenging the civic/ethnic and West/East Dichotomies in the study of Nationalism. *Comparative Political Studies* 35, 5: 554–85.

Smeekes, A. & Verkuyten, M. (2013). Collective self-continuity, group identification and in-group defense. *Journal of Experimental Social Psychology*, 49 (984-994).

Smeekes, A. & Verkuyten, M. (2014). When national culture is disrupted: Cultural continuity and resistance to Muslim immigrants. *Group Processes and Intergroup Relations*, 17, 45-66.

Stephan, W. G., Ybarra O. & Bachman G. (1999). Prejudice toward immigrants. *Journal of Applied Social Psychology*, 29 (11), 2221-2237.

Tajfel, H., & Turner, J. C. (1979). An integrative theory of intergroup conflict. W. G. Austin & S. Worchel (Ed.), *In The social psychology of intergroup relations* (33-47). Monterey, CA: Brooks/Cole.

Taşdemir, N. (2011). The Relationships between Motivations of Intergroup Differentiation as a Function of Different Dimensions of Social Identity. *Review of General Psychology*, 15(2), 125-137.

Taşdemir N. (in press). Ulusal Kimliğin Sınırlarını Tanımlama Biçimleri ve Türkiye'ye Gelen Suriyeli Sığınmacılara Yönelik Tutumlar. *Türk Psikoloji Yazıları*.

Taşdemir N. (under review). Sosyal Kimlik Motivasyonları ve Gruplar Arası Tutumlar. *Türk Psikoloji Dergisi*.

Taşdemir, N. & Öner-Özkan B. (2016a). Türk kimliği içerikleri: Sosyal psikolojik bir yaklaşım. *Türk Psikoloji Yazıları*, 38 (19), 35-49.

Taşdemir, N. & Öner-Özkan B. (2016b). Definitions of Turkish in-group boundaries: National participation and essentialism as predictors of inter-group attitudes in turkey. *Nations & Nationalism*, 22 (1), 143-164.

Thomas, W. E., Brown, R., Easterbrook, M. J., Vignoles, V. L., Manzi, C., D'Angelo, C., & Holt, J. J. (2017). Social Identification in Sports Teams: The Role of Personal, Social, and Collective Identity Motives. *Personality and Social Psychology Bulletin*, 43(4), 508-523.

Tunç, A. Ş. (2015). Mülteci davranışı & toplumsal etkileri: Türkiye'deki Suriyelilere ilişkin bir değerlendirme. *Tesam Akademi Dergisi*, 2 (2), 29 - 63.

Ufkes, E. G., Calcagno, J., Glasford, D. E., & Dovidio, J. F. (2016). Understanding how common in-group identity undermines collective action among disadvantaged-group members. *Journal of Experimental Social Psychology*, 63, 26-35.

Ünal, S. (2014). Türkiye'nin beklenmedik konukları: "Öteki" bağlamında yabancı göçmen & mülteci deneyimi. *Journal of World of Turks*, 6(3), 65-89.

Verkuyten, M. (2007). Ethnic in-group favoritism among minority and majority groups: Testing the self-esteem hypothesis among preadolescents. *Journal of applied social psychology*, 37(3), 486-500.

Verkuyten,M., (2009). Support for multiculturalism and minority rights: The role of national identification and out-group threat. *Social Justice Research*, 22, 31-52.

Verkuyten, M., & Martinovic, B. (2015). Behind the ethnic–civic distinction: Public attitudes towards immigrants' political rights in the Netherlands. *Social science research*, 53, 34-44.

Vignoles, V. L, Regalia, C., Manzi, C., Golledge, J. & Scabini, E. (2006). Beyond self-esteem: Influence of multiple motives on identity construction. *Journal of Personality and Social Psychology*, 90 (2), 308-333.

Yucesahin, M., & Sirkeci, I. (2017). Demographic gaps between Syrian and the European populations: What do they suggest?. *Border Crossing*, 7(2), 207-230. Retrieved from http://tplondon.com/journal/index.php/bc/article/view/988.

Yzerbyt, E., Castano, V. Leyens, M.P. & Paladino, S. (2000). The Primacy of the in-group: The interplay of entitativity and identification. *European Review of Social Psychology*, 11(1), 257-295.

Waldzus, S., Mummendey, A., & Wenzel, M. (2005). When "different" means "worse": In-group prototypicality in changing intergroup contexts. *Journal of Experimental social psychology*, 41(1), 76-83.

Wakefield, J. R. H., Hopkins, N., Cockburn, C., Shek, K., Muirhead, A., Reicher, S. & Rijswijk, W. (2011). The Impact of Adopting Ethnic or Civic Conceptions of National Belonging for Others' Treatment. *Personality and Social Psychology Bulletin*, 37(12), 1599-1610.

Wright, M. (2011). Diversity and the Imagined Community: Immigrant Diversity and Conceptions of National Identity. *Political Psychology*, 32 (5) 9221-2011.

APPENDIX

Measures of Social Identity Motives

Social Self Esteem Motive

Turkish identity is one of the most beautiful identities in the world

To have a Turkish identity means to be proud of being Turk

To have a Turkish identity is something to be pride of

Turkish identity has features to be ashamed of

Social Distinctiveness Motive

Turkish identity differentiates and distinguishes Turks from others

Turkish identity is not distinct from any other national identity in the world

Turkish identity has no features to distinguish Turks from others

Social Belonging Motive

To have a Turkish identity means to be in solidarity and unity

To have a Turkish identity feels oneself a part of wholeness

To have a Turkish identity means to share both sadness and joy

Social Continuity Motive

Turkish identity will exist forever

There has been a past and present of Turkish identity and so there will be future for it

Social Efficacy Motive

Turkish identity means having power to rule over the world

Turkish identity has an important influence over the countries in the World

Turkish identity has been in a leading position in the World throughout the history

Taşdemir

Table 1. Descriptive and Correlational Results

	Ort.	S	1.	2.	3.	4.	5.	6.	7.	8.	9.	10.	11.
1. In-group identification	5.64	1.87	1										
2. Social self esteem	5.37	1.58	.45**	1									
3. Social distinctiveness	4.63	1.93	.40**	.58**	1								
4. Social belonging	5.26	1.69	.51**	.66**	.58**	1							
5. Social continuity	5.80	1.49	.42**	.68**	.48**	.65**	1						
6. Social efficacy	4.22	1.79	.36**	.74**	.61**	.64**	.57**	1					
7. National participation	3.99	1.24	.39**	.55**	.35**	.53**	.48**	.48**	1				
8. National essentialism	2.86	1.51	.05	.18*	.12	.07	.17**	.25**	.19*	1			
9. Social distance	3.81	1.65	-.17*	-.41**	-.42**	-.35**	-.27**	-.35**	-.37**	-.22**	1		
10. Perception of threat	5.07	1.37	.19*	.38**	.41**	.34**	.27**	.34**	.45**	.20*	-.81**	1	
11. In-group favoritism	2.85	1.79	.30**	.56**	.43**	.50**	.44**	.41**	.43**	.17*	-.71**	.61**	1

*p< .05; **p< .01

Table 2. Predicting in-group identification, National participation and National essentialism

	In-group identification			National participation			National essentialism		
Independent variable	B	SD	β	B	SD	β	B	SD	β
Social self esteem	.20	.14	.17	.24	.09	.31**	.02	.13	.02
Social distinctiveness	.13	.09	.13	-.04	.06	-.07	-.01	.08	-.02
Social belonging	.36	.12	.33**	.20	.07	.27**	-.17	.11	-.19
Social continuity	.12	.13	.10	.06	.08	.06	.12	.12	.11
Social efficacy	-.12	.12	-.11	.05	.07	.08	.25	.11	.30*
R^2	.27			.34			.05		
R^2 change	.30			.36			.08		
F for $R^2 \Delta$	12.564***			16.839***			2.57*		

*p< .05; **p< .01; ***p<.001

Table 3. Predicting attitudes towards the Syrian refugees with in-group identification and boundary definitions

	Perception of threat			Social distance			In-group favoritism		
Independent variable	B	SD	β	B	SD	β	B	SD	β
In-group identification	.01	.06	.02	-.03	-.07	-.03	.15	.08	.16*
National participation	.46	.09	.42***	-.44	-11	-.33***	.51	.12	.35***
National essentialism	.11	.07	.12	-.17	.03	-.15*	.11	.09	.09
R^2	.20			.15			.20		
R^2 change	.21			.16			.22		
F for $R^2 \Delta$	13.66***			9.79***			14.00***		

*p< .05; **p< .01; ***p<.001

Figure 1. Proposed Model for Predicting Attitudes towards Syrian Refugees

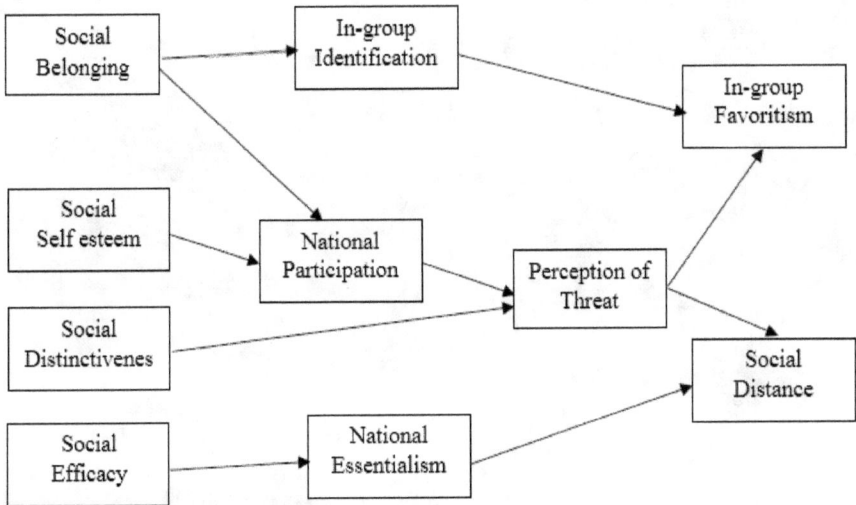

Figure 2. Measurement Model for Predicting Attitudes towards Syrian Refugees

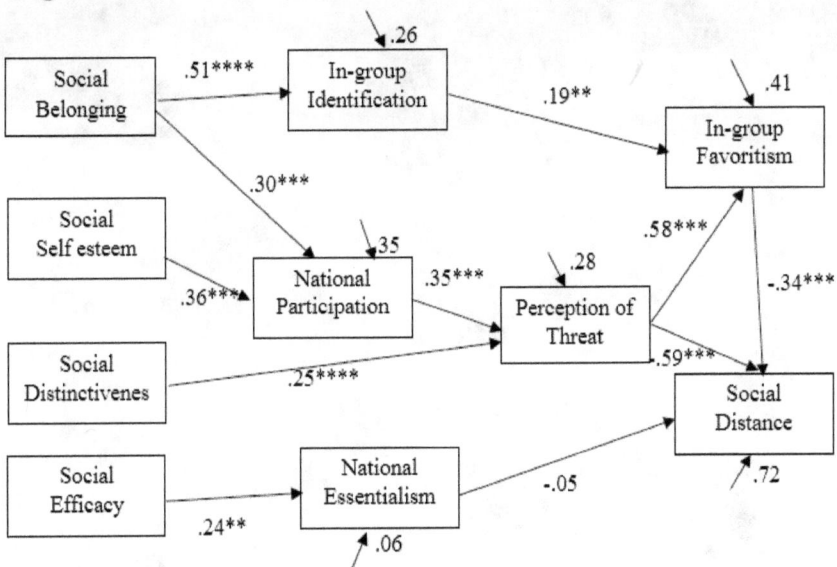

Taşdemir

PART 3

FUTURE PROSPECTS

Chapter Ten

Demographic Gaps between Syrian and the European Populations: What Do They suggest?

M. Murat Yüceşahin[Y], Ibrahim Sirkeci[Y]

Introduction

At least 6 million 148 thousand Syrians have been uprooted as a result of the crisis and conflict ongoing since 2011 in Syria. As of 6 August 2017, 5,165,502 have crossed the borders into neighbouring countries of Turkey, Lebanon, Jordan and Iraq whilst 983,876 moved further to Europe (UNHCR, 2017). A similar volume of population has been displaced within Syria too. This practically makes Syria one of the worst displacement cases in the history as more than half the contemporary population is displaced. Turkey with a long land border with Syria as well as historic links between populations, particularly in border provinces appeared as a favourite destination for Syrians who escape the conflict. As conflict grew and spread, in 2012 and onwards, a sharp increase in the number of Syrians arriving in Turkey was observed (Yazgan *et al.*, 2015; Sirkeci, 2017a). When Lebanon receiving proportionally the largest share of Syrian movers, Jordan, Egypt, and Iraq have also accommodated sizeable populations seeking refuge. Unlike the early days of the conflict when most movers preferred neighbouring countries, in later years, an increasing number of Syrians destined to Europe. There can be and are many factors moderating this behaviour. We can cite economic opportunities, democratic environment, as well as aspirations and cultures of migration among these factors. Certain political manoeuvres such

[Y] Murat Yüceşahin is Associate Professor of Geography, Ankara University, Faculty of Lanuages, History and Geography, Sıhhiye, Ankara, 06100, Turkey.
E-mail: mmyucesahin@gmail.com.
[Y] Ibrahim Sirkeci is Professor of Transnational Studies and Director of Regents Centre for Transnational Studies, Regents University London, Inner Circle, Regent's Park, London, NW1 4NS, UK. E-mail: sirkecii@gmail.com.
Acknowledgement: This is a reprint of the article published in *Border Crossing*, Vol.7, No.2 (July-December 2017). We appreciate the permission from the publisher.

as the German Chancellor Merkel's welcoming message in 2015 have also played a role.

In countries where sizeable Syrian communities emerged, debates about integration of movers have also been heightened in academia and general public. Being host for the largest population of Syrian movers, Turkey saw an exponential increase in academic interest in Syrians and migration in general. Nevertheless, most, if not all, of the research projects publicized have drawn conclusions based on small and non-representative samples. In the meantime, official data and summary releases remained primitive. Despite some interesting qualitative studies transpiring narratives of Syrian movers and non-movers in Turkey, there is a grave need for comprehensive analysis of trends in Syrian populations before attempting any conclusions about the future of this particular group and integration issues in waiting in Turkey and elsewhere.

Differences in demographic patterns and trends are as important as socio-economic and cultural differences between the movers and the non-movers in countries of destination. Nevertheless, apart from limited and often poor remarks that appear in discourses of politicians and in media, there has been no analysis of the demographic differences and projections for the future.

This sudden rise in interest in Syrians has resulted in an exponential growth in the number of research with poor quality, questionable methodologies, and controversial as well as unreliable analyses. This warrants robust and reliable analyses using representative and good quality data —as available. Our aim in this study is to offer a comprehensive analysis of Syrian population and demographic trends with reference to Demographic Transition Theory. Hence we may contribute to this gigantic task of filling the void with quality information. In this study, first, we delineate the demographic trends and changes in Syrian population from 1950 to 2015. Then we look at the projected trends from 2015 to 2100. We contrast these with the trends from selected key destination countries, Germany, Turkey and the United Kingdom. These analyses are based on the data from the World Population Prospects (UN, 2016). The conceptual point of reference for the analyses is Demographic Transition Theory which guides us in understanding the demographic changes which will be reflected in Syrian mover populations in destination countries in medium to long term.

Demographic Transition

The demographic transition is generally believed to be an unfinished process in the developing or less developed world, where rapid population growth is prevalent (Newbold, 2010). Mortality rates in the developing world have fallen rapidly from the mid-20th century, particularly due to much improved health provisions and technologies, better care and nutrition. However, fertility rates largely remained above the replacement level, and on average approximately three children per woman were reported. The rates in sub-Saharan Africa have been much higher than the average.

Within the "developed" world[1], shifts in mortality and fertility rates occurred towards the end of the 19th century and in early 20th century in relation to the Industrial Revolution and major improvements in public health provision. These led to a rapid decline in infant mortality rates while increasing the life expectancy (Bongaarts and Watkins, 1996; Weeks, 2002; Weinstein and Pillai, 2001; Rowland, 2012; Yaukey et al., 2007). In all developed countries today, fertility rates have been low for long enough to see populations in many developed countries are nearing to the end of the age transition, which brings up the challenge of population aging as a major concern. Populations in developed countries are largely characterized by relatively slow rates of population growth, low fertility levels, and controlled immigration. Some countries in Europe, and particularly in Eastern Europe, have been experiencing negative population growth rates for a while. In other words, their populations are on decline. According to the Population Reference Bureau projections, for example, Latvia's current population of 2.3 million will shrink to 1.9 million by 2050, thanks to low fertility levels. Germany's population, currently 82 million, is projected to decline to 71.4 million by 2050 (Newbold, 2010: 23). Due to its population momentum effect, Turkey's population is projected to increase until 2045-50. However, negative population growth attributed to low fertility rates is projected for the second half of the 21st century. However, this transition in fertility and mortality was observed in the 19th century and in the beginning of the 20th century in developed countries.

Despite the effectiveness of the global demographic transition, especially in the second half of the twentieth century (Reher, 2004; Caldwell, 2001; Caldwell and Caldwell, 2001), today there are still significant demographic differences between countries and population groups across the world.

---

[1] Here we are using "developed countries" to refer to highly industrialised countries with high average incomes.

Undoubtedly, our understanding of the demographic transition is deepened through comparing populations, especially between migrant sending and receiving countries. Every country or population experiences demographic transition in a unique fashion characterised by their own historic, social, cultural, economic and technological transitions (Lestheaghe, 1983; Coale and Watkins, 1986; Watkins, 1987; Caldwell and Caldwell, 2001). Therefore, no rate or percentage change can be deemed 'high' or 'low', and no set of characteristics can be considered 'more developed' or 'less developed', or 'traditional' or 'modern', for instance, without comparisons with other populations (Rowland, 2006: 120).

Concepts and theories, such as the demographic transition, provide a general comparative framework for research. These comparisons are necessary to draw conclusions and improve our understanding. Comparing data for different populations, at national, regional or local levels, is essential in gauging whether populations are distinctive, how much they have changed through time and whether their characteristics are adequately understood. Hence we can identify and explain the structural characteristics and changes in demographic trends over time.

The age and sex structure of a population is a commonly overlooked aspect of the social structure, yet it is one of the most influential drivers of social change in human society. The number of people at each age and of each sex is important to understand how a society is organized and how it operates (Rowland, 2012). The age composition is determined by the interaction of three demographic processes. Population movements can have a sizable impact, since movers tend to be concentrated in particular age groups and, in addition, movement is often selective of sex and age. Males in working ages are often more likely to move and this may have a significant impact on population change (Rowland, 2012; Newbold, 2010). Mortality has the smallest short-run impact on the age distribution. When mortality declines suddenly (as is the case in less developed countries), it turns the population to be more youthful and makes it grow rapidly. At the same time, a decline in mortality influences the sex structure by resulting in an increasingly larger number of females than males in older age groups (due to the fact that females usually have longer life expectancy than males and hence share of females in older age groups increases). Changes in fertility generally produce the biggest changes in a society's age structure, regardless of the level of mortality. High fertility, in general, results in a young age structure whereas low fertility leads to ageing of population.

Demographers examine the population processes that are likely to have an impact on future age and sex structure of a population based on various population projection scenarios. At the same time, examining past population trends allows us to understand behaviours of cohorts over time and in relation to social events and changes. Population projections help us to identify the direction of change. For example, it is possible to understand how a youthful population structure turns to an ageing population over time by examining the past demographic transition records of many developed countries. What matters is how fast or slow this transition takes place. These changes in age and sex structures of a population have a bearing on political, economic and social stability.

Countries with significant negative or positive net migration will face a change in age and sex structure of their populations after a while. For instance, it is useful to examine population movements and demographic transition in Germany, United Kingdom, USA, and Canada as these countries are characterised by strong net migration flows over a long period.

Overall, it is possible to spot the full variety of age groups among the movers. However, young adults are overrepresented among international and internal movers. For example, USA sees more inflows than outflows but those moving abroad are generally older than those arriving in the USA. This would certainly have, albeit a small, impact on age structure (Bouvier et al., 1997; Weeks, 2002). In the short run, the volume of young population declines in places marked by net emigration whereas in places of net immigration, the share of the young age groups increases in the total population. In the long run, the impact of migration is felt most in fertility patterns. This is due to the fact that most migrants are in prime reproductive ages (15-49 years old).

Therefore, movers' demographic features can be important for the receiving countries. Being concerned of the impact of population movements on demographic transition, many developed and developing countries have altered their population policies from anti-natalist to pro-natalist perspectives. More specifically, many developed countries have been applied a controlled or selective immigration policy within a pro-natalist perspective (Yüceşahin et al., 2016). Pro-natalist policies promote fertility to ensure population growth. By doing so, they aim to compensate their possible workforce deficit.

Data and Methods

There are no data sources that include country specific demographics of Syrian movers in the receiving countries. Therefore, in this study, we used the United Nations' (UN, 2016) country specific demographics to study the demographic differences among populations assuming that Syrians who moved to other countries would continue with similar demographic behaviour to what can be portrayed for the population of Syria. Here we should note that over time, some convergence is expected in demographic patterns of the movers and local populations. However, since mass Syrian population movements have only emerged in the last six years, the convergence is expected to be limited. To illustrate the demographic transition of Syrian population, we used crude birth rate (CBR) which is the ratio of births to the total population, crude death rate (CDR) which is the ratio of deaths to the total population, total fertility rate (TFR) which is an age-adjusted, period measure of lifetime fertility, derived by summing age specific birth rates in a given year for all ages of childbearing, and life expectancy at birth (LEB) which is the average number of years of life remaining to a group of persons who reached a given age, as key demographic indicators (for detailed definitions see Siegel and Swanson, 2004). We have also used population distribution by age and sex in 1950, 1980, 2010, and 2015 to explain the changes and transformations in age and sex structure of Syrian population. For this analysis, we selected roughly equal intervals (i.e. 30 years) as 1950, 1980 and 2010. On the other hand, we used the 2015 data for the distribution of population by age and sex in order to present the outflow effects on Syrian population between the 5-year-period from 2010 to 2015.

In the second part of this chapter, we focus on the potential future demographic differences between Syrian and European populations. Based on the current population movements since the beginning of the Syrian crisis, we have selected three destination countries: Germany, Turkey and the United Kingdom. These countries either received a large number of Syrian movers or have been popular destinations for movers in the last three decades. We used several demographic indicators produced by the United Nations (UN, 2016) for the period from 1950 to 2100. These include median age (the age at which a population is divided into two equal sized groups), total fertility rate, child dependency ratio, age dependency ratio and total dependency ratio (dependency ratios are relative size of an age group of interest to the number of persons in a different age group providing support for the former) (see Siegel and Swanson, 2004). We have also produced population pyramids of the four countries for 2015, 2025, 2050 and 2100 to illustrate the changes regarding age and sex distributions.

Background: Demographic Transition in Syrian Population, 1950-2015

Middle Eastern countries saw a shift from high fertility rates and high mortality rates towards lower rates in the second half of the 20th century. Similar to other developing regions, populations in the Middle East have gone through three major demographic stages especially during the second half of the twentieth century, in line with the Demographic Transition Theory (Winckler, 2003). The first is the pre-transition phase probably spanning from the early 20th century to the 1960s marked with high fertility and mortality rates. The second is the early transition phase from the 1960s to the 1990s, with rapid declines in fertility and mortality rates. This period saw high population growth rates (Allman, 1980; Omran and Roudi, 1993; Rashad, 2000). The third is the mid-transition phase from the late 1990s to 2010-15, during which the decline of fertility and mortality rates slowed down (Table 1). Thus, the demographic transition in the Middle East and/or Arab countries of Western Asia in general has been somewhat peculiar. Total fertility rose substantially before it began its historical decline in the 1960s. Life expectancy at birth rose rapidly.

Today in many countries of the Middle East, average total fertility is three or more children per woman. However, in general, fertility rates in Turkey, Tunisia and the Gulf countries are at about replacement level (i.e. 2.1 children per woman). Demographic transition in the Middle East and Near East seems likely to begin and continue at a declining pace, a unique fashion for the region. Syrian population in 1950 was 3.4 million and by 2010, it rose to 21.5 million. According to the United Nations (UN, 2016) Syrian population is expected to grow to 35 million by 2050. When compared to developed countries, Syrian population growth rate is significantly higher (Douglas, 2010: 50). With the exceptional small increases in 1965-70 and 1990-95 periods, crude birth rate has declined from 50.8 per thousand in 1950-55 to 24.1 in 2010-15. These high fertility rates along with low mortality rates resulted in increasing youth share in Syrian population. Also in general, across the region, crude death rates declined significantly to around 3.5 per thousand by 2005-10 (Table 1; Figure 1). This is even lower than the rates we would find in developed countries. However, by 2010-15, crude death rates increased slightly which is likely to be due to several wars and armed conflicts in the region (Figure 1).

Population growth changes in Syria were mostly negative from 1980 to 2015 (Figure 2). This shows that Syrian population growth slowed down and was destabilised due to wars and resulting mass displacements. As shown in Figures 1 and 2, crude death rate increased between 2005-10 and 2010-15 and average annual population growth rate changes turned negative at more remarkable rates. Conflicts and generally uncomfortable living circumstances pushed large segments of Syrian population to move to other countries in the region and beyond (Yazgan et al. 2015; Sirkeci, 2017a). This is particularly evident in the decline since 2010 corresponding to the intensive conflicts since 2011 (Figure 2).

Figure 1. Trends of crude birth rate, crude death rate, and population size in Syrian population from 1950-55 to 2010-15

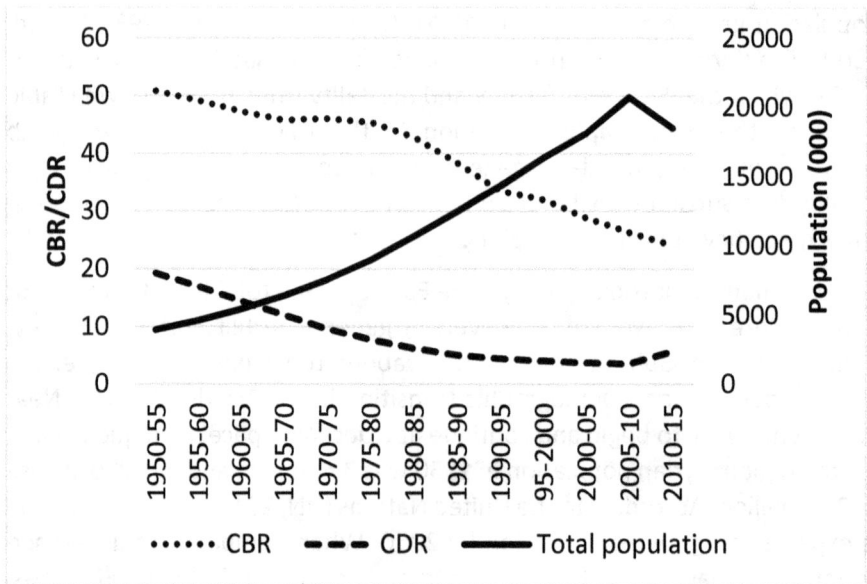

Data Source: UN (2016).

Contrary to many developing countries' experience with declining fertility in the early 1960s, the total fertility rate in Syria only started to decline significantly in the 1980s. Thus, despite rapid fertility transition seen in Syria, birth rates have remained high. The total fertility rate in Syria declined from 6.8 children per woman in 1980-1985 to 3.0 children per woman in 2010-2015 (Table 1).[2] In 1990-1995, the TFR declined to below 5 children per

---

[2] Taleb et al. (2015), with reference to the World Bank data, refer to different rates. For example, they state that total fertility rate was 3.6 in 2000 and declined to 2.9 in 2010.

woman for the first time. Therefore three distinct phases of fertility transition can be seen in Syria: the first is the 'pre-transition phase' spanning from 1950s to the early 1980s with very high fertility rates; the second is the 'early transition phase' from the early 1980s to the mid-2000s, with rapid fertility decline; and the third is the 'mid-transition phase' of the mid-2000s to 2010-2015 period (Figure 3). Approaching to the last phase(s) of the fertility transition, the third phase is characterised by slowing down of the decline in TFR. Unlike slightly below replacement level total fertility rates observed in many developing countries, the projections (UN, 2016) show that Syria's total fertility rate will reach the same levels no earlier than 2035-2040.

Figure 2. Trends in average annual rate of population change in Syrian population, from 1950-55 to 2010-15

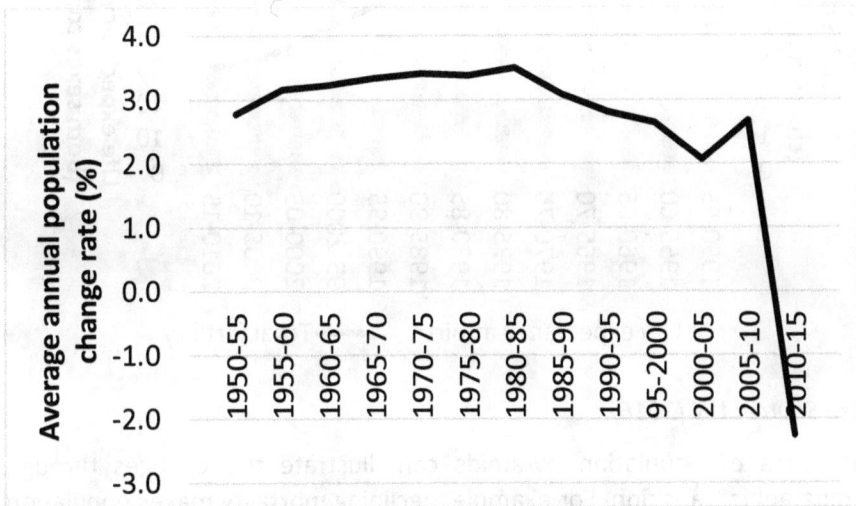

Data Source: UN (2016).

One of the important characteristics of the Demographic Transition is the increasing life expectancy depending on the primarily decreases in mortality in contrast to the decreases in fertility in due course. Life expectancy at birth in Syria increased 25.7 years from 1950-1955 to 2005-2010, increasing from 48.7 years to 74.4 years. It is expected to rise to 77.5 years by the 2050s (UN, 2016). Nevertheless, the civil war and conflicts in the country increasing since 2011, life expectancy at birth has declined to 69.5 years in Syria (Figure 3).

When child dependency ratio decreased from 100.8 percent in 1980 to 58.5 percent in 2010 in Syria, old-age dependency ratio also decreased from 6.1

percent to 5.8 percent. However, child dependency ratio bounced back to 63.1 percent and old-age dependency ratio to 6.9 percent in 2015. Total dependency ratio, therefore, decreased from 106.9 percent in 1980 to 64.3 percent in 2010, mainly due to the decrease in child dependency ratio (UN, 2016). The share of the population aged 65 and over first declined from 4.5 percent in 1950 to 3.0 percent in 1980, but increased to 3.5 percent in 2010 and to 4.1 percent in 2015 (UN, 2016).

Figure 3. Trends of total fertility rate and life expectancy in Syrian population between the periods of 1950-55 and 2010-15.

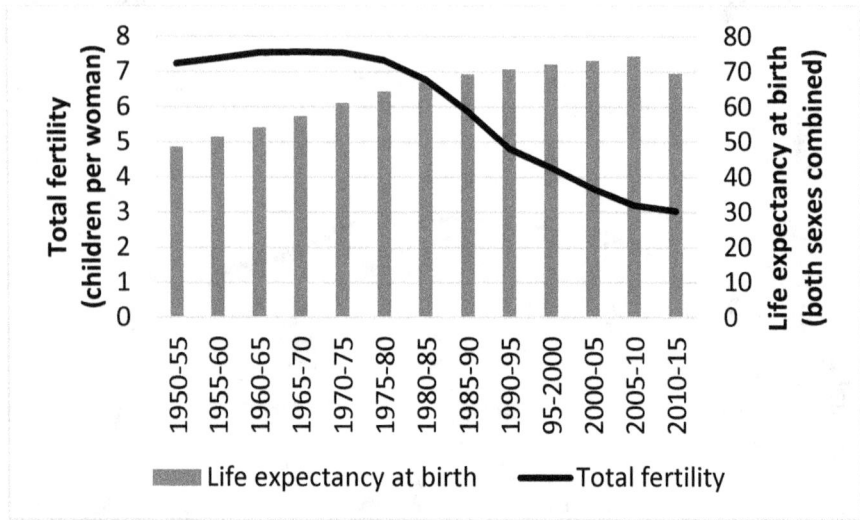

Data Source: UN (2016).

The types of population pyramids can illustrate the changes through demographic transition. For example, declining mortality makes population younger, since more children survive. This is reflected in wider based pyramids as the proportion of children increases early in the transition and leading young age profiles. Later in the transition, population ageing emerges as fertility declines reduces the share of children. Successive generations then become similar in size, as evident initially in the emergence of 'mature' age structures with similar numbers in parent and child generations. Ultimately 'old' age structures evolve in which the numbers in successive age groups are similar below the advanced ages where mortality is concentrated in post-transitional societies.

Table 1. Some selected demographic indicators of Middle East countries, from 1950-55 to 2010-15

	1950-55		1980-85		1990-95		2005-10		2010-15	
	CBR	CDR	CBR	CDR	CBR	CDR	CBR	CDR	CBR	CDR
Algeria	50.2	23.1	40.8	9.2	28.8	6.1	23.1	5.1	25.1	5.1
Bahrain	45.0	21.1	33.0	4.1	26.7	3.2	17.0	2.4	15.4	2.3
Egypt	50.6	25.4	39.0	11.4	29.8	7.9	25.2	6.4	28.5	6.2
Iraq	53.3	27.7	39.0	9.9	37.1	6.4	35.5	5.8	35.1	5.3
Iran	50.7	26.8	44.6	13.6	28.1	6.0	18.1	5.1	18.2	4.7
Jordan	47.4	20.4	39.7	6.5	34.0	4.8	28.7	3.9	27.9	3.9
Kuwait	43.7	13.6	36.3	3.6	19.9	2.6	23.2	2.7	20.6	2.5
Libya	51.0	30.6	37.0	6.5	25.4	4.8	22.9	4.8	21.7	5.3
Lebanon	40.2	12.9	28.8	7.2	23.3	6.6	12.7	4.7	15.0	4.6
Morocco	51.3	20.2	36.7	10.0	27.5	6.9	20.8	6.1	21.3	5.7
Oman	49.1	28.3	48.2	8.6	33.4	4.8	21.4	3.0	20.8	2.7
Palestine	45.9	20.0	44.9	6.8	45.7	4.8	34.0	3.7	33.1	3.6
Qatar	47.5	13.4	33.3	2.8	21.4	2.1	13.0	1.7	12.1	1.5
Syria	50.8	19.2	42.8	6.2	33.5	4.4	26.3	3.5	24.1	5.6
S. Arabia	47.8	23.2	42.5	7.2	33.1	4.5	22.6	3.5	20.8	3.4
Tunisia	45.5	26.6	33.1	7.8	22.9	5.8	17.0	6.0	18.4	6.6
Turkey	49.3	24.1	32.8	10.3	24.5	7.8	18.7	5.9	17.3	5.8
UAE	49.1	21.9	30.2	3.5	22.8	2.5	12.6	1.5	11.2	1.5
Yemen	48.4	30.3	54.7	15.1	49.8	11.1	35.8	7.8	33.2	7.1
	NI	TFR	NI	TFR	NI	TFR	NI	TFR	NI	TFR
Algeria	27.1	7.3	31.6	6.3	22.8	4.1	18.0	2.7	19.9	2.9
Bahrain	23.9	7.0	28.9	4.6	23.5	3.4	14.6	2.2	13.0	2.1
Egypt	25.2	6.6	27.6	5.5	21.8	4.1	18.8	3.0	22.3	3.4
Iraq	25.7	7.3	29.1	6.4	30.7	5.7	29.8	4.6	29.8	4.6
Iran	23.9	6.9	30.9	6.5	22.1	4.0	13.0	1.8	13.5	1.8
Jordan	27.0	7.4	33.2	7.1	29.2	5.1	24.8	3.6	24.0	3.5
Kuwait	30.1	7.2	32.7	5.0	17.2	2.4	20.6	2.6	18.1	2.2
Lebanon	27.3	5.7	21.6	3.8	16.8	2.8	8.0	1.6	10.3	1.7
Libya	20.4	7.1	30.5	6.7	20.5	4.2	18.1	2.7	16.4	2.5
Morocco	31.1	6.6	26.7	5.4	20.6	3.7	14.7	2.5	15.5	2.6
Oman	20.8	7.3	39.6	8.3	28.6	6.3	18.4	2.9	18.1	2.9
Qatar	34.1	7.0	30.4	5.5	19.2	3.7	11.3	2.2	10.6	2.1
Palestine	26.0	7.4	38.0	7.1	40.9	6.6	30.3	4.6	29.5	4.3
Syria	31.5	7.2	36.7	6.8	29.1	4.8	22.8	3.2	18.5	3.0
S. Arabia	24.6	7.2	35.3	7.0	28.6	5.6	19.2	3.2	17.4	2.9
Tunisia	18.9	6.7	25.4	4.8	17.1	3.0	11.0	2.0	11.8	2.2
Turkey	25.2	6.7	22.5	4.1	16.7	2.9	12.8	2.2	11.5	2.1
UAE	27.1	7.0	26.7	5.2	20.4	3.9	11.1	2.0	9.7	1.8
Yemen	18.1	7.4	39.6	8.8	38.7	8.2	28.0	5.1	26.1	4.4

Note: CBR: Crude birth rate (per 1,000 people); CDR: Crude death rate (per 1,000 people); NI: Natural increase (per 1,000 people); TFR: Total fertility rate (children per woman).

Source: UN (2016).

In sum, fertility decline has the greatest impact on the percentages in older age groups during the demographic transition, particularly because it reduces the relative numbers of children. In contrast, mortality decline has a smaller effect on the percentages in older age groups, but a dramatic impact on population size, bringing increased numbers through improved survival of infants and children (Rowland, 2012: 99-101). On the other hand, conflicts, wars and out- or in-migrations as a result of these conflicts could have an impact on the population structures because of the deaths, inflows or outflows (Courbage, 1999; Fargues, 2011). There are indirect relationships between demographic structures and economic and political crises (Courbage, 1994) and it was clearly evident in the Syrian case.

Population ageing has come as a rapid change in many developing countries especially in the 2000s. However Syria's population composition has been dominated by younger people. The population pyramids of Syria in 1950 and 1980 show a typical wide-based structure signalling a very young population (Figure 4).

Rapidly declining mortality and high fertility levels made Syria's population younger from 1950 to 1980 (Figure 3 and 4). However, from 1980s because of the rapid decreases in total fertility rates (Figure 3) between 1980 and 2010, shape of the population pyramid for Syria has changed dramatically. Although the pyramid for 2010 shows still a young profile, a narrowing trend on the base can be observed (Figure 4).

It can also be said that the population pyramid of Syria in 2010 was starting to converge to a rectangular shape. However, between 2010 and 2015, probably the most important change was reflected in the fact that the population pyramid turned to an asymmetrical shape. The population pyramid for 2015 shows that the share of female population was higher than that of males in all age groups. For the 2010-2015 period, the two-way transition process was probably the reason for the asymmetrical distribution of population by age and sex in Syria. Undoubtedly, the first reason is the demographic transition. However, the impact of the violent conflicts from 2011 to 2015 is also evident, particularly reflected in the population pyramid for 2015 (Figure 4).

Figure 4. Distribution of Syrian population by age groups and sex, 1950-2015

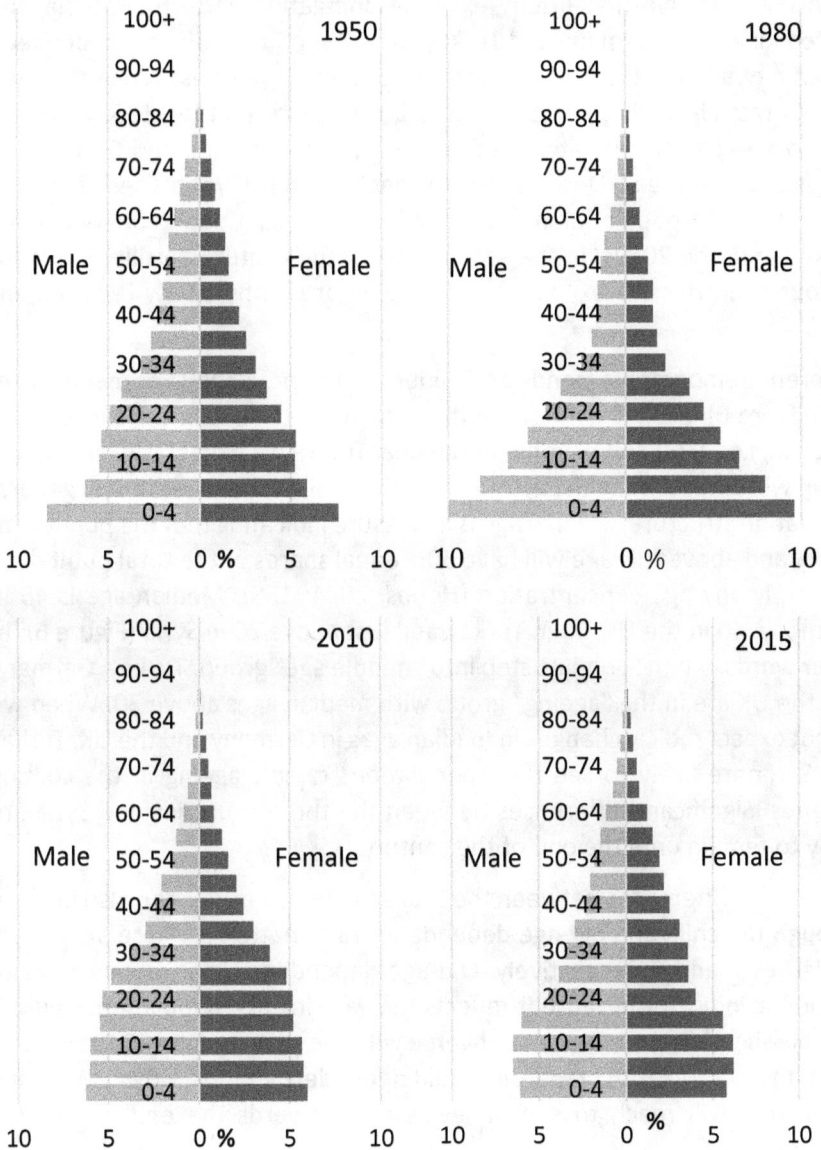

Data source: UN (2016)

Demographic Deficit and Potential Future Impact on Population

In this section, we first briefly examine population patterns in Syria, the United Kingdom, Germany and Turkey to reflect on the differences between Syrian movers and local populations in receiving countries. While the total fertility rates in Turkey and Syria were both very high in the 1950s, Turkish rates are expected to match that of the UK in about 2020 and Germany in about 2050 (Figure 5). Despite similarly declining fertility rates seen in Syrian population, the population momentum is likely to continue to be well above Turkey until the 2050s. In the second half of the century, fertility levels for all four countries are expected to converge at slightly below replacement level.

Different demographic trends are evident in the projections of median age, too (Figure 6). Even if we assume these patterns to remain the same in the long run, i.e. 2100 and beyond, in the near future we expect the largest age group will differ among these four countries. This will be reflected in general population structure. Median age is a measure indicating that the population below and above this age will have 50% equal shares of the total but it does not imply any age concentration (Hobbs, 2004: 158). Median age is 45 in Germany, 40 in the UK, 30 in Turkey and just above 20 in Syria (Figure 6). In other words, when Syria just step into "middle age" group, Turkey, Germany and the UK are in the "ageing" group with median ages above 30. When we do not expect radical changes in median ages in Germany and the UK, Turkey and Syria are likely to see their populations rapidly ageing in the coming decades. Significant differences between the three countries and Syria are likely to remain until the end of the century.

Age profile differences between the four selected countries can also be seen through the child and old-age dependency ratio patterns. These are shown in Figures 7 and 8, respectively. Old-age dependency ratio is also a socio-economic indicator because it reflects the working age population. Figure 7 roughly shows that Turkey will converge with the UK in around 2040 and with Germany in about 2065 regarding child dependency ratios. However, Syrian population will reach to similar levels only towards the end of the 21st century.

Share of the population under 15 in Syria has started to decline in about the same period as it did in Turkey but this was reversed towards the 1980s, since when it has been in decline. This fluctuation can also be explained by the conflicts in the Middle East as Syria has historically received significant number of movers from neighbouring countries in trouble. Those aged 15-

Figure 5. Total fertility rates in selected countries: 1950-2100

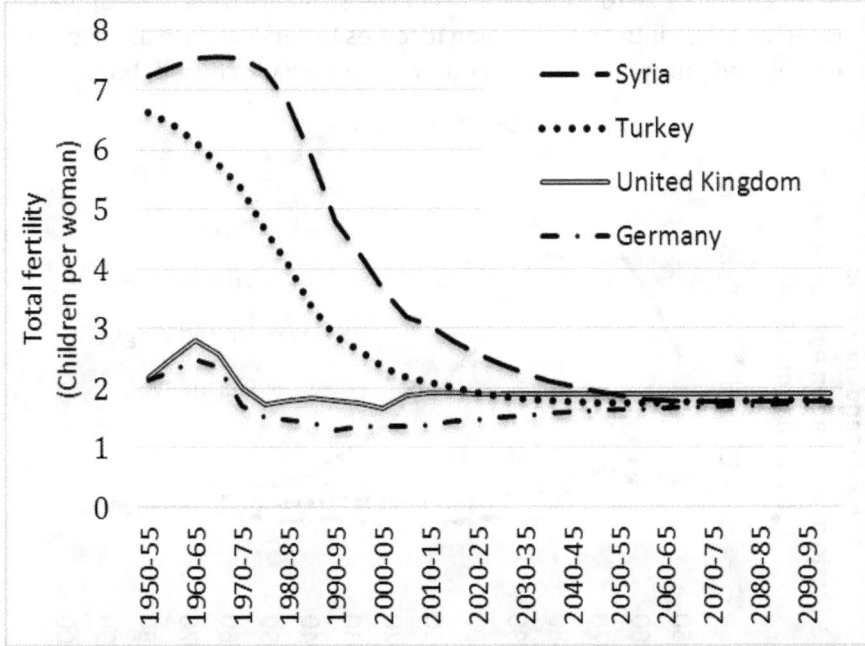

Data Source: UN (2016).

Figure 6. Median age trends in selected countries: 1950 – 2100

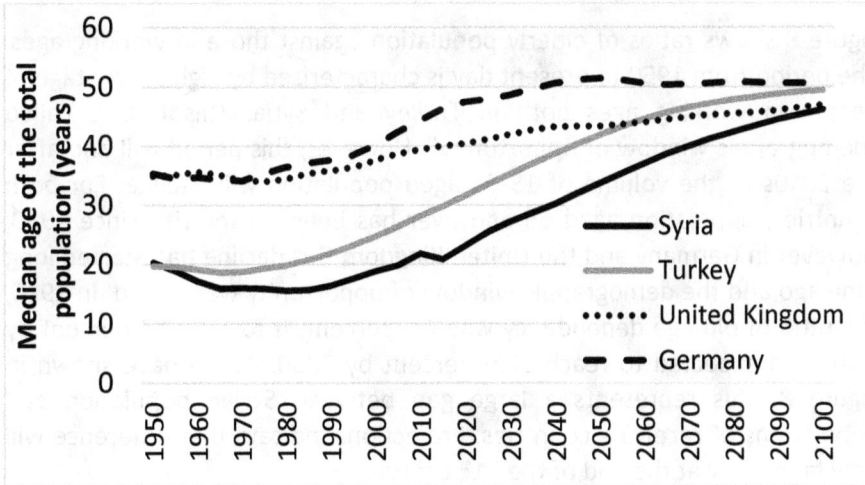

Data Source: UN (2016).

64 comprised 48.3 percent of population in Syria in 1980 and this figure rose to 60.5 percent by 2010. These trends in age structure of Syrian population needs to be taken into account when it comes to services such as child care, schooling, and job creation in the countries and areas of destination.

Figure 7. Child dependency ratios, 1950-2100

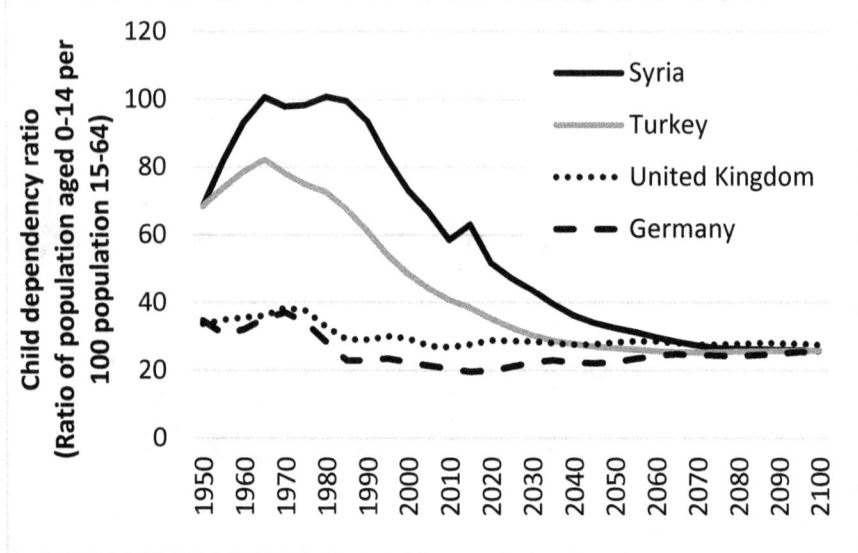

Data Source: UN (2016).

Figure 8 shows ratios of elderly population against those in working ages. The period from 1950 to present day is characterised by high percentage of people in working ages both in Turkey and Syria. This is also called "demographic window of opportunity". However, this period will end after the 2040s as the volume of 15-64 aged population will decline. For both countries, population aged 65 and over has been on the rise since 1980. However in Germany and the United Kingdom this decline had started long time ago and the demographic window of opportunity was closed. In 1980, the ratio of old-age dependency was 2.9 percent. It rose to 3.7 percent by 2010 and expected to reach 12.9 percent by 2050. As we have shown in Figure 8, this represents a large gap between Syrian population and populations of receiving countries. Projections indicate that difference will only fade away at the end of the 21st century.

In figures 9a to 9d, we present population pyramids for the four selected countries. Different shapes of population pyramids and changes expected over time support our argument above. It is clear that a significant decline is expected in working age populations in Germany and the United Kingdom. Turkey's age and sex structure is also expected to converge rapidly with the trends seen in these two developed countries. It is important to note that all age groups up to 35-39 are about the same size in Turkey. Nevertheless, Syria differs from other three countries with its very large children and adolescent age groups. Over the course of the century, Syrian population is expected to be transformed into a shape similar to developed countries. Turkey's population will be ageing faster than others while children population will further shrink in Germany and the United Kingdom.

Figure 8. Old-age dependency ratios, 1950-2100

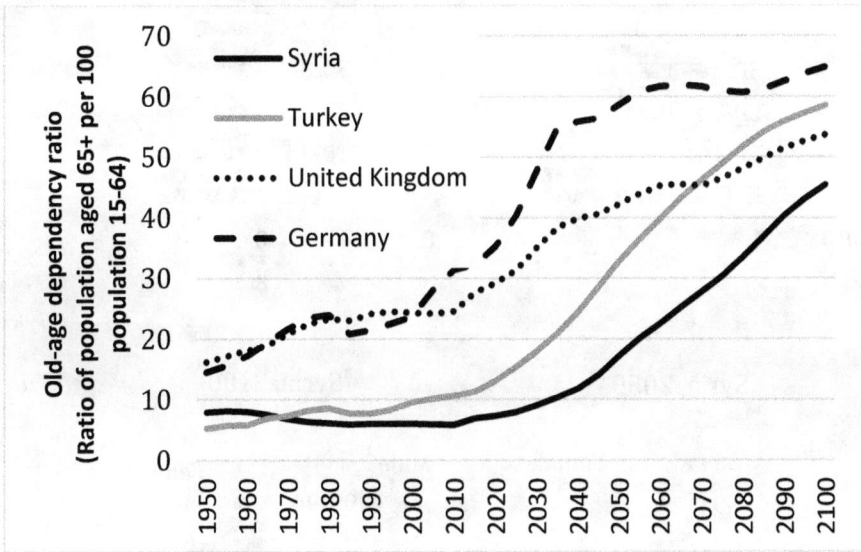

Data Source: UN (2016).

By 2050, the lower age groups, particularly children, will decline in their share of the total population in all four countries. In the same period, we expect the share of the groups aged 40 and over to gradually increase. However, this process will be much slower for the Syrian population. By the end of the 21st century, we predict that population pyramids will significantly converge as differences in demographic processes and patterns will decrease among these selected countries. Low fertility rates, ageing populations and relatively high mortality rates due to elderly population will characterise the demographic profiles of the countries by the end of the century (Figures 9a to 9d).

Figure 9a. Population pyramids for Syria, 2015-2100

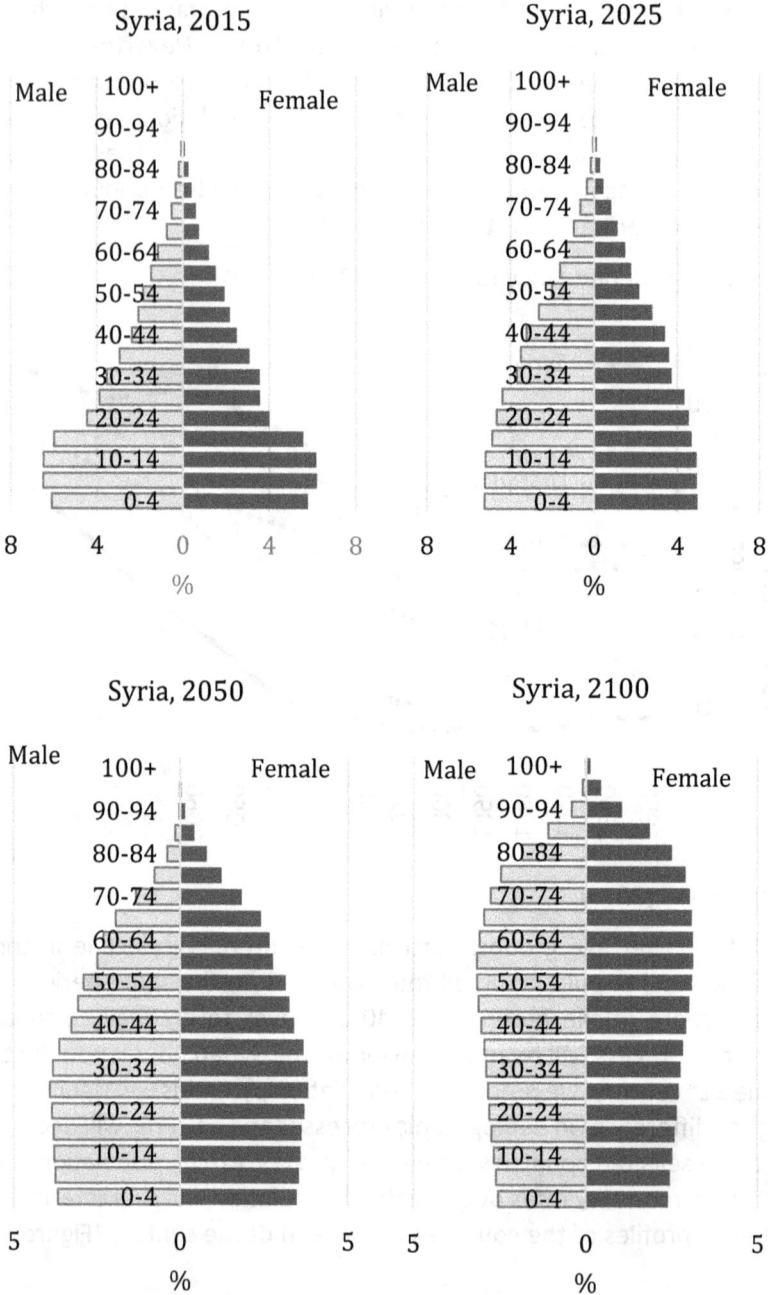

Syria, 2015

Syria, 2025

Syria, 2050

Syria, 2100

Data source: (UN, 2016)

Figure 9b. Population pyramids for Turkey, 2015-2100

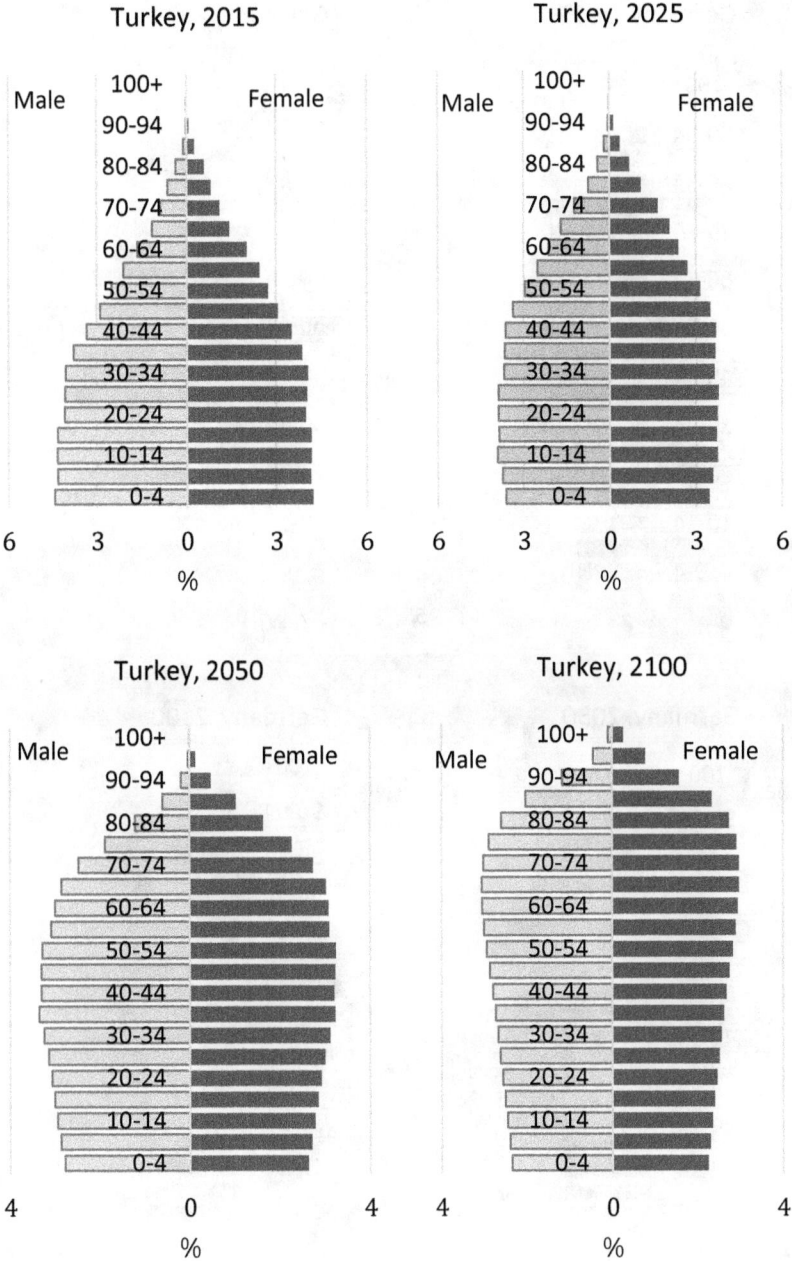

Data source: (UN, 2016).

Figure 9c. Population pyramids for Germany, 2015-2100

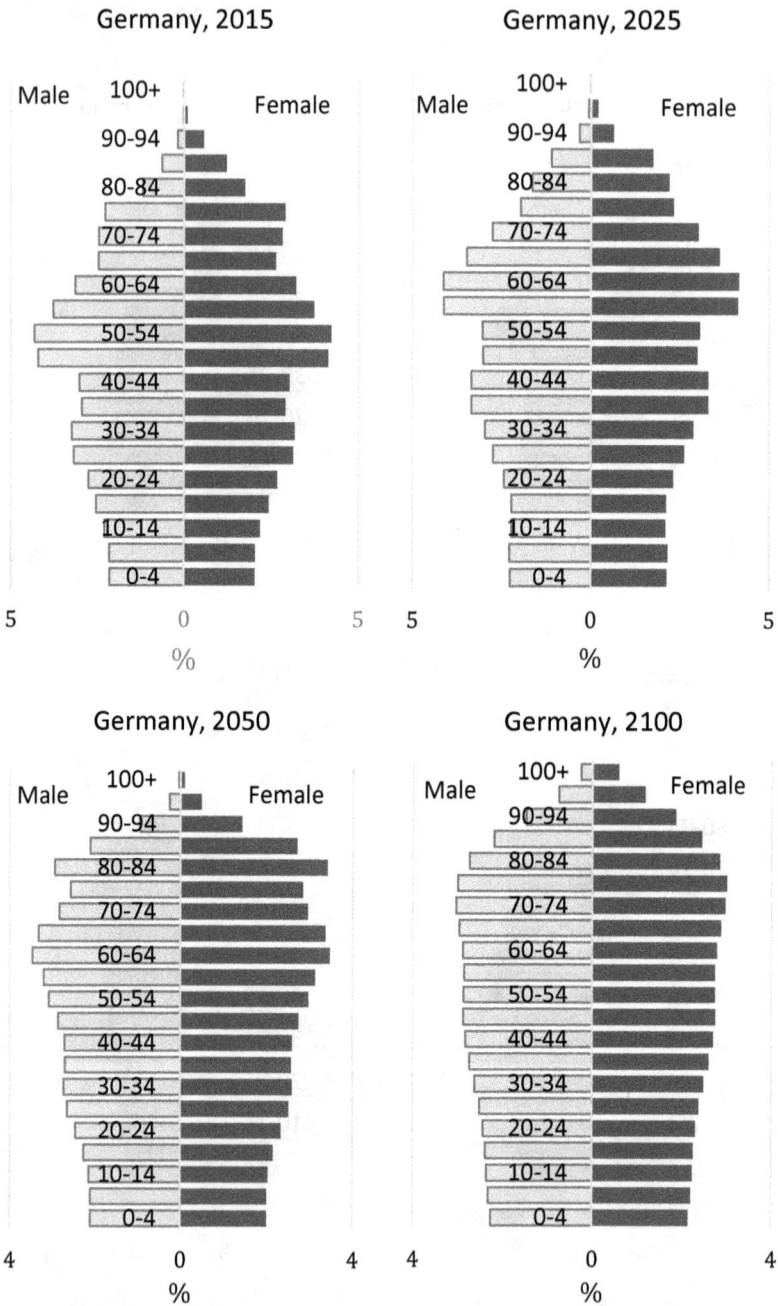

Germany, 2015

Germany, 2025

Germany, 2050

Germany, 2100

Data source: (UN, 2016).

Figure 9d. Population pyramids for United Kingdom, 2015-2100

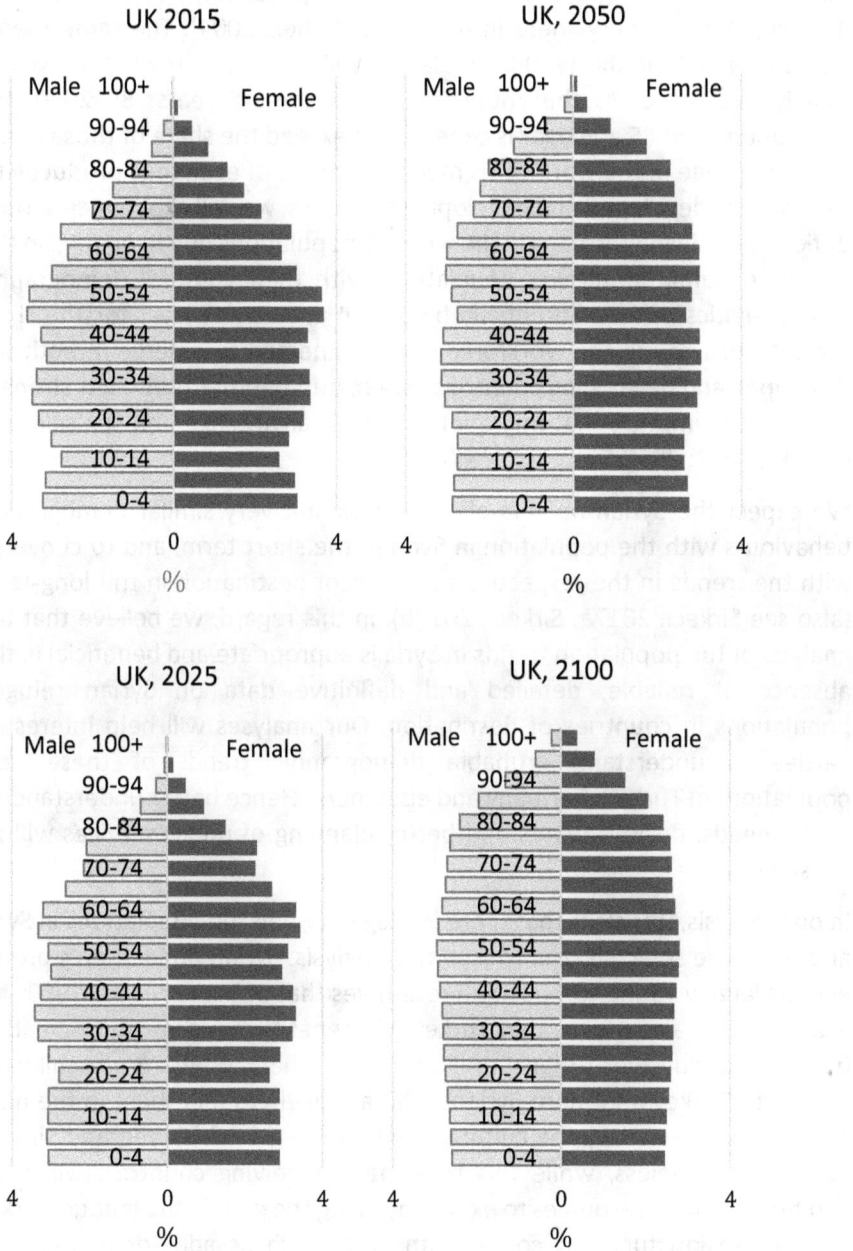

UK 2015

Male 100+   Female

90-94
80-84
70-74
60-64
50-54
40-44
30-34
20-24
10-14
0-4

4   0   4
%

UK, 2050

Male 100+   Female

90-94
80-84
70-74
60-64
50-54
40-44
30-34
20-24
10-14
0-4

4   0   4
%

UK, 2025

Male 100+   Female

90-94
80-84
70-74
60-64
50-54
40-44
30-34
20-24
10-14
0-4

4   0   4
%

UK, 2100

Male 100+   Female

90-94
80-84
70-74
60-64
50-54
40-44
30-34
20-24
10-14
0-4

4   0   4
%

Data source: (UN, 2016).

Conclusion

According to Demographic Transition Theory, fertility rates have been declining almost everywhere in the world (Reher, 2004). The same theory also suggests that the world population will continue growing as well as rapidly ageing across the countries in the coming years. By 2050, the population aged 65 and over is expected to exceed the share of those under 15 years of age in the world. This means, in terms of economic productivity, especially in developed and developing countries, we will experience serious difficulties in filling the gaps in the working populations due to ageing. In this regard, dynamic immigrant populations with their youthful demographic characteristics offer a potentially beneficial answer, at least for the short term, to this gap in the workforce that is expected to emerge in both the developed and developing countries. Again, our arguments also get strength with the assumption that migration is almost always age and sex selective (Weeks, 2002: 255-257).

We expect the Syrian movers abroad to exhibit very similar demographic behaviours with the population in Syria in the short term, and to converge with the trends in the respective countries of destination in the long-term (also see Sirkeci, 2017a; Sirkeci, 2017b). In this regard, we believe that the analysis of the population trends in Syria is appropriate and beneficial in the absence of reliable, detailed and definitive data on Syrian refugee populations in countries of destination. Our analyses will help interested parties to understand probable demographic trends of these new populations in Turkey, Germany and elsewhere. Hence better understanding of the needs, desires, wants and better planning of public services will be possible.

In our analysis, it is clear that there is a lag between the populations in Syria and the three selected countries in this analysis. Syrian population's profile with its largely young composition resembles that of Turkey in the 1980s for example. This also means that Turkey will benefit from a young population because already more than 3 million Syrians (half of whom are children) moved to Turkey and more Syrians who are likely to join them in the near future as suggested by the culture of migration model (Cohen and Sirkeci, 2011). Nevertheless, while this may mean receiving countries will have additional human resources to exploit by filling the gaps in the labour market and in pension funds, it comes with costs such as additional resources needed for schools, hospitals and other public services. For example, the number of additional school places needed in Turkey might be as high as one million and a large number of Syrian refugee children were still not enrolled at schools as of the end of 2016. Similarly, the number of children born to Syrian refugee mothers in Turkey has probably already exceeded 200,000 as by September 2016, the total number of children born to Syrians was nearly 180,000 according to Turkey's health ministry (Al Jazeera, 2017). Thus a young profile often means higher birth rates and that much healthcare and prenatal care needed.

As they are likely to stay on and more movers from Syria are to follow (i.e. culture of migration model (Cohen and Sirkeci, 2011; Sirkeci and Cohen, 2016) predicts further mobility even after the initial triggers of mobility disappears over time), one further issue of concern is sociocultural, political and economic integration of Syrian movers in destination countries. For example, in Turkey, despite the presence of a sizeable Arabic speaking minority population prior to the arrival of Syrians, anxieties about the arrival of this large additional Arabic speaking population need to be addressed to avoid conflicts and facilitate cohesion. Different cultural practices including religious nuances need to be understood and accommodated. The process of settlement and integration will be complicated and not without hurdles (Özservet and Sirkeci, 2016).

References

Allman, J. (1980). The demographic transition in the Middle East end North Africa. *International Journal of Middle East Studies*, 12: 277-301.

AlJazeera (2017, January 19). UNICEF: 40% of Syrian children in Turkey not in school. http://www.aljazeera.com/news/2017/01/unicef-40-syrian-children-turkey-school-170119175018121.html (accessed 21/06/2017).

Bongaarts, J. and Watkins, S.C. (1996). Social interactions and contemporary fertility transitions. *Population and Development Review*, 22: 639-682.

Bouvier, L., Poston, D. L. and Zhai, N. B. (1997). Population growth impacts of zero net international migration. *International Migration Review*, 31: 294-311.

Caldwell, J.C. (2001). The globalization of fertility behaviour. *Population and Development Review*, 27: 93-115.

Caldwell, J.C. and Caldwell, P. (2001). Regional paths to fertility transition. *Journal of Population Research*, 18: 91-117.

Coale, A.J. and Watkins, S.C. (1986). *The Decline of Fertility in Europe*. Princeton: Princeton University.

Cohen, J. H., and Sirkeci, I. (2011). *Cultures of Migration: The Global Nature of Contemporary Mobility*. Austin: University of Texas Press.

Courbage, Y. (1999). Economic and political issues of fertility transition in the Arab World—answers and open questions. *Population & Environment, 20* (4), 353-379.

Courbage, Y. (1994). Fertility transition in Syria: From implicit population policy to explicit economic crisis. *International Family Planning Perspectives*, 20 (4): 142-146.

Douglas, A. P. (2010). *Syria (Modern World Nations)*. New York: Chelsea House Publishers.

Fargues, P. (2011). International migration and the demographic transition: A two-way interaction. *International Migration Review, 45* (3), 588-614.

Hobbs, F. B. (2004). Age and sex composition. In: *The Methods and Materials of Demography*. Siegel, J.S. and Swanson, D.A. (ed.). Londra: Elsevier Academic Press, pp. 125-173.

Lestheaghe, R. (1983). A century of demographic and cultural change in Western Europe: An explanation of underlying dimensions. *Population and Development Review*, 9: 411-435.

Newbold, K. B. (2010). *Population Geography: Tools and Issues*. Lanham: Rowman & Littlefield Publishers, Inc.

Omran, A. R., and Roudi, F. (1993). The Middle East population puzzle. *Population Bulletin, 48* (1): 1-40.

Özservet, Y. Ç., and Sirkeci, I. (2016). Editörden: Çocuklar ve göç. *Göç Dergisi, 3* (1): 1-4.

Rashad, H. (2000). Demographic transition in Arab countries: A new perspective. *Journal of Population Research, 17*(1): 83-101.

Reher, D. S. (2004). The demographic transition revisited as a global process. *Population, space and place, 10* (1): 19-41.

Rowland, D. T. (2012). *Demographic Methods and Concepts*. New York: Oxford University.

Sirkeci, I. (2017a). Turkey's refugees, Syrians and refugees from Turkey: a country of insecurity. *Migration Letters, 14* (1): 127-144.

Sirkeci, I. (2017b). Bir güvensizlik ülkesi olarak Türkiye'nin mültecileri, Suriyeliler ve Türk mülteciler. *Göç Dergisi, 4* (1): 21-40.

Sirkeci, I., and Cohen, J. H. (2016). Cultures of migration and conflict in contemporary human mobility in Turkey. *European Review, 24* (3): 381-396.

Taleb, Z. B., Bahelah, R., Fouad, F. M., Coutts, A., Wilcox, M., and Maziak, W. (2015). Syria: health in a country undergoing tragic transition. *International journal of public health, 60* (1): 63-72.

UN (United Nations) (2016). *World Population Prospects, the 2015 Revision Data Base*. United Nations, Department of Economic and Social Affairs, Population Division, USA. Accessed from https://esa.un.org/unpd/wpp/; on 18.09.2016.

UNHCR (2017). Syria Regional Refugee Response. Inter-agency Information Sharing Portal. Accessed from http://data.unhcr.org/syrianrefugees/regional.php; on 12.08.2017.

Watkins, S.C. (1987). The fertility transition: Europe and the Third World compared. *Sociological Forum*, 2: 645-673.

Weeks, J. R. (2002). *Population: An Introduction to Concepts and Issues*. Belmont: Wadsworth Thomson Learning.

Weinstein, J. and Pillai, V.K. (2001). *Demography: The Science of Population*, Boston: Allyn and Bacon.

Winckler, O. (2003). Fertility transition in the Middle East: The case of the Israeli Arabs, *Israel Affairs*, 9: 39-67.

Yaukey, D., Anderton, D.L. and Lundquist, J.H. (2007). *Demography: The Study of Human Population*. Illinois: Waveland.

Yazgan, P., Eroğlu Utku, D. and Sirkeci, I. (2015). Syrian crisis and migration. *Migration Letters*, *12* (3): 181-192.

Yüceşahin, M. M., Adalı, T. and Türkyılmaz, S. (2016). Population policies in Turkey and demographic changes on a social map. *Border Crossing*, 6 (2): 240-266.

Yucesahin, M., & Sirkeci, I. (2017). Demographic gaps between Syrian and the European populations: What do they suggest?. *Border Crossing*, 7(2), 207-230. Retrieved from http://tplondon.com/journal/index.php/bc/article/view/988.

Yüceşahin, Sirkeci

Chapter Eleven

Integration of Syrians: Politics of Integration in Turkey in the Face of a Closing Window of Opportunity

K. Onur Unutulmaz[¥]

Introduction

Integration has become one of the most popular concepts in today's daily, political, and academic discussions. Countries of all sorts with a large number of immigrants and sizable communities with 'immigrant-origins' are now conceptualising several issues and challenges related to immigration and the ensuing ethnic and cultural diversity as matters of integration. While both what they mean by the term and how they are trying to achieve it vary widely, the political nature of the whole process and the hegemony of the concept of integration are beyond discussion.

This chapter, firstly, provides a brief selective analytical background for the significance of the concept of integration by describing how the current 'backlash against diversity' has come into being. Secondly, the concept of integration is discussed briefly with reference to some common facets that could be identified in effective integration schemes. Thirdly, integration of Syrian communities in Turkey is discussed as a particularly big challenge. Lastly, the chapter makes a case for urgency in adopting a sound integration vision and creating effective integration policies in Turkey. Relatively low level of politicisation of immigrant integration issue is then discussed as a context conducive to develop such policies. Finally, the ways in which this politicisation has been rapidly changing recently and the restrictive impact of such politicisation over controversial issues on governance is discussed.

[¥] K. Onur Unutulmaz Social Sciences University of Ankara, Turkey. E-mail: onur.unutulmaz@asbu.edu.tr

A Conceptual Background: Integration and Its Discontents

Backlash against Diversity

It seems evident that in Turkey, like in many other countries, international migration has become more visible, politically salient, and controversial than ever. However, contrary to a quite common perception of immigration growing exponentially with every passing year as a major aspect of world's apparent globalisation (Ghemawat 2011), the share of international migrants in world population remains low at 3.4 per cent despite an increase over the last few decades (Sirkeci, 2017, 129). Similarly, de Haas (2005, 2008) repeatedly suggests that the public outcry and intensified debates over international migration are often influenced by myths rather than facts: a myth of growing, unstoppable invasion of immigrants draining national sources and abusing the welfare state.

These myths, ever so masterfully exploited by extreme right political movements, have become the ideological justification to what has been termed a 'backlash against diversity' (Grillo 2005; Vertovec et al. 2010). The actual dynamics that created this backlash, particularly in the Western European context, were manifold and, in fact, a separate inquiry would be necessary to understand it in each different national context. There are, however, some common factors that contributed in the emergence of such a backlash can be identified. As can be seen below, many of these factors and dynamics are inter-related and they are caused by various other important factors. Yet, it would be beneficial to underline these factors anyway:

Emergence of super-diversity in the West: While probably no human society has ever had complete ethnic and cultural homogeneity, the level of diversity in the contemporary Western societies seems to be unprecedented in history. It also differs from its historical precursors in essence as well since it is marked by "a dynamic interplay of variables, including: country of origin (comprising a variety of possible subset traits such as ethnicity, language, religious tradition, regional and local identity, cultural values and practices), migration channel, and legal status (including myriad categories determining a hierarchy of entitlements and restrictions)" (Vertovec 2007, 7). While the idea that "unstoppable floods of immigrants are invading all Western countries" is a myth (Haas 2008), the fact that Western societies have become such visibly super-diverse is one of the reasons why this myth exists and has so much traction. It needs to be also remembered that a vast majority of mass immigration in Western European countries occurred in the latter half 20th century, following the end of the Second World War. Thus, the most intense immigration flows that would change the European social fabric forever, took place in a rather short amount of time which, coupled with some other factors described below, significantly adds to the identity concerns of Europeans citizens.

End of post-war economic boom and economic crises: In line with "inter-group conflict" theories, immigration and diversity seemed to cause the perception of threat and negative attitudes towards immigrant and minority groups particularly when the groups seem to compete for same scarce resources (Blalock 1967; Olzak 1992; Quillian 1995). Therefore, when the economy is in a dynamic growth period where unemployment is low and the immigrants usually fill jobs that are deemed undesirable by the natives, such perceptions of threat and emergence of negative stereotypes are not very likely. It is when economy is in stagnation and unemployment levels are high, however, that such negative developments become more likely. Indeed, the fact that the backlash against diversity has intensified in 1980s and 1990s appear to confirm this prediction. While until mid-1970s European economies had displayed dynamic growth rates with very low unemployment rates as they were undergoing a largely US-sponsored economic reconstruction in the aftermath of WWII, following 1974 OPEC crisis the economic growth came to a halt and unemployment soared (Eichengreen 2007; Aldcroft 2001). Therefore, the end of post-war economic boom and occurrence of periodic large-scale crises need to be highlighted as a significant factor contributing in the politicization of migration and emergence of a strong societal backlash against diversity in many European countries.

Demographic factors- Ageing and declining populations: Another important component of the contemporary backlash against migration-related diversity is the demographic transformation the Western world has been undergoing. There are three main aspect of this transformation that had caused significant concerns related to cultural and national identities in different countries. The first is the changing demographic profiles of the native populations in the West related to decreasing fertility rates. As it is well known, in order for a population to remain stable the fertility rate needs to be 2.1 which is called the 'replacement level'. Fertility rate can be defined as the total number of children that are born to a woman over her lifetime. When we look at the fertility rates in Europe, we see that in all European countries the rate is well beyond the replacement level (Coale and Watkins

1986; Fargues 2011). In fact, the average total fertility rate in the EU-28 is 1.58 while it gets as low as 1.3 in many countries (see Table 1).

Table 1: Total Fertility Rates in Europe, 1960-2015

	1960	1970	1980	1990	2000	2010	2013	2014	2015
EU-28 ([1])	2.58	2.36	1.87	1.66	1.46	1.62	1.55	1.58	1.58
Belgium ([2])	2.54	2.25	1.68	1.62	1.67	1.86	1.75	1.73	1.70
Bulgaria	2.31	2.17	2.05	1.82	1.26	1.57	1.48	1.53	1.53
Czech Republic	2.09	1.92	2.08	1.90	1.15	1.51	1.46	1.53	1.57
Denmark	2.57	1.95	1.55	1.67	1.77	1.87	1.67	1.69	1.71
Germany	2.37	2.03	1.44	1.45	1.38	1.39	1.42	1.47	1.50
Estonia ([3])	1.98	2.17	2.02	2.05	1.36	1.72	1.52	1.54	1.58
Ireland	3.78	3.85	3.21	2.11	1.89	2.05	1.96	1.94	1.92
Greece	2.23	2.40	2.23	1.39	1.25	1.48	1.29	1.30	1.33
Spain	2.86	2.84	2.20	1.36	1.23	1.37	1.27	1.32	1.33
France ([1])	2.85	2.55	1.85	1.77	1.89	2.03	1.99	2.01	1.96
Croatia	2.29	1.98	1.88	1.63	1.39	1.55	1.46	1.46	1.40
Italy	2.37	2.38	1.64	1.33	1.26	1.46	1.39	1.37	1.35
Cyprus	3.50	2.61	2.35	2.41	1.64	1.44	1.30	1.31	1.32
Latvia	1.94	1.96	1.86	2.02	1.25	1.36	1.52	1.65	1.70
Lithuania	2.56	2.40	1.99	2.03	1.39	1.50	1.59	1.63	1.70
Luxembourg	2.29	1.97	1.50	1.60	1.76	1.63	1.55	1.50	1.47
Hungary	2.02	1.98	1.91	1.87	1.32	1.25	1.35	1.44	1.45
Malta	3.62	2.03	1.99	2.04	1.70	1.36	1.38	1.42	1.45
Netherlands	3.12	2.57	1.60	1.62	1.72	1.79	1.68	1.71	1.66
Austria	2.69	2.29	1.65	1.46	1.36	1.44	1.44	1.47	1.49
Poland ([4])	2.98	2.20	2.28	2.06	1.37	1.41	1.29	1.32	1.32
Portugal	3.16	3.01	2.25	1.56	1.55	1.39	1.21	1.23	1.31
Romania	2.34	2.89	2.43	1.83	1.31	1.59	1.46	1.52	1.58
Slovenia	2.34	2.23	2.06	1.46	1.26	1.57	1.55	1.58	1.57
Slovakia	3.04	2.41	2.32	2.09	1.30	1.43	1.34	1.37	1.40
Finland	2.72	1.83	1.63	1.78	1.73	1.87	1.75	1.71	1.65
Sweden	2.17	1.92	1.68	2.13	1.54	1.98	1.89	1.88	1.85
United Kingdom	2.69	2.44	1.90	1.83	1.64	1.92	1.83	1.81	1.80
Iceland	4.29	2.81	2.48	2.30	2.08	2.20	1.93	1.93	1.80
Liechtenstein	:	:	:	:	1.57	1.40	1.45	1.59	1.40
Norway	2.85	2.50	1.72	1.93	1.85	1.95	1.78	1.75	1.72
Switzerland	2.44	2.10	1.55	1.58	1.50	1.52	1.52	1.54	1.54
Montenegro	3.60	2.74	2.24	2.08	1.72	1.70	1.73	1.75	1.74
FYR of Macedonia	3.84	3.16	2.49	2.21	1.88	1.56	1.49	1.52	1.50
Albania	6.49	4.91	3.62	2.98	2.16	1.65	1.70	1.79	1.67
Serbia	2.5	2.3	2.1	1.8	1.48	1.40	1.43	1.46	1.46
Turkey	6.30	5.56	4.36	3.08	2.48	2.04	2.08	2.17	2.14

([1]) 2014 and 2015: break in series.   ([3]) 2015: break in series.
([2]) 2014: break in series.   ([4]) 2000 and 2010: break in series.

Sources: World Bank and Eurostat. Available at http://ec.europa.eu/eurostat/statistics-explained/index.php/Fertility_statistics and https://data.worldbank.org/indicator/ SP.DYN.TFRT.IN/ (last accessed on 19.10.2017)

It should also be pointed out that the fertility levels in Europe used to be much higher a few decades ago. When we look at 1960s and 1970s, for instance, the fertility rates in many European countries appear to be well above the replacement level. In 1990s and 2000s, however, this demographic shift seems to have become very apparent which means that literally all Western European countries and most others in other parts of the continent have demographically decreasing populations (Coale and Watkins 1986) (Table 1).

Another important implication of the falling fertility rates is that the structure of existing populations is also undergoing a remarkable structural change. This process is called ageing and it involves the shrinking of younger strata of the population while the older age groups are getting progressively more crowded (Alvardo and Creedy 1998; Davoudi, Wishardt, and Strange 2010; Walker and Maltby 1997). In fact, while the number of new individuals joining the society is continuously decreasing due to aforementioned fall in the fertility rates, the number and share of older people in the population tends to increase due to a corresponding fall in the mortality rates. In other words, while less and less babies are being born, less and less people die due to improved life standards, advancements in medicine, and overall lowered risk of death in the contemporary developed world. This shift has many significant implications for the countries concerned. For example, due to growing elderly population and declining population in working ages, welfare systems face a challenge because contributions to welfare funds and pension funds decline. Hence the systems face funding crisis in serving inactive populations. Moreover, because changing such demographic indicators is considerably difficult if not impossible, impact of these demographic transitions are projected to continue in the near future (Davoudi, Wishardt, and Strange 2010; Alvardo and Creedy 1998) (Figure 1).

These two demographic trends, i.e. low fertility and ageing of populations, have been somewhat countered by mass immigration (Alvardo and Creedy, 1998). In other words, through immigration mostly young and economically active individuals arrive in these countries to offset the impact of low fertility as shown in Syrian case by Yucesahin and Sirkeci (2017). Moreover, immigrant communities in most countries tend to have a higher fertility rate than the host society which further helps offset the ageing (Coleman 1994). However, all these demographic trends have given rise to serious anxieties about identity amongst host societies who seemingly perceive their ethnic, cultural, and national identities to be under risk. Extreme far-right political leaders exploit this idea that due to continuing (and "unstoppable") immigration flows and very high fertility rates of immigrant communities, they will become the majority in the near future which will make the current dominant ethnic group (in the host country) a minority in their own lands (Unutulmaz 2012).

Figure 1: Population Pyramids EU-28, 2016 and 2080

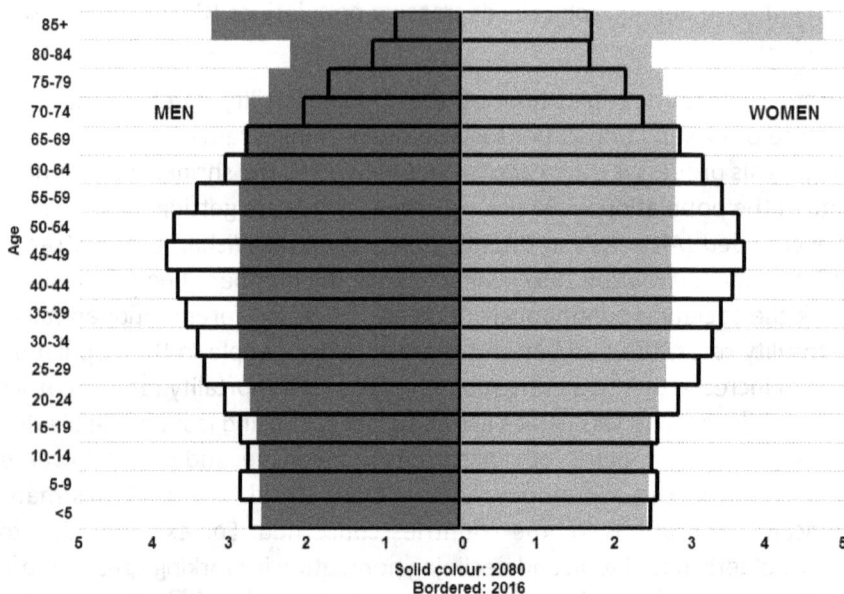

Source: Eurostat. Note. 2016: provisional estimate. 2080 projections (EUROPOP2013).

Available at http://ec.europa.eu/eurostat/statistics-explained/index.php/Population_ structure_and_ageing

Securitization of migration in post 9/11 world: A further development which significantly exacerbated the backlash against diversity in the Western world in general and in Europe in particular was the impact of the September 11 terrorist attacks in the US (Bourbeau 2011; Buonfino 2004). These attacks, which involved hijacking of commercial airplanes and crashing them to the twin towers of World Trade Center in New York as well as to Pentagon, were carried out by the fundamentalist terrorists and this created a global reaction. Most significant was the reaction of the US who declared a war against the global Islamic terror (Bourbeau 2011, 106). The truly tragic terminology used by the American administration provided ample opportunity for xenophobes and Islamophobes by referring to the perceived religious aspect of the attacks and their perpetrators (Saeed 2016). What is more, George W. Bush, then the President of the US, went so far as to use the term 'crusades' when referring to their fight against these Islamist terrorists. This was beginning of a period with intensified debates over the 'clash of civilizations' (Huntington 1992) where individuals of immigrant origin would now be confronted with questions about their loyalty and allegiances to the host countries even more frequently (Bourbeau 2011; Aksoy 2006).

The Concept of Integration

As a result of all these and some other factors, the aforementioned backlash against diversity, liberal immigration policies, and multiculturalist social frameworks were created. The rise of populist and/or nationalist politics that we are witnessing today, a particular defining characteristic of which is an anti-immigration discourse, can also be seen as the continuation of the above-summarised processes. Another outcome of the above-discussed factor has been the growth, both in prominence and popularity, of the concept of integration (Castles et al. 2002; Favell 1998). Integration emerged as a very useful notion that symbolizes a compromising position for the liberal democrats: although they were not prepared to partake in the anti-immigrant and xenophobic fervour of the far right, they conceded the necessity on the part of immigrants to make an effort to become a part of the society and share at least some basic societal values. Therefore, integration was meant to reject both the assimilationist demands put forth by the far right, on the one hand, and the too expansive multicultural rights granted previously by countries like the UK and the Netherlands, on the other (Unutulmaz 2017). This undoubtedly positive sounding concept that seems to be simultaneously able to soothe the general public's above described anxieties and provide policy-makers with a vague, hence flexible, vision to mobilize people and resources in adopting policies managing diversity (Unutulmaz 2012, 2017, Favell 1998, 2001).

The concept of integration has become an almost universal point of reference in public, academic, and political debates (Castles et al. 2002; Unutulmaz 2017). As suggested above, it is possible to identify many points of criticism against the inherent vagueness of the concept as well as the tendency it seems to embody for many people to put a disproportionate responsibility on the shoulders of immigrants. Some people even suggest that integration is nothing but a sugar-coated version of assimilation (Vasta 2009, 2007). Differences in political visions of what should integration mean and how should it be achieved notwithstanding; it needs to be pointed out that the basic yearning for effective integration policies seems to be a fairly justified one. That is if we define integration policies as the ones to create a framework in which newcomers are provided with necessary opportunities for becoming fully functional members of the society who are bound with the rest of the society by feelings of mutual belonging and shared values.

What is 'the Best' Integration Policy?

There have been explicit efforts for constructively managing ethnic and cultural diversity as well as integration programmes in most countries receiving mass immigration for the past several decades (Unutulmaz 2017). Moreover, there have been an extremely wide-ranging set of visions, policies, institutional frameworks, legal precautions, and political instruments used in these countries. Surely, one may be inclined to look at these different policies to try to measure them with respect to their effectiveness and identify 'the best one'. Such an endeavour, however, would be futile for several reasons. First, the integration visions, i.e. what is meant by the concept and hence what the policy objectives are, are ultimately political constructs that emerge through intricate processes in each context (Unutulmaz 2012). Therefore, the effectiveness and overall success of each integration policy needs to be assessed in reference to its own objectives and vision. In other words, it would be analytically fallacious to compare the effectiveness of different integration policies with so diverse visions.

Secondly, integration policies are not adopted or implemented in a vacuum. They are rather the products of lengthy historical processes in terms of both how the question of integration is posed and how it is responded. In other words, the very understanding of what needs to be done and how are shaped by the social, political, legal, and institutional structure of a country that had been shaped for over centuries. What some authors call "national philosophies of integration" emerge in a dynamic interplay with the rest of public philosophies of such countries (Favell 1998).

Lastly, even if it were possible to recognize a policy or a specific programme to be perfectly effective or the best compared to all others with similar stated objectives, this would not automatically mean that the same policy would work in other contexts in the same way. In other words, just as the policy is dependent on the political vision and historical context, so would its outcomes be dependent on the context. While an integration policy might work perfectly in one country, in whatever way 'the perfect' is defined; it may just cause more problems in another country.

Does that mean it is of no use to look at the experiences in other countries to come up with some useful tips on how to develop effective integration policies? Certainly not. In fact, what is suggested here is that the context and its peculiarities are to be taken into account before defining not only the answers but, perhaps more importantly, the questions. It is appropriate and potentially very useful, to review the existing integration policies as well as the literature on these policies, to try to highlight common elements in the effective policies. There are two key aspects in integration policy debates: first, the vision of integration (essential features) and instruments used in realising the vision.

The essential features of successful integration policies include, firstly, an emphasis on the requirement of fostering a common identity and sense of belonging among immigrants and the host society members. Particularly in the above described context of securitised immigration debates and backlash against diversity, this emphasis of creating certain common norms and values gluing the whole society together in all of its complexity and diversity came to dominate the agenda. Secondly, a solid and explicit rejection of assimilation as a political objective is now an invariable and essential aspect of effective integration policies. This may sound somewhat tautological yet it is not: the conceptual vagueness of integration coupled with the negative reaction against contemporary diversity have meant that certain 'integration policies' could mostly concentrate on immigrants' acquisition of new values, norms, and knowledge even at the expense of their existing ones. More recently, however, integration policies are built on the solid understanding that people could adopt a strong identity (of belonging to the host society) without forfeiting their existing cultural norms and values. Lastly, a common element of successful integration initiatives is a strong emphasis on mainstreaming. Mainstreaming refers to a strategy of preventing social marginalisation of immigrants and minorities by bringing them closer to the centre of society. In other words, mainstreaming immigrants means making every effort to make them and their culture a part of the mainstream society and culture instead of pushing them towards a socially and culturally isolated position. Mainstreaming can also be described as making minorities a part of 'us' rather than 'them' or 'others', both in the eyes of the host society and the immigrants themselves[1] (see Figure 2).

Figure 2: Common Elements in Effective Integration Policies

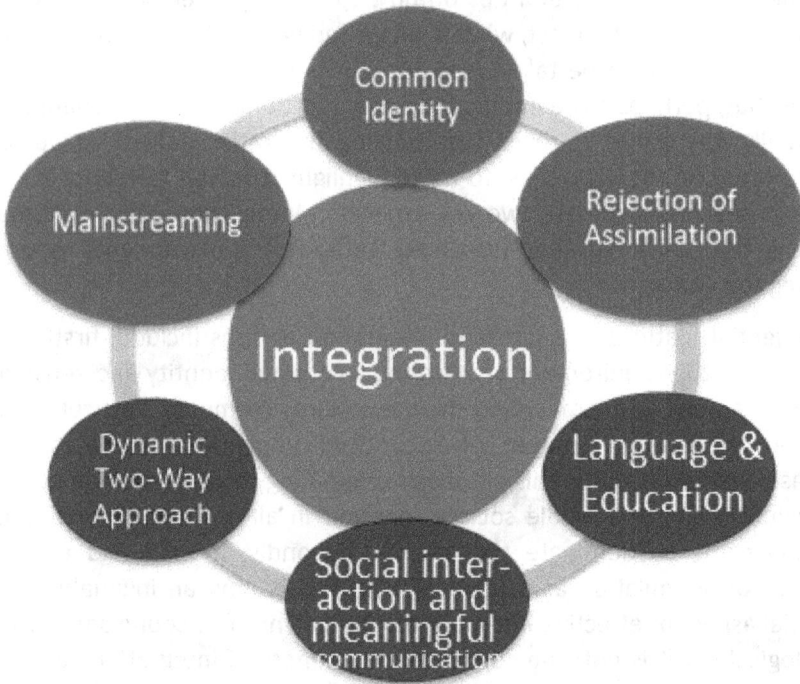

Source: Created by the author based on the discussion presented above. The green circles represent essence-related objectives and blue ones potential instruments.

There are also instrumental aspects of effective integration policies. Firstly, the vital importance of language instruction for newcomers and their children could not be over-stressed. The countries with well-developed language instruction programmes that include language support throughout school life of immigrant children are more successful in effective integration (SIRIUS 2013). Equally important is creating an education system, which does not accommodate diversity in a passive manner, but places diversity at the centre of the system to try to maximise potential benefits of it. This perspective is reflected in the multicultural composition of the teaching staff and the curriculum as well as incorporation of cultural elements such as religious festivals (of immigrant groups) in the education system (Brown

---

[1] See for instance, https://www.gov.uk/government/publications/2010-to-2015-govern-ment-policy-community-integration

2015; Crul 2004). Secondly, it needs to be emphasised that effective integration policies appear to require adopting a dynamic two-way and multilateral approach, instead of a top-down and static perspective (Castles et al. 2002, 11). The latter considers integration as the responsibility, or rather obligation, of the immigrants to integrate into the society, which would be facilitated by national integration policies. By adopting a dynamic two-way and multilateral approach, integration is understood as a mutual process of adaptation for all segments of the society. Lastly, increasing the volume and quality of social interaction between different segments of society, particularly including immigrants and minorities is important. Both for creating common values and norms and for ensuring mainstreaming of minority cultures, this is of critical importance (see Figure 2).

Why are Integration Policies Particularly Essential in Turkey?

It is clear that integration policies, as generally defined above, are essential for any country with an ethnically and culturally diverse population. It should further be underlined, however, that effective integration policies are even more vital in today's Turkey (Şeker, Sirkeci, and Yüceşahin 2015; Sirkeci, Şeker, and Çağlar 2015; Erdoğan 2014). Before elaborating on the various risks and challenges as well as opportunities and potential benefits specific to the Turkish case, it would be useful to very briefly reiterate the context in Turkey.

Turkey has faced a very quick and unprecedented insertion of mass immigration. In the course of less than six years, more than 3 million Syrian refugees have arrived in Turkey. According to the official figures released by the Directorate General of Migration Management (DGMM), there were more than 2.9 million Syrians who are registered as 'persons under temporary protection' (see Figure 3). This is obviously a mass population movement making Turkey the country with the largest refugee population in the world (IOM 2015: 2). While Turkey has long been a country of immigration as well as emigration, the immigration of Syrians has certainly been unmatched with respect to its volume, pace, and complexity (Erdoğan and Kaya, 2015). Moreover, it needs to be remembered that this immigration was perceived to be temporary for a long time, which had meant that no systematic or long-term preparation for their effective integration existed. As it is discussed in the below section on increasing politicisation of the issue, it has only recently been acknowledged that at least a significant part of the Syrians will be permanent residents in Turkey.

Unutulmaz

In addition to the large volume of the Syrian immigrant community, its demographic and socio-economic profile also makes it imperative for Turkey to develop effective policies and mechanisms for integration. Some key statistics are worth mentioning in the context of a discussion over integration. The first and foremost is the fact that the Syrian community in Turkey is very young. Almost half (45.6%) of all registered Syrians are under the age of 18, with around 350 thousand are between the ages of 0 and 4 indicating that they were either born in Turkey or moved here as infants. When we look at the young age group of under the age of 35, it constitutes a staggering 78% of the whole Syrian population (see Table 2). Therefore, this very young population should be integrated into the social, economic, legal structures in Turkey very carefully. This is in line with our analyses of the Syrian demographics overall (see Chapter by Yucesahin and Sirkeci in this book; also Yucesahin and Sirkeci, 2017).

Figure 3: Number of Officially Registered Syrians in Turkey, 2011-2017

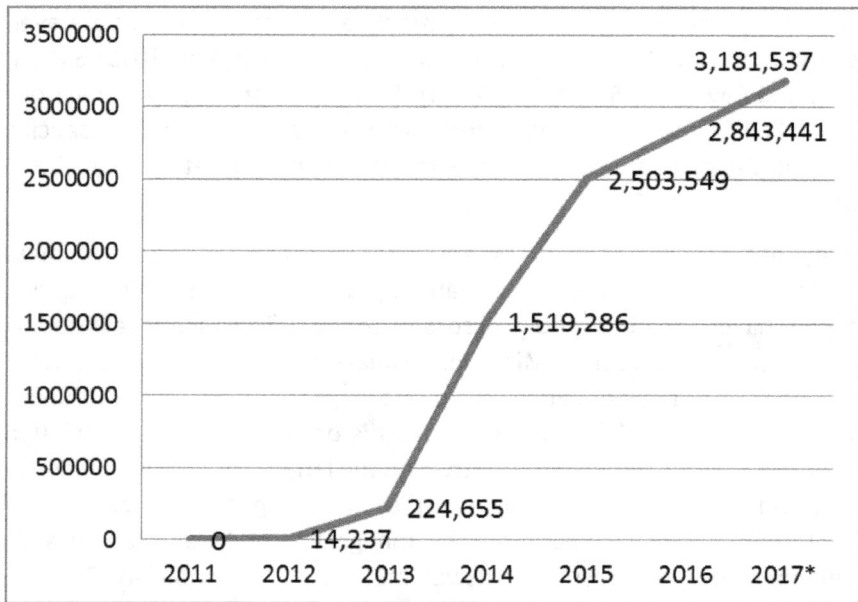

Source: DGMM Official Web Page (*by the date 14.09.2017)

http://www.goc.gov.tr/icerik6/gecici-koruma_363_378_4713_icerik (last accessed on 20.09.2017)

Secondly, it needs to be pointed out that the socio-economic and educational attainment levels of the Syrians in Turkey are quite low. The existing information on the educational attainment levels of Syrians indicates that almost half (46%) of them are either illiterate or literate but not graduate of any formal schools. The combined ratio of those who are graduates of primary and secondary schools are around 28% while there is no information on more than a quarter of the community (see Figure 4).

Table 2: Syrians Under Temporary Protection by Age and Gender

Yaş Grubu	Erkek	Kadın	Toplam	%
0-18	695.334	637.020	1.332.354	
0-4	179.572	166.898	346.470	
5-9	216.619	204.180	420.799	45.6
10-14	164.380	151.693	316.073	
15-18	134.763	114.249	249.012	
19-34	535.813	416.830	952.643	
19-24	243.368	187.117	430.485	32.6
25-29	158.471	124.262	282.733	
30-34	133.974	105.451	239.425	
35-59	283.718	256.479	540.197	
35-39	95.266	78.849	174.115	
40-44	67.047	62.765	129.812	18.4
45-49	51.727	47.539	99.266	
50-54	41.689	39.398	81.087	
55-59	27.989	27.928	55.917	
60 +	47.728	51.121	98.849	
60-69	32.439	33.228	65.667	
70-79	11.213	12.800	24.013	3.4
80-89	3.499	4.376	7.875	
90 +	577	717	1.294	
TOPLAM	1.562.593	1.361.990	2.924.583	100

Source: DGMM Official Web Page

http://www.goc.gov.tr/icerik6/gecici-koruma_363_378_4713_icerik (last accessed on 15.04.2017, age breakdown for the 14.09.2017 figure not available)

The studies conducted on Syrians as well as reports produced by the NGOs working in the field overwhelmingly suggest that socio-economic profile of the population tends to be low with majority of them suffering from economic problems (Erdoğan 2014; Icduygu 2015; Kirisci 2014; Emin 2016). The low educational attainment and skill repertoires coupled with rampant economic problems experienced by the Syrian population in Turkey further complicate the question of integration as well as making it vital for the social and economic stability in the country.

Unutulmaz

Figure 4: Syrians in Turkey According to their Educational Attainment

Source: Ministry of Development, March 2016[2]

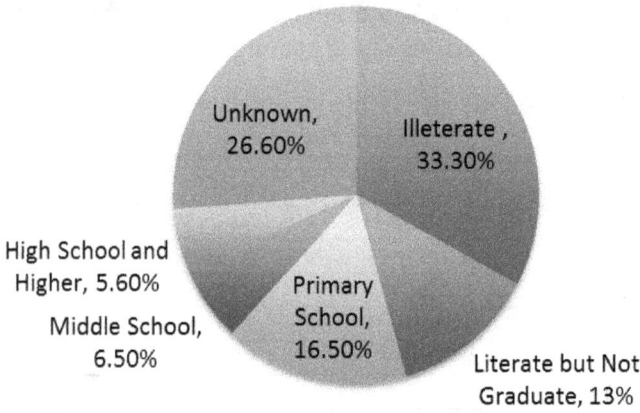

- Illeterate, 33.30%
- Unknown, 26.60%
- Primary School, 16.50%
- Literate but Not Graduate, 13%
- Middle School, 6.50%
- High School and Higher, 5.60%

Figure 5: Syrians in Turkey According to Where They Live

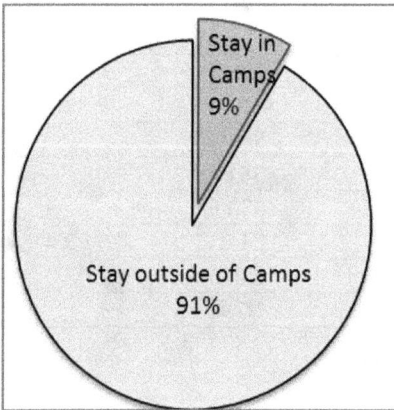

- Stay in Camps 9%
- Stay outside of Camps 91%

Source: DGMM Official Web Page: http://www.goc.gov.tr/icerik6/gecici-koruma_363_378_4713_icerik (last accessed on 15.04.2017)

Last but not least, the fact that a huge majority of Syrians are not only scattered across Turkey but also are leading quite mobile lives frequently moving from one city to another further accentuates the necessity of well-designed and standardised integration policies at the national level. Out of the 2.9 million registered Syrians, more than 2.7 million live as dispersed to all 81 provinces of Turkey, only 254 thousand live in camps, which corresponds to around 9% of the population (see Figure 5).

---

[2] Figures are obtained by Prof. Murat Erdogan from the Ministry and used with his permission.

This mobile and scattered living situation of the Syrian community in Turkey naturally makes it more difficult to manage them as well as ensuring smooth provision of public services such as education and health to Syrians as well as the wider society.

Politics of Immigration and Integration in Turkey: A Fleeting Window of Opportunity

Politicization of immigration and integration policies, which could be defined as the process through which issues related to immigration and immigrants move upwards in political salience and importance, has a tremendous impact on how integration matters are handled in a given context. In Turkey, ethnic and cultural diversity have always been at the centre of political debates. Further, it can be argued that, in terms of its historical experiences and legal, institutional and social structure, Turkey is not well prepared to manage suddenly emerging "super-diversity" (Vertovec 2007). It has been a migration country for a long time, yet the mass Syrian immigration has caught the country off guard. Besides, ethnic and cultural diversity has never been welcomed in the country, which was established on very strong republican ideals of a unified nation embodied in the imagination of a modern Turkish citizen. While Turkey failed in handling the 'Kurdish question', a basic question of integration remains unanswered: how to foster a sense of belonging among a minority ethnicity to the country while retaining their distinctive ethnic and cultural identity? How can they be integrated in all national public institutions and economy while responding to their cultural demands? How will they be integrated into national education while granting them the very basic right of education in mother tongue?

Now the questions remain the same: How can a nation which has struggled for decades with a similar question without success be expected to effectively deal with an emerging Syrian diaspora?' Yet, surprisingly, Turkish government as well as the wider Turkish society appears to be much more welcoming and constructive in responding to the various challenges arising from the presence of Syrians. The government appears keen on establishing a longer-term integration vision and strategy. While this issue is regularly covered in annual Migration Reports published by the DGMM-Directorate General of Migration Management there have also been projects commissioned by the DGMM and conducted by the International Organisation for Migration (IOM) and United Nations High Commissioner for

Refugees (UNHCR) for this specific purpose[3]. In everyday life, too, one can be surprized to see how relatively easily, for instance, Arabic is incorporated in official plates on hospital walls or public transportation system while any use of Kurdish language would have created a public uproar. Why, then, does it seem easier at the moment to take constructive steps towards Syrians and what are the implications?

While the answer to the first question requires a sophisticated comparative historical analysis of Turkey's Kurdish question and the displacement caused by the Syrian crisis; a large part of the answer seems to be related to the fact that the Kurdish question in Turkish politics is extremely securitised while the case of Syrian refugees appears to enjoy a much lower, yet increasing, level of securitisation (Aydin 2003, 176-179). In fact, there are studies which empirically substantiate the argument that 'the peace process' between the Turkish government and the PKK made some significant progress when the AKP government was able to 'de-securitize' the Kurdish issue and this process came to the brink of utter and complete breakdown when the issue became 're-securitized' (Geri 2016; Weiss 2016). As it is the case with the Kurdish question in Turkey and Muslim immigrants and refugees in many European countries, the heightened political debates and security-oriented perception of an issue significantly reduces the ability of policy-makers to effectively govern it (Bourbeau 2011, 18-30).

In democratic systems this usually works in the following way: an issue comes to occupy a very central place in the political agenda, any action the policy-makers take will be more closely followed by public and reported by the media, they immediately become more politically risky, any move they make will also be criticized and abused by their political opponents, the policy-makers will become more and more reluctant to move, they face increasing pressure to move in the meantime, the prospects of approaching elections will further make policy-makers who wish to be re-elected move with more caution, and so on and so forth (Balzacq 2011; Rychnovska 2014). Politicization of an issue has the additional politically destructive and dangerous effect of polarizing the society. Usually, the more politicized it is, the stronger will the people feel about it and more bitter the polarization will be (Hammerstad 2012). In cases of certain ethnic communities and social

---

[3] One of the most relevant such projects is the "Project to Support Development of Turkey's Harmonization Policy" which includes a "Harmonization Strategy Document and National Action Plan" (for details, see: http://www.goc.gov.tr/icerik6/uyum-strateji-belgesi-ve-ulusal-eylem-plan)i-gelistirme-komisyonu-1-toplantisi-gerceklestirildi_350_359_9031_icerik)

groups being in the centre of such debates, this polarization tends to create victimization of certain groups as well as an increase in social perils of racism and xenophobia. This has been certainly the case with politicization of immigration and integration issues (Bourbeau 2011).

It is possible to argue that the issue of Syrian refugees has not been politicized to the extent that it makes it difficult for the policy-makers to effectively produce solutions to different challenges including integration. It is, however, becoming increasingly clear that the issue is moving rapidly upwards in the political agenda in Turkey and it is only a matter of time before it reaches a fully politicized status. In the following, an analysis is presented on why this issue has been able to escape the fate of politicization and securitization in the Turkish context. Next, the quickly transforming social and political dynamics will be listed to suggest that Turkey has indeed a small window of opportunity before the issue will move to become a much more difficult one to manage.

Why has the issue of Syrian refugees not been politicized in Turkey?

To clarify, it is not argued here that the issue of Syrian refugees in Turkey has not been political at all. Of course it has always been so and it still is. The point is, however, it has not been very central in political discussions so far and it has not created a significant social polarization for the majority of time it has existed. Now, the situation is changing, yet what were the reasons that shielded this issue to become such an important and controversial political debate?

Firstly, the humanitarian aspect of the open door policy, i.e. extending a helping hand to a neighbouring people who are devastated by civil war and escaping violence, has shielded it from initial harsh criticisms. The presentation of the policy with strong reference to this humanitarian motivation has effectively silenced any opposing views and prevented the issue to be perceived as a polarizing political preference. Any comment made on the government policies or Syrian refugees themselves have had to first acknowledge the difficulty of the situation, nobility of Turkey's response which has humanitarian responsibility, communicate a message of sympathy, and only then could proceed to criticize one or the other aspect of the policies' implications.

Secondly, an enormously influential factor complementing the humanitarian aspect has been the perception of temporariness. In fact, the presentation of the policy as a humanitarian response based on good conscience and historical sense of responsibility was mostly as effective as it had been because it was also presented to be a temporary nuisance. Accordingly, the Syrians were displaced by a civil war and political oppression which were to come to an end in Syria soon with an upcoming change of government/regime. All the Syrians would then happily go back to their countries and Turkey would have been a country which has delivered what it seems to be promising in the region and it would obtain more influence. Indeed, in the initial stages of the Syrian crisis, the Turkish government seems to have been expecting the crisis to be over in a short few months. This perception was also reflected in the official discourse for the initial couple of years when the Syrian movers were called 'guests' and not given any other stable official status.

Thirdly and perhaps most importantly, the heavy political investment of a strong government seems to have shielded the issue from being easily manipulated. The above described political calculation of a swift transfer of power in Syria became the cornerstone of AKP government's foreign policy. While the calculation has proven to be wrong in the 6th year of the civil war with no change in Syrian government seems viable, admitting this would harm the credibility of government as a whole. Therefore, the AKP government, which has had a strong electoral support and a single party government for over a decade, has been the main actor framing the discussions related to Syrians in Turkey. It needs to be added that media outlets in Turkey have been under a significant level of pressure and all the mainstream media channels are now largely under the control of government. Therefore, the way all the news and information concerning the Syrians are framed has been under the control of government, too. In many Western countries where the aforementioned backlash against diversity and the rise of far-right political currents on anti-immigrant discourses have been witnessed, there are considerable media coverage of anti-immigrants views and inflammatory stories (Brookes 1999; Khosravinik 2009; Holland 2010; Clare and Abdelhady 2010). Particularly many tabloid newspapers have been able to exploit such increasing xenophobic and anti-immigrant sentiments. When we look at the mainstream media outlets, this has mostly not been the case in Turkey.

Closing window of opportunity: politicization of Syrian migration in Turkey

It seems apparent, however, that the issue of Syrian immigrants in Turkey has recently been undergoing a quick process of politicisation. The first reason accounting for this is related to the growing numbers and visibility of this community in Turkey. As stated earlier, more than 90% of around 3 million Syrian refugees live across all 81 provinces of Turkey.[4] Therefore, in all these cities their visibility in the daily life has been progressively increasing over the past few years. This increasing visibility coupled with a growing economic stagnation and increasing unemployment rates are likely to contribute to a rising anti-immigrant (i.e. anti-Syrian in Turkey) sentiment.

Secondly, there is a growing realisation that Syrians' presence in Turkey will not be temporary as it was initially expected, but rather a significant proportion would be very likely to be permanent. When the immigrants were perceived to be temporary asylum-seekers who would return to their homes as soon as the war finishes, the level of tolerance of the host society is expectedly higher (Erdoğan 2014). Not preparing the mentality of society for the long-term presence of immigrants would be very harmful and this is one of the reasons accounting for the quick politicisation of the issue in Turkey.

Thirdly, the intense political atmosphere in Turkey over the past few years inflamed by a series of local and national elections as well as, most recently, a constitutional referendum caused an increase in politicisation of the issue. This is mostly because, considered in conjunction with the political investment of the governing party in this issue, during every election campaign certain gossips and conspiracy-theories surface about government plans to have Syrians vote in the elections. It has been assumed that, since it was the AKP government under the leadership of Recep Tayyip Erdogan that applied the open-door policy towards the Syrians, they have a great sympathy toward him and that they would vote for his party[5].

Fourthly, several politicians from major opposition parties have recently started to use anti-immigrant discourses to gain political support. In a widely popular speech, Sinan Ogan an MP from the ultranationalist National Action

---

[4] By the way, it is important to underline that Turkey has always been home to a small Arabic speaking minority, especially in the southern provinces (Sirkeci, 2000; Sirkeci, 2006) and Sirkeci argues that this might be one of the reasons why Syrians (outside camps) have been dispersed around the country so easily because there are Turkish citizen friends and perhaps relatives with whom they may want to be nearby.

[5] For some examples, see: "Will the Syrians vote? A Response from the Government" http://www.haber7.com/guncel/haber/2264173-suriyeliler-oy-kullanacak-mi-hukumetten-cevap ; "Will 10 Thousand Syrians Cast Their Votes in the Referendum? Deputy Prime-Minister Answered"http://t24.com.tr/haber/basbakan-yardimcisi-cevapladi-10-bin-suriyeli-referandumda-oy-kullanacak-mi,386349 ; "Will Syrians Vote in the Referendum?" http://odatv.com/referandumda-suriyeliler-oy-mu-kullanacak-0802171200.html ; "Will the Syrians Vote?" https://www.cnnturk.com/video/turkiye/suriyeliler-oy-kullanacak-mi

Unutulmaz

Party (*Milliyetçi Hareket Partisi*-MHP) created public uproar by suggesting that while the Turkish soldiers were fighting in Syria (in the context of the Shield of Euphrates Operation), Syrian young men were harassing Turkish women by their gazes on Turkey's Mediterranean beaches[6]. Similar remarks came from a Deputy Chairman of the main opposition Republican People's Party (*Cumhuriyet Halk Partisi*-CHP), Ozturk Yilmaz[7]. Other politicians have made similar comments, albeit not using an as strongly racist, patriarchal, and provocative language. Obviously, such comments echo those of similar ones made by political figures such as Geert Wilders of the Netherlands or Nigel Farage of the UK, among others, indicating how strongly the issue is entering into the political arsenal of particularly nationalist politicians.

Concluding Remarks

Managing ethnic and cultural plurality and/or superdiversity against a backlash of declining multiculturalism and increasing securitisation of migration and integration is an extremely complex challenge. While there is a wide range of integration policies and programmes implemented in different countries, it is possible to identify some common key features in devising effective integration policies and mechanisms. Integration of more than 3 million Syrians now living all around Turkey is not only an inevitable public policy challenge, but it is vital for the social and political stability in the future. Turkey needs to act urgently as it has a quickly closing window of opportunity due to relatively low level of politicisation of the issue of Syrian migration. It has been shown that while many of the factors that prevented politicisation of the issue in the Turkish context are still prevalent, the issue is quickly becoming a divisive political issue exploited by nationalist politics.

The well-known tendency of far right political circles to exploit people's fears does not change the fact that international human mobility brings with itself a number of risks and challenges that really need to be addressed. It is true that the language and discourse people use with respect to immigration and immigrants do carry significant political implications. Therefore, one should

---

[6] "While they were staring at Turkish girls at beaches…" (Hurriyet, 3 March 2017, http://www.hurriyet.com.tr/sinan-ogandan-soke-eden-sozler-40383629 ; Sozcu, 3 March 2017, http://www.sozcu.com.tr/2017/gundem/sinan-ogan-suriyeliler-sahilde-turk-kizlarini-dikizliyor-1712208/)

[7] "Our Mehmets are becoming martyrs in Syria while Syrians are strolling around with Turkish girls" (Hurriyet, 31 January 2017, http://www.hurriyet.com.tr/mehmedimiz-el-babda-sehit-olurken-suriyeliler-turk-kizlariyla-geziyor-40352135 ;Sozcu, 1 February 2017, http://www.sozcu.com.tr/2017/gundem/mehmedimiz-suriyede-sehit-oluyor-suriyeliler-turk-kizlariyla-geziyor-1653857/)

be very careful while talking about 'terror and immigrants' or 'crime rates at times of mass immigration'. However, this does not necessarily mean that various risks related to human mobility should be ignored. Instead, they should be openly addressed in a politically careful and constructive fashion so that they cannot be exploited for racist or discriminatory purposes manipulating ignorance and fears.

One particular risk facing countries without effective integration mechanisms is that of marginalizing particularly younger immigrants and future generations born to immigrant families. Dramatic examples of this were seen in Europe. What was common in the dramatic incidents erupted in the suburbs of Paris in 2005 and in the very heart of London in 2011 was the image of young people clashing with police, harming public properties, and displaying a complete disregard for the public order and law. Another commonality was that most of these young people were coming from immigrant and minority communities. In the aftermath of the 2011 riots in London, the overwhelming feeling was that these young people have been left at the margins of society without any feeling of belonging or ownership and the solution was to give these young people a steak in the society. The way to do that was suggested to involve improving community engagement and cohesion, giving these young people hopes and dreams, and let them get involved in meaningful social interactions (Riots Communities and Victims Panel 2011). This is just another way of describing an effective integration policy.

As it has been argued in detail above, the young Syrian community in Turkey, a significant part of whom has been traumatised by the on-going bloody conflict, makes this risk even more crucial. Therefore, Turkey needs to adopt effective integration policies and programmes that:

- aim to create a common denominator in terms of shared norms and values which in time would create a base of a common identity;

- absolutely and clearly reject assimilation as a political objective and respect the cultural and ethnic identity of all immigrants; and,

- emphasise mainstreaming of its immigrant population by adopting a welcoming approach to cultural diversity.

In order to realise these general objectives, a wider perspective change is necessary. In other words, the above listed policy objectives could not be achieved in themselves through adoption of any particular set of legislation or establishment of any institutions. Their existence could only be hoped when, and only when, a long-term transformation of mentality and vision takes place. Lastly, it is argued and needs to be underlined again that Turkey has a brief window of opportunity where the issue of Syrian immigrants is not completely politicized and abused by extremist political movements.

References

Aksoy, A. (2006) . Transnational Virtues and Cool Loyalties: Responses of Turkish-Speaking Migrants in London to September 11. *Journal of Ethnic and Migration Studies* 32 (6): 923–46. doi:10.1080/13691830600761487.

Aldcroft, D. H. (2001) . *The European Economy 1914-2000*. 4th ed. London and New York: Routledge.

Alvardo, J., & Creedy, J. (1998) . *Population Ageing, Migration and Social Expenditure*. Edward Elgar Publishing.

Aydin, M. (2003). Securitization of history and geography: understanding of security in Turkey. *Southeast European and Black Sea Studies* 3 (2)

Balzacq, T. (2011). A theory of securitization. In Balzacq, T. (ed.) *Secutitization Theory: How security problems emerge and dissolve*. London and New York: Routledge

Blalock, H. M. (1967) . *Toward a Theory of Minority Group Relations*. New York: John Wiley and Sons.

Bourbeau, P. (2011) . The Securitization of Migration: A Study of Movement and Order. London and New York: Routledge.

Brookes, R. (1999). Newspapers and National Identity: the BSE/CJD crisis and the British press. *Media, Culture and Society* 21 (2)

Brown, C. S. (2015) . The Educational, Psychological, and Social Impact of Discrimination on the Immigrant Child. Washington DC: Migration Policy Institute.

Buonfino, A. (2004) . Between Unity and Plurality: The Politicization and Securitization of the Discourse of Immigration in Europe. *New Political Science* 26 (1): 23–49.

Castles, S., Vasta, E., Vertovec S., & Korac, M. (2002) . *Integration: Mapping the Field*. Oxford: COMPAS, University of Oxford.

Clare, M. & Abdelhady, D. (2016). No longer a waltz between red wine and mint tea: the portrayal of the children of immigrants in French newspapers (2003-2013). *International Journal of Intercultural Relations*. 50

Coale, A.J., & Watkins, S.C.. (1986) . *The Decline of Fertility in Europe*. Princeton: Princeton University Press.

Coleman, D. A. (1994) . Trends in Fertility and Intermarriage among Immigrant Populations in Western-Europe as Measures of Integration. *Journal of Biosocial Science* 26 (1): 107–36.

Crul, M. (2010) . How Do Educational Systems Integrate? Integration of Second Generation Turks in Four Institutional SettingsIn . Harvard University.

Davoudi, S., Wishardt, M., & Strange, L. (2010). The Ageing of Europe: Demographic Scenarios of Europe's Futures. *Futures* 42 (8).

Eichengreen, B. J. (2007). *The European Economy since 1945: Coordinated Capitalism and Beyond*. Princeton: Princeton University Press.

Emin, M. N. (2016). Türkiye'deki Suriyeli Çocukların Eğitimi: Temel Eğitim Politikaları. SETA.

Erdoğan, M. M. (2014). *Syrians in Turkey: Social Acceptance and Integration Research*. Ankara: Hacattepe University Migration and Politics Research Centre.

Erdoğan, M. M. & Kaya, A. (2015). *Türkiye'nin Göç Tarihi: 14. Yüzyıldan 21. Yüzyıla Türkiye'ye Göçler*. İstanbul: İstanbul Bilgi Üniversitesi Yayınları.

Fargues, P. (2011). International Migration and the Demographic Transition: A Two-way Interaction. *International Migration Review* 45 (3): 588–614.

Favell, A. (1998). Philosophies Of Integration: Immigration and The Ideal Of Citizenship In France and Britain. Basingstoke: Macmillan.

Favell, A. (2001). Citizenship Today: Global Prespectives and Practices. In *Integration Policy and Integration Research in Europe: A Review and Critique*, edited by T. Alexander Aleinikoff and Doug Klusmeyer. Washington, DC: Brookings Institute.

Geri, M. (2016). The securitization of the Kurdish minority in Turkey: ontological insecurity and elite's power struggle as reasons of the recent re-securitization. *Digest of Middle East Studies*

Ghemawat, P. (2011). *The World 3.0: Global Prosperity and How to Achieve It*. Boston: Harvard Business Review Press.

Goodhart, D. (2004). Too diverse? *Prospect* 95

Grillo, R. D. (2005). Backlash against Diversity? Identity and Cultural Politics in European Cities. University of Oxford *COMPAS Paper*.

Haas, H. d. (2005). International Migration, Remittances and Development: Myths and Facts. *Third World Quarterly* 26 (8): 1269–84.

Haas, H. d. (2008). The Myth of Invasion: The Inconvenient Realities of African Migration to Europe. *Third World Quarterly* 29 (7): 1305–22.

Hammerstad, A. (2012). Securitization from below: the relationship between immigration and foreign policy in South Africa's approach to the Zimbabwe crisis. *Conflict, Security and Development*. 12 (1)

Holland, A. (2010) Shooting the Messenger: Mediating the public and the role of the media in South Africa's xenophobic violence. *Africa Development*. 35 (3)

Huntington, S. P. (1992). The Clash of Civilizations? *Foreign Affairs* 72: 22–49.

Icduygu, A. (2015). *Syrian Refugees in Turkey: The Long Road Ahead*. Istanbul: Migration Policy Institute.

IOM. (2015). *World Migration Report 2015*. International Organization for Migration.

Khosravinik, M. (2009). The representation of refugees, asylum seekers and immigrants in British newspapers during the Balkan conflict (1999) and the British general election (2005). *Discourse and Society*. 20 (4)

Kirisci, K. (2014). Syrian Refugees and Turkey's Challenges: Going Beyond Hospitality. Washington DC: Brookings Institute.

Olzak, S. (1992). *The Dynamics of Ethnic Competition and Conflict*. Stanford, CA: Stanford University Press.

Unutulmaz

Quillian, L. (1995). Prejudice as a Response to Perceived Group Threat: Population Composition and Anti-Immigrant and Racial Prejudice in Europe. *American Sociological Review* 60 (4): 586–611.

Riots Communities and Victims Panel. (2011). *After the Riots: The Final Report of the Riots Communities and Victims Panel*. http://webarchive.nationalarchives. gov.uk/20121003195935/http:/riotspanel.independent.gov.uk/wp-content/uploads/2012/03/Riots-Panel-Final-Report1.pdf.

Rychnovska, D. (2014). Securitization and the power of threat framing perspectives. *Perspectives* 22 (2)

Saeed, T. (2016). Islamophobia and Securitization: Religion, Ethnicity and the Female Voice. Palgrave Macmillan.

Şeker, B. D., Sirkeci, I., & Yüceşahin, M. M. (2015). *Göç ve Uyum*. London: Transnational Press London.

SIRIUS. (2013). European Policy Network on the Education of Migrant Children and Young People with a Migrant Background- Literature Review. SIRIUS Network.

Sirkeci, I. (2017). Turkey's refugees, Syrians and refugees from Turkey: a country of insecurity. *Migration Letters*, 14(1), 127-144.

Sirkeci, I. (2000). "Exploring the Kurdish population in the Turkish context", GENUS, an International Journal of Demography, 56(1-2): 149-175.

Sirkeci, I. (2006). The Environment of Insecurity in Turkey and the Emigration of Turkish Kurds to Germany. New York: Edwin Mellen Press

Sirkeci, I., Şeker, B. D., & Çağlar, A. (2015). *Turkish Migration, Identity and Integration*. London: Transnational Press London.

Unutulmaz, K. O. (2012). Gündemdeki Kavram: Göçmen Uyumu- Avrupa'daki Gelişimi ve Britanya Örneği. In *Küreselleşme Çağında Göç: Kavramlar, Tartışmalar*, edited by Asli Sirin and Suna Gulfer Ihlamur. Istanbul: Iletisim Yayinlari.

Unutulmaz, K. O. (2017). Batı Dünyasında Farklılıkların Yönetimi Ve Azınlıkların Entegrasyonu. In *21. Yüzyılda Din ve Uluslararası İlişkilerde Dönüşüm*, edited by Filiz Çoban. Istanbul: Nobel Yayınları.

Vasta, E. (2007). Accommodating Diversity: Why Current Critiques of Multiculturalism Miss the Point? University of Oxford COMPAS Working Papers.

Vasta, E. (2009). Accommodating Diversity: Understanding Multiculturalism. *Confluence*, 1–2.

Vertovec, S. (2007). New Complexities of Cohesion in Britain: Super-Diversity, Transnationalism and Civil-Integration. London: Commission on Integration and Cohesion.

Vertovec, S., Wessendorf, S. & others. (2010). Multiculturalism Backlash: European Discourses, Policies and Practices. Routledge.

Walker, A., & Maltby, T. (1997). *Ageing Europe*. Bristol: Open University Press.

Yucesahin, M.M. and Sirkeci, I. (2017). Demographic gaps between Syrian and the European populations: What do they suggest?, *Border Crossing*, 7(2): 207-230.

CONCLUSION

K. Onur Unutulmaz[¥], Ibrahim Sirkeci[Υ], Deniz Eroğlu Utku[±]

Conflicts, tensions, discomforts, dissatisfaction and frustration over resources and representation are feeding into the perception of human insecurity around the world (see Sirkeci, 2003, 2006; Sirkeci and Cohen, 2016). These individual level insecurities meet national level insecurities and securitisation of migration and migration policy is simply a, somehow inevitable, side effect. Turkey, once known as a source country for mass labour migration, is now firmly placed on the map of immigration destinations marked by over 3 million Syrian refugees and about half a million refugees from other parts of the world. The country has also been in the receiving end of sizeable numbers of returnees and immigrants from the traditional destination countries of Turkish emigrants such as Germany as a result of emerging cultures of migration over these corridors (Cohen and Sirkeci, 2011; Sirkeci and Zeyneloglu, 2014). Human mobility across Turkey's southern border has always been peculiar because of the ethnic mix, close ties, and historical baggage. Turkey, after the collapse of the Ottoman Empire, remained home to a large Arabic speaking population who were dominantly living in provinces across the Syrian border. A very porous border that allowed practically free movement of people, relatives, and friends on both sides for decades. The tensions between the two countries' governments marked and disturbed this status quo. Disputes and tensions since the end of the Empire made this border between the Syrian Arab Republic and Turkey unstable and prone to conflicts. Since 2011 this border has witnessed a vast mobility as a result of one of the biggest tragedies of human history because of the aggravation of *Demographic Deficit*, *Development Deficit* and *Democratic Deficit (3D)* happening in Syria. A rising environment of insecurity as well as conflicts involving several different

¥ K. Onur Unutulmaz, Social Sciences University of Ankara, Turkey. E-mail: onur.unu-tulmaz@asbu.edu.tr
Υ Ibrahim Sirkeci, Regent's Centre for Transnational Studies, Regent's University London, United Kingdom. E-mail: sirkecii@regents.ac.uk
± Deniz Eroğlu Utku, Department of Public Administration, Trakya University, Edirne, Turkey. E-mail: denizeroglu@trakya.edu.tr

armed groups paved the way for Syrian influx into the neighbouring countries. While a detailed analysis of this conflict requires several volumes of separate study and hence was not in the scope of the present book, this study tried to turn its gaze towards the displaced millions of Syrians who had to leave their homes. Turkey has become one of the top countries for those seeking refuge due to its geographic proximity to the war zone as well as the aforementioned historical background.

By the third quarter of 2017, there were almost 3.5 million Syrians living in Turkey. Millions of Syrian refugees in Turkey bring about major implications for the present as well as for the future. Some of these are significant challenges while others present remarkable potential for the future in all spheres of life. Neither responding to the complicated challenges at present, nor managing the risks or mustering the potential associated with the current conundrum is possible without developing an in-depth understanding of social, political, economic and psychological dynamics of human mobility and that of Syrians who have been uprooted for reasons uprooting millions around the world day in day out.

Content of the Book

This book arose from a desire to understand the Syrian communities in Turkey drawing on research from a variety of disciplines and perspectives. We present original research and pose new questions and share new insights. We begin with tackling some theoretical issues and present works that critically review government policies towards Syrians and integration issues in Turkey. Chapters in the opening part explore several key concepts and categories that are used to define Syrians in Turkey.

Conceptual discussions are followed by case studies in part one. Accounts and primary data gathered and analysed by academics and activists shed light onto issues that are often overlooked. In this part, problematic aspects of refugees' lives in both big cities and small towns and the background to Turkey's "generous" open door policy are discussed. What is more, this part offers methodologically diversified studies, as there are both qualitative and quantitative data analyses here.

As the war in Syria continues and the stays of Syrians in Turkey are extended, a vital question emerged about the future of Syrians. Therefore we have reserved the last part to focus on the future for Syrians in Turkey. It is important to profile Syrians in Turkey accurately drawing on reliable data. Demographic analysis offered in this book aims to do exactly that. It allows us to see past and present features and patterns and offer information on which one may contemplate and project future trends. This is much needed in the current climate of misinformation and noise about Syrians and refugees from elsewhere. Such analyses are very much needed to understand patterns of integration and develop policies to foster and facilitate integration. Despite politics around Syrians, their stay in Turkey should be seen as long term and therefore our effort here is to underline the urgency of integration policies to be developed.

As we stressed a few times, this book is a collection of work examining Syrian population in Turkey from various disciplinary perspectives. Each chapter reflects such nuances as well as perceptions of the contributing authors. We purposefully avoided imposing our or any specific discipline's terminology. What to call people fleeing from persecution or conflict in general or discomfort or tension is a universal open debate and even more so if one studies asylum in Turkey. Cohen and Sirkeci (2011) have long argued that we are looking at movers (aka migrants) who avoid conflicts, difficulties, tensions, conflicts, discomforts and so on and who pursue some kind of human security, relatively better than what they do or used to experience at the place of origin. Calling them labour migrant, irregular migrant, or refugee is just a legal and administrative technicality. In this book, we did not make a choice between administrative terminology or motives for migration. Therefore each contributing author has used the terminology of their own choice as it suited to their particular contribution and discussion.

There is considerable xenophobia and discriminatory attitude towards Syrians in Turkey. This is evident in some contributions included in this book and published elsewhere. Authors of this edited book seemingly share the view that there is still ambiguity about the future of Syria and Syrians in Turkey and the need for developing policies to deal with these challenges arose from the arrival and settlement of millions since 2011. We open a debate on the future by highlighting few questions and observations in the closing passages. We do hope these contributions will be received positively as an addition to the growing literature on Syrian refugees in Turkey and elsewhere.

Future Prospects

Talking about future prospects of socio-political phenomena that are as multi-dimensional, as complicated and as dynamic as the ones centred around the Syrian population in Turkey is not easy. Without attempting to engage in fortune telling, however, it is still possible to talk about certain potential trends and transformations that are likely to take precedence in Turkey. Many of the individual chapters in this volume have done this in their respected areas of focus. In this final section, we would like to take a much more general and necessarily brief look at what to expect in the Turkish context related to Syrians. We see five key areas to observe challenges and changes and would like to draw attention to certain aspects.

The Challenge of Developing Migration and Integration Policies: While it has always been a significant country of immigration and emigration, Turkey today is increasingly under an unprecedented amount of pressure to effectively govern its borders and manage population mobility within, across, to and from its territory. Given the current trends and patterns, we believe migration pressure and the challenge of developing migration policies will continue and grow. In the same vein, despite being home to diverse ethnic groups, the current level of diversity which suddenly grew by international population movements requires Turkey to develop a more pro-active stance on governing diversity through effective integration policies while also sporting a stronger stance on preventing discrimination, racism and xenophobia.

Demographic Transformations: As shown in the chapter by Yucesahin and Sirkeci, demographic differences between Syrians and general population in Turkey are significant and indicate a time lag in the course of demographic transition. The empirical evidence, the demographic structures of the general population in Turkey as well as the population of Syrian communities in the community display potential for dynamic change in the coming decades. It is essential for Turkey to closely monitor these processes of demographic transformation and develop a long-term approach to respond to the additional implications in terms of various public policy domains such as education and health as well as for the economy in general.

Politicization and Securitization of Migration: As various chapters have touched upon, the framing of the Syrian refugees in Turkey has been somewhat suppressed not to become a contentious political and security matter in the mainstream media and political debates. It is, however, also suggested that this situation is quickly changing, as the issue is quickly becoming politicized and securitized under the pressures coming from various segments of society, media, and politics. In the highly polarized political climate of the country, the politicians from opposition parties have begun frequently emphasising the Syrians' presence in their campaigns. Similarly, while they are not often reported in the mainstream media, there is also an increase in the number and scale of incidents across the country at grass roots level manifesting an increase in xenophobia towards Syrians and foreigners. There is brewing potential for ethnic conflict and growing hatred against which serious precautions must be taken.

Required Institutional and Legal Changes: To be able to affectively deal with the issues stated above requires not only a political will and vision, but also the development of the necessary legal and institutional instruments. Turkey has already taken several significant steps in the right direction including the establishment of the Directorate General of Migration Management and the adoption of the Law on Foreigners and International Protection. It needs to be remembered that both of these developments have their roots prior to the arrival of Syrian refugees in the European Union accession negotiations. While there are several units established under various ministries to coordinate public policies and services toward Syrian refugees, the sheer scale of the current predicament suggests that Turkey will need to create more effective institutions equipped with authority and resources that are clearly assigned to them by legal regulations.

Field of Migration Studies in Turkey: Until recently, migration studies in Turkey has been an obscure subfield with very few pioneering academics doing research and publishing on a regular basis (see Sirkeci and Yüceşahin, 2014). Although there was an observable growth in interest as quite a few universities launched research centres dedicated to migration studies and equally strong interest raised abroad, the exponential growth in the field was seen after the arrival of Syrians in the 2010s. The Turkish migration conferences held at Regent's University London in 2012 and 2014 followed by 2015 in Prague and 2016 in Vienna were clear indicator as hundreds of academics from various disciplines participated in these events (see www.migrationcenter.org). Clearly, this recent hype over migration studies as well as the inflow of significant funding to conduct research on migration helped to make migration an attractive field of study for academics, students and other parties across many disciplines. While it is healthy to have more people interested in migration research, it is equally important to sift through the noise to reach reliable information and robust analysis. In the current climate the growth in research on migration and particularly on Syrian movers comes largely from make-shift expertise and many careless accounts with little or no methodological skills fill the knowledge pool. If effective communication and coordination amongst stake holders is achieved, development of such a diverse, strong and more engaging academic field of migration studies would help Turkey in the difficult task of responding to the challenges posed by human mobility today and in the future.

References

Cohen, J.H. & Sirkeci, I. (2011). Cultures of Migration: Global nature of contemporary human mobility. Austin, TX: University of Texas Press.

Sirkeci, İ., & Yüceşahin, M. (2014). Editörden: Türkiye'de göç çalışmaları. Göç Dergisi, 1(1), 1-10. http://www.tplondon.com/dergi/index. php/gd/ article/view/2 adresinden erişildi.

Sirkeci, I. (2003a). Migration Ethnicity and Conflict, unpublished PhD thesis, University of Sheffield, UK.

Sirkeci, I. (2006). The environment of insecurity in Turkey and the emigration of Turkish Kurds to Germany. New York & Lampeter: Edwin Mellen Press.

Sirkeci I and Cohen J. H. (2016). Cultures of Migration and conflict in contemporary human mobilitiy in Turkey. European Review, 24 (3): 381-396.

Sirkeci, I. and Zeyneloglu, S. (2014). Abwanderung aus Deutschland in die Türkei: Eine Trendwende im Migrationsgeschehen? In: Alscher, S. & Krienbriek, A. (eds.) Abwanderung von Türkeistämmigen: Wer verlässt Deutschland und warum?. Germany: BAMF, pp. 30-85.

www.ingramcontent.com/pod-product-compliance
Lightning Source LLC
Chambersburg PA
CBHW050420280326
41932CB00013BA/1939